LANGUAGE DEMOGRAPHY

Language Demography presents, exemplifies, and develops linguistic concepts involved in demography and the demographic concepts involved in sociolinguistics.

The first introductory guide of its kind, it is presented in a way that is accessible to non-specialists. The book includes numerous examples of the sources and types of data used in this field, as well as the various factors affecting language demography. Taking a global perspective supported by examples, it gives explanations of how demolinguistic analyses are performed and their main applications in relation to minority and majority languages.

Language Demography will be of interest to students from a range of disciplinary backgrounds, from linguistics and modern languages to sociology, anthropology, and human geography.

Francisco Moreno-Fernández is Alexander von Humboldt Professor at Heidelberg University, Germany, Director of the Center for Ibero-American Studies, and honorary Research Professor at the University of Alcalá, Spain. He is a full member of the Academia Europaea and the Academia Norteamericana de la Lengua Española, and a corresponding member of the Cuban, Mexican, and Chilean academies of language, as well as the Real Academia Española. He directed the Cervantes Institute centers in São Paulo and Chicago. He was academic director of the Instituto Cervantes (Madrid) and director of the Observatory of Spanish and Hispanic Cultures of the Instituto Cervantes at Harvard University, USA.

LANGUAGE DEMOGRAPHY

Francisco Moreno-Fernández

In collaboration with Héctor Álvarez-Mella

Spanish List Advisor
JAVIER MUÑOZ-BASOLS

LONDON AND NEW YORK

Designed cover image: aelitta / Getty Images

First published 2024
by Routledge
4 Park Square, Milton Park, Abingdon, Oxon OX14 4RN

and by Routledge
605 Third Avenue, New York, NY 10158

Routledge is an imprint of the Taylor & Francis Group, an informa business

© 2024 Francisco Moreno-Fernández

The right of Francisco Moreno-Fernández to be identified as author of this work has been asserted in accordance with sections 77 and 78 of the Copyright, Designs and Patents Act 1988.

All rights reserved. No part of this book may be reprinted or reproduced or utilised in any form or by any electronic, mechanical, or other means, now known or hereafter invented, including photocopying and recording, or in any information storage or retrieval system, without permission in writing from the publishers.

Trademark notice: Product or corporate names may be trademarks or registered trademarks, and are used only for identification and explanation without intent to infringe.

British Library Cataloguing-in-Publication Data
A catalogue record for this book is available from the British Library

Library of Congress Cataloging-in-Publication Data
Names: Moreno Fernández, Francisco, author. |
Schimel, Lawrence, translator. | Benitez-James, Layla, translator.
Title: Language demography / Francisco Moreno-Fernández ;
[translated by Lawrence Schimel and Layla Benitez-James].
Description: Abingdon, Oxon ; New York, NY : Routledge, 2023. |
Includes bibliographical references and index.
Identifiers: LCCN 2022060868 (print) | LCCN 2022060869 (ebook) |
ISBN 9781032355382 (paperback) | ISBN 9781032355399 (hardback) |
ISBN 9781003327349 (ebook)
Subjects: LCSH: Linguistic demography.
Classification: LCC P40.5.D45 M67 2023 (print) |
LCC P40.5.D45 (ebook) | DDC 306.44–dc23/eng/20230531
LC record available at https://lccn.loc.gov/2022060868
LC ebook record available at https://lccn.loc.gov/2022060869

ISBN: 978-1-032-35539-9 (hbk)
ISBN: 978-1-032-35538-2 (pbk)
ISBN: 978-1-003-32734-9 (ebk)

DOI: 10.4324/9781003327349

Typeset in Bembo
by Newgen Publishing UK

To Jaime Otero
Translated by Lawrence Schimel and Layla Benitez-James

CONTENTS

List of Figures ... ix
List of Tables ... x
List of Graphs ... xii
List of Maps ... xiv
Acknowledgements ... xv

Introduction ... 1

1 Demography and Demolinguistics ... 6
   Demolinguistics and Geodemolinguistics 8
   Demolinguistics and Geography 10
   Denominations for Demolinguistics 11
   The Precursors of Demolinguistics 17
   Summary 21

2 Linguistics for Demographers ... 23
   Fundamental Linguistic Concepts 25
   Geographic Considerations 33
   Psychosocial Considerations 36
   Social and Ethnic Considerations 46
   Language Vitality 53
   Summary 56

3 Demography for Linguists ... 62
   Population 63
   Composition of the Population 65

Population Distribution 77
Demographic Changes 78
From Facts to Theories 86
Summary 87

4 Demolinguistic Data and Sources 91
 Data 91
 Sources 93
 Administrative Registers 95
 Censuses 96
 Surveys 101
 International and Digital Sources 112
 Encyclopedias, Catalogs, and Other Sources 115
 Summary 120

5 Demolinguistic Factors 130
 Speakers and Their Communities 130
 Speaker Profiles 143
 Explanatory Factors 149
 Summary 167

6 Demolinguistic Analyses 171
 Objectives and Levels of Demolinguistic Analysis 171
 Qualitative and Quantitative Analysis 176
 The Statistical Elements of Demography 181
 Errors, Biases, and Changes in Criteria 193
 Graphic Representations 199
 Summary 215

7 Applications of Demolinguistics 219
 Ethnic, Local, and Social Minority Languages 221
 Immigrant Minority Languages 235
 Regional and National Languages 238
 Transnational Majority Languages 243
 Summary 250

Conclusion 256

Index 259

FIGURES

3.1	Concentric levels of identity.	69
3.2	Pyramid of the integration process.	85
4.1	Evolution of the discussions regarding the wording of the question about main languages in the Swiss surveys.	104
4.2	Fragment referring to languages from the questionnaire used in the Third Census of Native Communities of Peru.	104
4.3	Section on education from the questionnaire used in the Third Census of Native Communities of Peru.	105
4.4	Questions on languages in the censuses of the United Kingdom (2011) and the United States (2014).	106
4.5	Fragment of the survey on the social situation of Valencian.	108
5.1	Linguistic questions in Switzerland.	134

TABLES

2.1	Glottonymic distinction of languages.	32
2.2	Levels of vitality according to the SUM Model.	54
2.3	Degrees of vitality of languages according to UNESCO.	56
3.1	Identification of ethnicity, language, and religion in 27 EU countries.	71
3.2	Class scheme.	75
3.3	Generations of immigrants.	84
4.1	Dates and types of censuses in Ibero-America by country and decade in the 2000s and 2010s.	98
4.2	Subjective vitality questionnaire.	111
4.3	Questionnaire for the project "The Vitality of Indigenous Languages in Mexico: A Study in Three Contexts".	112
4.4	Demolinguistic sources.	121
4.5	List of sources mentioned.	123
5.1	Treatment of questions about languages in 17 European Union countries.	132
5.2	Overview of (set of) census questions in four multicultural countries.	133
5.3	Disadvantages of criteria for defining and identifying population groups in a multicultural society.	135
5.4	Number of native speakers of nine languages according to different sources (1964–2015).	137
5.5	Entropy and number of speakers of various languages.	142
5.6	Typology of languages of demolinguistic interest.	150
5.7	Coding of ISCED levels.	157

6.1	Basic typology of demolinguistic analysis.	177
6.2	Paradigms in ethnographic and demographic research.	178
7.1	Estimate of Romani speakers in Europe.	234
7.2	Use of Asturian/Bable in formal and semi-formal situations by bilingual speakers.	242

GRAPHS

1.1	Ngram Viewer results for *demolinguistics*, *linguistic demography*, and *language demography* (volume usage).	13
1.2	Ngram Viewer results for *démolinguistique* and *démographie linguistique* (volume usage).	14
1.3	Ngram Viewer results for *demolingüística* and *demografía lingüística* (volume usage).	16
2.1	EGIDS diagnosis considering the youngest generation with some proficient speakers.	55
4.1	Sources and types of information.	94
5.1	Levels for the categorization of speakers.	146
5.2	Educational diagram of Spain.	156
5.3	Characteristics of language as an economic good.	160
5.4	Global presence of science across different linguistic fields.	164
5.5	Presence of English, Spanish, Portuguese, French, and German on digital platforms.	166
6.1	Relationship between age of migration to Santiago [de Chile] and fluency in Mapudungun.	173
6.2	Interactive continuum of qualitative-quantitative philosophy.	179
6.3	Schematic representation of positive (A), negative (B), and "no correlation" (C) correlations.	179
6.4	Projections of communities of native speakers of Spanish, French, and English in 2012, 2050, and 2100.	190
6.5	Projection of the Hispanic population in the United States between 2020 and 2060.	191
6.6	Simplified scatter diagram for intergenerational disruption scale.	192

6.7	Naturalizations of Spanish-speaking migrants in Germany (1991–2019), based on data from the *Statistisches Bundesamt* (2020).	201
6.8	Descendants of migrants in Germany (1/1/2019) (typical development), based on data from the *Statistisches Bundesamt* (2020).	202
6.9	Oral use at home and with friends. Prevalence of Valencian / Spanish / other languages or indistinct use.	203
6.10	Bar graph (left) and histogram (right).	204
6.11	Evolution of the Basque-speaking population by age group. CAE (Comunidad Autónoma de Euskadi) 1991–2016 (%).	205
6.12	Competence in Mapudungun of members of Mapuche communities in Santiago de Chile.	205
6.13	Varieties of Spanish in Germany and their speakers: distribution by federal state, based on data from the *Statistisches Bundesamt* (2020).	206
6.14	Basic types of pyramids.	207
6.15	Population that speaks indigenous languages in Mexico, 1990 and 2010. Superimposed pyramids.	208
6.16	Population pyramids of the Spanish-speaking immigrant population in Germany according to their origin (1/1/2019), based on data from the *Statistisches Bundesamt* (2020). Juxtaposed pyramids.	209
6.17	Coleman diagram for social mechanisms of demography.	210
7.1	Knowledge of Totonac in Mecapalapa by age group.	222
7.2	Population pyramids of persons self-ascribed as indigenous in Mexican censuses of 2000 and 2010.	223
7.3	Ecology of pressures in minority language contexts.	228
7.4	Population of Miranda do Douro according to the censuses of 1964–2011.	231
7.5	2009 population pyramid of Palenque de San Basilio. Sociolinguistic self-diagnosis.	232
7.6	EU residents not born in the EU, by country of origin.	237
7.7	Main nationalities of people who applied for asylum in the EU for the first time. 2020.	238
7.8	Comparison of the relative positions of languages according to their IL from 1995 to 2015 and from 2015 to 2020.	248

MAPS

4.1	Population census methodology in the 2010s.	100
5.1	US states where English is official, with an indication of the kind of recognition, in 2021.	152
5.2	Main models of primary education (ISCED 1) and the first stage of secondary education (ISCED 2) in Europe, 2020 / 21.	155
6.1	Point map of languages in a critical situation in Africa, Oceania, and South Asia.	211
6.2	Map of origins of Hispanics in Europe.	212
6.3	Map of areas of the population that self-identifies as indigenous or native to the Andes according to districts of Peru (2017).	213
6.4	Students of Spanish by federal state (2018/19 academic year), based on data from the *Statistisches Bundesamt* (2020).	214
7.1	Map of differences in the number of threatened languages between 2060 and 2100.	225

ACKNOWLEDGEMENTS

This work has been made possible by the work, involvement, and support of very generous and brilliant people. First of all, I must mention the closest and most committed collaborator in the development of the task: Héctor Álvarez Mella. His technical skills have ensured, on the one hand, that the illustrations are harmonious and effective and, on the other hand, that the writing has become clearer. This contribution has been happily joined by Andrés Castro, a demographer by profession and vocation, who has not only helped me to avoid mistakes and clarify concepts but has also helped me to shake my fear of presenting this work to a multidisciplinary audience. On the other hand, Óscar Loureda Lamas has reviewed the text and provided valuable suggestions, beyond our shared projects. My gratitude to these three colleagues is enormous. I am similarly grateful to Routledge publishing house for trusting in the potential of this work to have a good reception internationally, and am especially grateful to Javier Muñoz-Basols, editor of the publishing house's collections, whose interest, support, and advice have been a definitive cornerstone for giving the book its final form. Of course, comments from anonymous reviewers have also been of great help in detecting the weak points in a text that aspires to be useful to students and experts across very different disciplines.

INTRODUCTION

When Michael Krauss published "The World's Languages in Crisis" in 1992, international public opinion turned its attention toward linguistic diversity. Krauss predicted that half of the world's languages would disappear in the twenty-first century, and only 10% seemed safe in the long term. This meant all of humanity would shift from having 7,000 languages to just 700 within a few decades.

In the wake of this moment, many initiatives which were already concerned with cataloging, quantifying, or vindicating the world's languages received a boost in support whose effects are still noticeable to this day. Important research teams across the Americas, Europe, and the Pacific were tasked with cataloging languages. The work of classification found itself reinforced by many countries' interests in the coexistence of languages within their territories, and the protection of linguistic and cultural minorities became part of many governments' political agendas around the globe. The planet's loss of linguistic diversity could only be compared to another phenomenon of gigantic proportions: the deterioration of its biodiversity.

Still vivid in humanity's collective conscience, this pessimistic panorama served as a good excuse for developing various lines of study concerned with the world's languages and their communities, both in their own right and from a more comparative perspective. This interest was not new: since the eighteenth century, there have been catalogs of languages; since the nineteenth century, there has been an insistence on identifying and delimiting the languages of each nation; and since the twentieth century, many governments have focused their political attention on the linguistic diversity of their populations.

The differences among studies carried out in the twenty-first century and those of earlier periods lie, on the one hand, in the added relevance gained through identity claims which usually placed languages center stage and, on the other hand,

DOI: 10.4324/9781003327349-1

2 Introduction

in the quality and quantity of technical resources currently available to undertake investigations. As could be expected, underlying questions exist. Though they are overwhelmingly conceptual, they sow doubts about our understanding of linguistic diversity: What is a natural language? Where are the boundaries among variations? How does one count a multilingual speaker? These are all good questions, but equally important is the fact that today's available sources and means ensure that studies are undertaken with greater guarantees than those of just half a century before.

Interest in linguistic diversity has developed across different fields and, as a result, reflects heterogeneous perspectives and positions in terms of the epistemology and aims of investigations. Ethnography has had one of the greatest traditions in this field and, together with anthropology, has consistently concerned itself with languages as the cultural and social expression of peoples. Since the 1990s, ecological linguistics or ecolinguistics merged with ethnographic traditions in its interest in indigenous or native communities, their languages, and the dynamics of their conservation or shift (Haugen, 1972). In this same period, the sociology of language and sociolinguistics concerned itself with minority languages, coexistence and contact between languages, and the social functions these perform for their respective communities (Bright, 1966). From the twentieth into the twenty-first century, the field of the economics of language has developed a model of study that centers its interest in the economic function of languages within societies and its relevance for social communication, as a technology of social communication, as a factor of socialization, and as a creative support (Grin, 1996; Alonso, 2006).

Naturally, such diversity of perspectives and interests has led to a varied bibliography concerned with very different, though often complementary, aspects of the diversity of languages and their communities of speakers, aspects approached from qualitative and quantitative methodologies combined in different ways. Nevertheless, these perspectives all reveal a common denominator, an unavoidable factor upon which a great deal of their justification and reasoning is built. That common denominator is none other than the study of populations of speakers through demography. When demography has as its subject the populations that speak some languages or others, the demography of languages or demolinguistics arises. This is the center of vital interest for *Language Demography,* in which these two labels will be used interchangeably.

Demolinguistics, defined as the study of the relationship between the social use of languages and the demographic reality of its speakers, is a discipline that cuts across all those works which have been interested in linguistic diversity. By its demographic nature, one could argue that the quantitative basis of demolinguistics does not fit easily within the qualitative perspective that prevails in ethnographic or ecolinguistic works, but the truth is that these methods never renounce the elemental task of counting and recounting speakers, which is how their demographic dimension is shown. In fact, the development of demolinguistics is not unconnected to the main lines of diversity analysis, as it quite naturally incorporates fields of study such as linguistic vitality, regional linguistic minorities, migrant communities, or the international dynamics of languages, always with demography as the shared foundation, which illuminates, rather than muddies, the analysis of other aspects of languages and their speakers.

In the study of the world's linguistic diversity, there are three fundamental components that can acquire greater or lesser importance according to the initial epistemology and the particular interests of each investigation. These components are the populations of speakers, the linguistic varieties, and the territories. The speakers are of interest collectively and individually, the varieties are important in all their manifestations, and the territories matter for their distinct configurations and dimensions. Nevertheless, demolinguistics never forgets that the main focus always falls on the populations and their identifying characteristics.

This book, *Language Demography*, is written with the goal of serving as an introductory text for those linguists who wish to delve into the field of demography and those students of social sciences who wish to explore linguistic questions; in both cases the aim is studying populations in relation to their languages, territories, and groupings. For this reason, once the general framework of demolinguistics has been outlined, the text will offer one chapter of linguistic questions and concepts of interest for demographic analysis and another chapter of demographic questions and concepts oriented towards linguistic and sociolinguistic concerns. Understandably, the result might unite students' interests across fields as diverse as sociology, economy, or (of course) ethnography. The work offers numerous examples stemming from different international areas, though it pays particular attention to European and American contexts.

The conceptual outline explained in the first chapters of this book is essential for understanding the factors with greatest influence on the social life of languages and the dynamics of populations and how they function. There's no question that births, deaths, and migrations form the basis of communities of speakers' composition and evolution. However, other factors can affect the vitality of languages, their prestige, their usage, and, in short, the possibilities of their endurance or disappearance. Logically, among the concepts and terms analyzed, "language" and "speaker" stand out, but many others prove to be essential, such as "vitality," "community," or "native speaker," this last term being understood from an updated perspective.

The book's central chapters present the technical core of the demographic layout, detailing both the nature of the data typically handled in the research as well as the sources from which those data are collected. Data and sources are this building's foundations, so much so that any faults found with them have direct repercussions on the sustainability of the research as a whole. The chapter devoted to demolinguistic analysis is fundamental in understanding how to manage, in practical terms, all the concepts and factors presented, keeping in mind both their qualitative dimension and quantitative development. A demographer would most likely find the information offered about demographic facts and ideas to be too simple, along with the graphic representations, with the most common mistakes and biases in demolinguistic practice. However, demographers are not used to focusing their instruments of analysis upon the multiple and, at times, ethereal realities of languages and their speakers. All of this is presented as clearly and rigorously as possible with the goal of mitigating the image projected by the expression "the happy figures of demolinguistics" (Salvador, 1992).

The final chapter offers some of the primary applications of demolinguistics in relation to several basic types of minority and majority languages: ethnic, regional, local, or social minority languages; and national or transnational majority languages. It might be interpreted that placing these sections on the applications of demolinguistics at the end reflects the concession of a lesser importance for that aspect of the research. Nothing could be further from reality. Their position at the close of the work signifies that their applications are the colophon of the studies because, for the most part, they determine the studies. The ultimate goal of demolinguistics is not simply to describe the populations of speakers of some languages, however commendable that task might be; the final goal is to present the results of the analysis in such a way that they have a use, directly or indirectly, within social or community goals, generally through the exercise of linguistic planning and politics. From this perspective, demolinguistics is not a descriptive discipline, but an essential and instrumental one: a resource for linguistic, educational, social, and cultural planning.

Despite the fact that this book presents its contents in the order that's been previously described, the truth is that its chapters and epigraphs enjoy a certain autonomy, such that it's possible to proceed with a non-linear reading, adapted to the needs or conveniences of each person. In this way, those readers who come from the field of linguistics, but who are not familiar with demolinguistics, can begin the book with chapter 1, continue with chapter 5, and then proceed with 3, 4, and 6. If, on the other hand, readers come from the social sciences, they might begin their reading with chapter 7, focused on applications of demolinguistics, and continue with chapter 2 before proceeding with chapters 5 and 6. In the case of demographers and other social scientists, beginning with chapter 7 and then continuing with chapters 5 and 6 is also recommended. In short, if one's interest lies in acquiring knowledge of methodological viewpoints, one can proceed directly to reading chapters 4 and 5. Moreover, the text allows for a "surgical" reading in which it is possible to jump directly from the indexes to the sections or chapters that are of interest at a particular moment. The needs of each reader and the convenience of the instructors who guide students' reading are given the final word on which itinerary to follow.

Finally, *Language Demography* is presented with the clear intention of serving as a bridge between disciplines with distinct epistemological roots. No one denies the differences between minority, regional, national, or transnational languages; no one denies the distance that exists between the language used in a small indigenous community and the use of a language in international forums. However, some languages and others, some situations and others, some populations of speakers and others are bound together, in theory, through the connection of demography and, in practice, by censuses and questionnaires. This introduction has sought to highlight that fact. Indeed, it's possible to present a unifying vision of the multiple ways that exist of understanding linguistic diversity in relation to populations. That vision is based simply on the concepts and methods shared within the space of demolinguistics.

References

Alonso, José Antonio (2006): *Naturaleza económica de la lengua*. Madrid: ICEI.
Bright, William (ed.) (1966): *Sociolinguistics: Proceedings of the UCLA Sociolinguistics Conference 1964*. The Hague: Mouton.
Grin, François (1996): "Economic approaches to language and language planning: an introduction". *International Journal of the Sociology of Language*, 121: 17–44.
Haugen, Einar (1972): *The Ecology of Language*. Stanford: Stanford University Press.
Krauss, Michael (1992): "The world's languages in crisis". *Language*, 68: 4–10.
Salvador, Gregorio (1992): *Política lingüística y sentido común*. Madrid: Istmo.

1
DEMOGRAPHY AND DEMOLINGUISTICS

Demography was born as a discipline in the seventeenth century with Londoner John Graunt's (1662) *Natural and Political Observations*, but it did not receive its current name until the nineteenth century (Schweber, 2006). These milestones don't overshadow the existence of speaker and population censuses from the Roman Empire, especially during the rule of Augustus. Nor do they diminish the relevance of Ibn Khaldun's writings. A Tunisian of Andalusian origin, Khaldun was the author of a universal history whose first volume (*Muqaddima*: Khaldun, 1377) is considered to be a valuable precursor to sociology, the philosophy of history, and demography. Likewise, the emergence of modern demography doesn't undermine the descriptions collected in the Spanish military orders' *Libros de visitas* (ca. 1500) or the censuses instituted by the Spanish monarchy since the sixteenth century called *Vecindarios* (ca. 1500–1700) whose purely demographic components are essential. With all these predecessors, and building upon the experience of John Graunt and Johann Süssmilch (1741), England's Thomas Robert Malthus (1798) came to be considered the father of modern demography with his publication of *An Essay on the Principles of Population* (1798).

In general terms, the very word *demography* conveys the discipline's interests: the study or description (Gr. *graphos*) of peoples (Gr. *demos*). Therefore, its frame of reference is incredibly broad given that the "study" can be undertaken with different goals and methods, and "peoples" can be diverse and analyzed from different perspectives. Nevertheless, demography's primary interest since its beginnings has been the analysis of the size, territorial distribution, and composition of populations, as well as those changes produced as a result of births, deaths, and migrations of peoples.

Demography has received numerous definitions with varying degrees of specification. Most of them have "population" as a central point of reference

DOI: 10.4324/9781003327349-2

and refer to its characteristics with special attention to its size, distribution, and structure, as well as the processes or changes it experiences (Rowland, 2003: 16). The interest in these factors explains why Dudley Kirk (1972) defined demography as a discipline with strong roots in sociology and important ties to economics, statistics, geography, human ecology, medicine, and genetics. Therefore, it is a discipline positioned among different fields rather than an autonomous subject area. In fact, disciplines with the capacity for connecting with demography are even more numerous than those mentioned by Kirk.

It is precisely the interdisciplinary and transversal nature of demography which explains how the ways of developing and applying it are so varied (Reques Velasco, 2011). Thus, there is an "economic demography," which is concerned with the relationships between population and economics: the effects of economic circumstances upon the population, the effects of the population's dynamics upon the economy, the economic implications of migrations, or the consequences for populations due to economic policies, among other aspects. Likewise, there is a "social demography," which is concerned with the relationship between populations and each society's manner of living: the social consequences of population dynamics, such as the increase in life expectancy or the effects of pandemics; the consequences of different ways of life on populations such as those derived from religious beliefs or the effects of changing value systems. In general, social demography is interested in family cycles, given that natality, aging, and mortality are elements strictly tied to societies, their structures, and their dynamics.

Another interesting expression of the subject matter is "historic demography," devoted to the study of ancient populations and their evolution over time, with special attention paid to periods in which there are no registers nor concrete population data. When the conditioning factor is geography, one speaks of "demographic geography," "geodemography," or "demogeography," where the interest lies in all aspects relating to populations in relation to how they appear or are distributed across certain geographies or specific spaces. This task implies both analyzing the processes of population across different territories and representing them cartographically.

When putting any of these possible demographies into practice, the task can be undertaken from two basic but not exclusionary positions: the application of a "qualitative demography" or using a "quantitative demography." In the first case, qualitative analysis allows for precision as to the realities and basic concepts for the demographic study, both in the periods before the analysis and in its discussion and the extraction of conclusions. In the latter, the focus centers on the numeric dimension of the populational factors, so it is also called "mathematical demography." Likewise, demographers usually distinguish between "population studies" and "mathematical or formal demography." The latter includes an area called "demographic analysis," which is interested in a population's stimulation and correction of vital statistics or natural movements (Wachter, 2014).

It could be said that the vast majority of demographic studies include a quantitative component as they are based on specific observations which are often quite detailed. In these cases, statistics is the most helpful discipline for analyzing and interpreting data. When data are scarce or non-existent, mathematics helps create models which aid in understanding or accessing hidden realities. If one keeps in mind the difference between "mathematical models" and "statistical models," it can be said that formal demography relies primarily on the former, whereas population studies work mainly with the latter.

As it is across other disciplines, the aims of each investigation and various approaches open the door to adding supplementary adjectives to demography. Therefore, there is a "theoretical demography" interested in abstract population processes, a "descriptive demography" interested in the description of specific population realities, and an "explicative demography" or "analytical demography" interested in finding the causes of population dynamics and the ways they manifest. On the other hand, geography affects the manner of applying demography, by which one can distinguish between international, national, regional, and local demographies; at the same time, the time frame considered allows for establishing a distinction between population changes over the long term ("slow demography") and those more immediate changes in fecundity and mortality ("fast demography") (Billari, 2022).

Demography's versatility also derives from the nature of the trends that demographic methods reveal. The French demographer Jean Bourgeois-Pichat (1971) adroitly explained that demography is affected by biological phenomena that influence all levels of life (cells, organs, individuals) while it is implicated in sociocultural realities and psychological phenomena. This means that the population processes of fertility, migration, births, and deaths have a clear social dimension, given that they affect the lives of people and societies, which value, appreciate, or interpret them according to specific social and cultural guidelines. These sociocultural guidelines, in turn, can condition population processes. Likewise, the psychological perception of demographic events affects their evolution, just as the nature of those events affects their perception.

Of the three kinds of events highlighted by Bourgeois-Pichat (biological, sociocultural, and psychological), biological events are modified most slowly while psychological experiences are altered most easily and quickly. Sociocultural events present an inertia which, while it doesn't make their modification impossible, does contribute to their greater stability over time. Furthermore, among the most relevant sociocultural experiences, one finds languages are clearly affected by demography given that they are an ability of individuals and an essential driver of social dynamics.

Demolinguistics and Geodemolinguistics

Let us accept, like Bourgeois-Pichat, that demographic structures and dynamics involve biological, sociocultural, and psychological factors. Hence, sociology and anthropology have generated numerous studies that explain how religions, economic cycles, political regimes, education, lifestyles, traditions, and/or family relationships affect demography: the ways of organizing families, of understanding birth and death, as well as of passing down ways of living. Social and cultural factors with the capacity to influence the processes of reproduction, birth, mortality, or migration are very diverse and intimately tied to the psychological perception (individual and collective) of demographic factors.

Within phenomena of a sociocultural nature, language, through numerous languages and the varieties in which they manifest, is one of the most interesting and complex. This is true without its social dimension taking any importance away from its biological and psychological dimensions. When the interests of demographic studies are combined with those of linguistic studies, the opportunity arises to speak of *linguistic demography* or *demolinguistics*. If "sanitary demography," "political demography," "religious demography," or "psychiatric demography" exist, the existence of "linguistic demography" is another dimension which fits perfectly and naturally within demography. In his book *Methods and Models in Demography* (1988) Colin Newell states:

> It is exactly the strongly interdisciplinary nature of demography that makes it so interesting, fertile and productive.
>
> *Newell, 1988*

Demolinguistics has been defined as the study of the relationship between the sociolinguistics of a language and the demographic reality of its real or potential speakers (Ruiz, Sanz, & Solé, 2001). Often, this kind of definition is proposed from the study of minority languages, which is very attentive to the evolution of their numbers of speakers, to the conditions of their social use, and to their possible substitution or shift, usually as a call to attention or a denunciation. Nonetheless, the application of demolinguistics need not restrict itself to minority languages: in fact, it can be applied to any language, whether minority, majority, or international. Additionally, any language can have a majority use in some contexts and a minority one in others: English, while unquestionably very international, can also occupy minority spaces, as is its situation in Egypt, in the same way that Spanish is in the minority in a German context or in Morocco, as Portuguese is in Andorra, or Mandarin Chinese in New York. Likewise, the sociolinguistic determinants can vary greatly for each of the varieties in which the same language manifests. The goals of demolinguistics, therefore, need not be limited to the analyses of the processes of substitution, displacement, or abandonment of languages by one population, but it offers many other possibilities: in principle, all those that have to do with the dynamism, growth, or distribution of the population that is expressed in a particular language or in any of its varieties (Kandler, 2009).

Languages and their uses have a great impact upon human relationships, among other reasons, because the latter are built upon the former. This means that languages can intervene in demographic processes such as the formation and development of homes or migrations: the possibility of communicating in a certain language is one of the factors that receives most weight in the decision to migrate to one geographic area and not another. In this way, languages are a primary element of identity for populations, which is clear when different ethnic groups must coexist, whether within the same community or in border situations. Additionally, ethnic, religious, racial, or social minorities acquire relevance through the maintenance of their heritage languages or their corresponding varieties. But, at the same time, languages help to construct social spaces on an international scale, creating demographic dynamics of continental or transcontinental reach.

The psychological dimension of language also establishes a strong relationship with demography. In this respect, it's worth mentioning questions relating to social and personal bilingualism (its formation and maintenance) or bilingual practices in community life, as well as learning foreign languages (Ó Riagáin, 2002), phenomena which all have important psychological implications, and are present in the lives of individuals, communities, and, in short, the population.

The demographic study of languages needs to go beyond births, deaths, and migrations in order to develop in an adequate way. Languages can be acquired or forgotten, lost or maintained in many different personal and social circumstances which must be kept in mind when practicing demography. There are cases of linguistic acquisition, of maintenance through cultural heritage, and of learning through school that are not directly tied to the factors of birth, death, or migration. In short, languages (and the knowledge and use of them) are not phenomena that are necessarily constant nor homogeneous within the dynamics of populations.

Likewise, in studying the relationship between populations and languages, one observes that there are linguistic attitudes and opinions that have a direct impact on social dynamics, including on demographic events: marriages, adoptions, migrations… etc. Related to beliefs, these attitudes and opinions can either be stable, when they have sufficient sociocultural support, or more short-lived, when they depend on personal or group circumstances. Therefore, linguistic opinions can change quickly within a population.

There are even more connections between languages, psychology, and demography, such as those referred to in the application of IQ tests (these tests include a linguistic component) (Ballantyne, 2002) or those that link a society's language(s) of instruction with poverty rates or birthrates in various social sectors. However, these connections won't be addressed deeply at this stage: firstly, because they are thankfully infrequent; and secondly, because they are topics that belong more properly to sociolinguistics rather than demolinguistics.

Demolinguistics and Geography

Natural languages, as opposed to artificial ones, are those acquired and used in a natural way by speakers and their communities. Therefore, these languages manifest in connection with specific geographies, as happens with events, rates, or demographic variables which adhere to specific areas or geographies, whether these are neighborhoods, a rural or urban center, a province or district, a region, or a country... While it's true that social media and digital communications have allowed languages to be used in an atypical fashion, it's no less true that speakers are still usually bound by certain geographic factors in the construction of their discourses, and their physical contexts condition their communicative resources.

The geographic dimension of social factors and linguistic realities presents some parallels that deserve highlighting; not in vain are individuals/speakers the reference for their mutual analysis. Thus, the population is located within a territory, an area, or a residence, which also implies the placement of language(s) or varieties which that population knows and uses. Likewise, the demographic significance of the distinction between rural and urban is naturally combined with linguistic significance. Similarly, if urbanization and rural depopulation are phenomena of a demographic nature, their linguistic repercussions are no less significant, especially for the appearance or development of new urban varieties and the disappearance or minoritization of specific rural varieties. What's more, mobility between urban centers and their peripheries, as well as intra- or interregional or intra- and international mobility, entails a clear connection between demographic dynamism and linguistic variation and change. Finally, as has already been mentioned, those population movements par excellence (migrations) usually have linguistic repercussions in one way or another, even when questions of language don't figure directly among their causes.

The importance of the link between population and geography becomes evident in the creation and development of a specialty called *geodemography*. It has already been noted that geodemography involves the way in which populations and demographic factors are distributed or produced by a specific geography or space, giving rise to differentiated processes deserving of specific and comparative analysis. By the same turn, the importance of the link between language and geography, tied to the link between language and demography, allows us to speak of *geodemolinguistics*. If every demolinguistic variable or process is located within a geographic space, there is no obstacle to giving priority to the term *geodemolinguistics* over *demolinguistics*, but the latter is much less unwieldy, as is the case with *demography* versus *geodemography*.

Denominations for Demolinguistics

The term *demolinguistics* appears and becomes widespread in the second half of the twentieth century, most notably in the 1970s and '80s. However, the term has not evolved on its own but hand in hand with the phrase *linguistic demography*. The history of these terms can be explored through the graphics and data offered by the online search engine *Ngram Viewer*, which analyzes printed resources published between 1500 and 2018. It is worth briefly reconstructing that history in order to compare the discipline's terminology in English, French, and Spanish.

a. English Denominations

Historically, the English language has used three overlapping terms which come close to the actual meaning of demolinguistics. These variations have been *linguistic demography, language demography,* and *demolinguistics.* For these three terms, the *Ngram Viewer* search engine offers the evolution reflected in the graph (the vertical axis of coordinates indicates frequency of appearance in printed resources). In the graph, it can be observed that the use of three variants began to be quantitatively notable in the 1970s and that *demolinguistics* is clearly the most recent of the three to appear in English.

Among the oldest uses in the English language, one finds *linguistic demography,* which appeared in 1877, a few years after the use of *demography* in the modern sense. The term appeared in a New York publication (*Frank Leslie's Illustrated Newspaper*: 20 October, p. 107), included in an advertisement for an anthropological exhibit that would include maps and charts related to "*linguistic demography.*" This specific use brings us back to a discipline interested in languages, generally indigenous ones, in relation to speaker populations and their geographies. This anthropological interpretation of *linguistic demography* also appears in later works as significant as the first volume of the magazine *Anthropological Linguistics* (1959), which explains:

> Issues of *linguistic demography* are also addressed, including the percentage of Inuit who still speak their native language to be found in each settlement and geographic area.

The term *linguistic demography* has endured over time within the field of anthropology and in reference to minority languages: in 1978, for example, Geoffrey Pullum used it in his article "Language and genocide," at a time when its properly demolinguistic meaning was beginning to prevail, as well as the variations *demolinguistics* and *language demography.* This latter term had its greatest usage in the first decade of the twenty-first century, but it finally seems to have ceded its position to *linguistic demography* and, finally, to *demolinguistics.*

b. French Denominations

The rise in frequency of use of English terms for demolinguistics coincides with that of the alternatives used in French: *démographie linguistique* and *démolinguistique.* The latter term arose in the 1970s and reached its peak in the '90s, although it currently remains the preferred term. As for *démographie linguistique,* it was popularized principally during the 1980s, but its use can be traced back to the

Demography and Demolinguistics 13

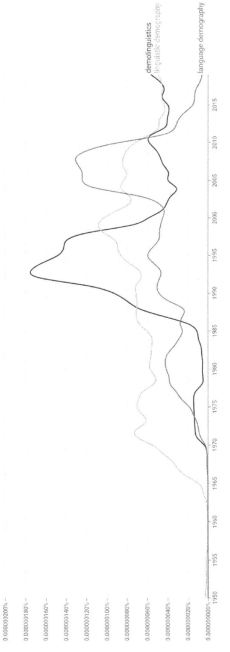

GRAPH 1.1 Ngram Viewer results for *demolinguistics*, *linguistic demography*, and *language demography* (volume usage).

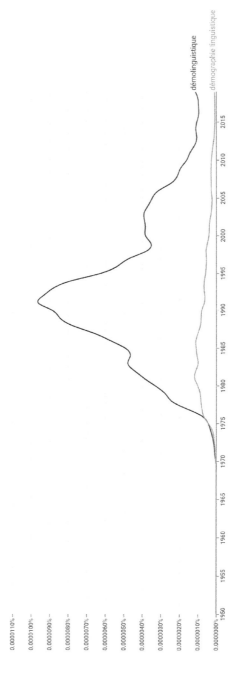

GRAPH 1.2 Ngram Viewer results for *démolinguistique* and *démographie linguistique* (volume usage).

1940s and '50s, with a meaning tied to anthropology and therefore closely related to its English equivalent (*linguistic demography*).

Coinciding dates in the expansion of English and French denominations in the 1970s prove relevant as we'll also see the same trend in Spanish. What is the reason for this coincidence? The explanation has its origin in Canada's linguistic situation, specifically that of the province of Québec. The 1960s were a significant decade for the forging of Canadian identity. During this period, what's referred to as the "Quiet Revolution" took place in which languages and identities played a special role. In 1965, the Canadian flag with the maple leaf in its center was officialized, and in 1963 the "Royal Commission on Bilingualism and Biculturalism" (also called the "Bi and Bi Commission") was constituted with the goal of investigating Canada's linguistic and cultural situation. Its recommendations were published between 1965 (preliminary) and 1970, and as of 1971, the government began their implementation. In that same period, the separatist movement of Québec intensified through the actions of the Parti Québécois political party. Finally, in 1968, the Official Languages Act (Loi sur les langues officielles) concerning English and French came into effect, turning Canada into an officially bilingual country (De Vries, 1994).

Among its immediate consequences, this sociopolitical situation inspired the beginnings and further development of studies devoted expressly to linguistic demography, given that one of the goals of the "Bi and Bi Commission" was to investigate and analyze the state of bilingualism and biculturalism in Canada. The commission's report used the term *démographie linguistique* (1967), but this hotbed of development was ideal for the generalized dissemination of the term *démolinguistique* which easily spread to the English language with its equivalent. In 1974, the work *Linguistic Composition of the Nations of the World*, edited by Heinz Kloss and Grant McConnell, was already expressly referring to the "domaine de recherche nouveau d'une science appelée *démolinguistique*."

c. Spanish Denominations

The terms used in Spanish (*demolingüística* and *demografía lingüística*) run parallel with French and English usages. As happened in those other languages, Spanish began to use these variations in the 1970s. However, in the case of European Spanish, contributing circumstances related to the plurilingual state of Spain also arose. The death of Francisco Franco in 1975 gave rise to what is called the "Spanish Transition" (transición política española) in which both the bilingual territories of Spain and their respective languages played a significant role. This circumstance led to publications about the linguistic situation of Spain in which "demolinguistic" questions immediately flourished, especially after 1983, the year in which laws of linguistic normalization in communities such as Catalonia, Galicia, the Basque Country, Navarra, Valencia, and the Balearic Islands came into effect. With the influence of the Canadian experience, these circumstances

16 Demography and Demolinguistics

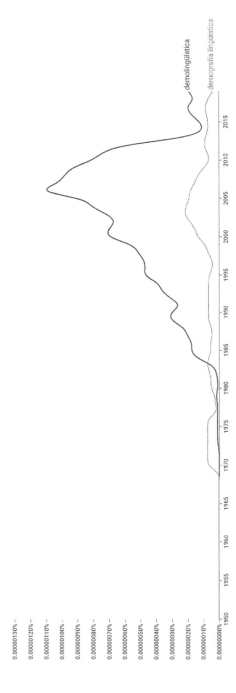

GRAPH 1.3 Ngram Viewer results for *demolingüística* and *demografía lingüística* (volume usage).

favored the use of the concept of "demografía lingüística" and opened the door to the term *demolingüística*, related primarily to the knowledge and use of Spain's minority languages or, in other words, the historic languages of each of its territories (Siguán, 1992).

It's interesting to observe that the peak of the use of *demolingüística* in Spanish takes place in the first decade of the twenty-first century. This high point coincides with that of the term *language demography* in English. However, the reasons don't seem to coincide. In the case of English, the frequency of use reflected the publication of studies dedicated to diverse linguistic and cultural situations around the world, as well as an interest in aspects of international educational and communication. In the case of Spanish, the publication of the *Anuario del Instituto Cervantes*, starting in 1998, played a role, as it was systematically interested in demographic questions. Of similar influence was the launch of the project "El valor económico del español" (The Economic Value of Spanish), coordinated by José Luis García Delgado, José Antonio Alonso, and Juan Carlos Jiménez, whose results began to be published in 2007. In projects such as this, demolinguistics shows its utility for understanding the situation of international languages, in combination with that of minority languages (García Delgado, Alonso, & Jiménez, 2007; Moreno-Fernández & Otero Roth, 2009).

A very brief note about Italian must be added to these observations on English, French, and Spanish terms. It relates to the use of *demolinguistica* to refer to questions that affect the relationship between dialectal varieties and popular culture, or the social history of culture, without the express intention of quantifying populations of speakers. From the perspective of a group of Italian scholars (Toschi, 1962; Bronzini 1978), popular culture is an area of operations common among "demologists" (experts in popular culture) and "dialectologists" (experts in popular speech), in a natural convergence between "demolinguistics," also called "ethnolinguistics," and "demodialectology," which is interested in popular traditions and dialects or, more specifically, in the dialectal dimension of the popular world. As can be easily deduced, this connotation of the Italian term *demolingüística* remains somewhat outside our main area of interest.

The Precursors of Demolinguistics

The history of culture reveals many episodes of interest surrounding the knowledge of languages within territories. Each year during the Zhou dynasty in China, the feudal lord sent a man in a light cart pulled by horses to visit every corner of the Chinese territory with the goal of gathering the words and linguistic usages characteristic of each region. This information made it possible (a few centuries later in year 9 during the Han dynasty) for a Chinese writer, philosopher, and poet named Yan Xiong to create what is perhaps the world's first work of historical dialectology. This work was called *The Fāngyán*, although its complete title would be equivalent to "Local expressions of other countries in times immemorial explained by the Light-Carriage Messenger." It is the first known case in the history of humanity of a field investigation of actively spoken languages and linguistic variations which also includes demolinguistic information.

It's obvious that many population censuses made in antiquity or the Middle Ages allowed for deductions to be made about languages spoken by one people or another. In this same sense, much of the information offered by the geographic and statistical dictionaries of the nineteenth century, like the one made by Pascual Madoz for Spain (1846–1850) would be useful. However, it could be said that linguistic demography didn't begin to take shape as a specialty with aspirations of scientific rigor until the conceptual inclusion of languages in population censuses. As has already been mentioned, population censuses are the fundamental meeting point between linguists, demographers, and statisticians.

Belgium was the first country to introduce "language(s) of the speaker(s)" as a category on its official census. This was in 1846, and the initiative was followed by Prussia and Switzerland in 1850. The International Conference on Statistics held in Brussels in 1853 organized a session on the topic of "spoken language" (*langue parlée*), which it proposed as one of the items that should be obligatory for inclusion in a standardized census questionnaire. However, the primary intention of that interest wasn't in the languages themselves, but in the definition of the concept of "nationality," which was crucial at the time (Kertzer & Arel, 2001). The interpretive possibilities were diverse: the French, in keeping with the spirit of their revolution, conceived of the nation as a unified political entity; later it spoke of territory delimited by frontiers; whereas the Germans advocated for the nation understood as a cultural community. In all these interpretations, languages appear as a determining factor, hence the interest in the study of linguistic communities. This was considered true to such a degree that in the Conference on Statistics held in Saint Petersburg in 1866, it was concluded that language was the most important deciding factor of nationality.

While it's true that the first recommendation of statisticians was to use the phrase *langue parlée* to refer to the language of the censuses, it was soon seen that the formulation didn't distinguish between the familiar and public uses of language. This ambiguity inspired them to propose "language spoken in habitual interaction" as an alternative. In some cases, this has been interpreted as "mother tongue," as happened in Russia; in other cases, it was interpreted as "language of use," to give an example from Austria. In any event, neither of these options used on various censuses managed to resolve the controversy.

It could be said that many of these initiatives were contemplated by demolinguists *avant la lettre*, even if their primary concern was statistics, politics, or engineering. But there has also historically been an interest in the relationship between languages, populations, and geography in the field of linguistics after its emergence as a modern discipline in the nineteenth century, although in most cases this interest doesn't, strictly speaking, take a demographic perspective.

Linguistics has taken an interest in the origin and distribution of languages throughout the world (Ruhlen, 1994). Thus, the spread of languages in prehistory has been explained as a succession of population waves that originated in central western Asia. According to the linguist Mauricio Swadesh (1966), around the year 25 million BCE, there were a dozen protolanguages scattered across the world, among which would be Indo-European in Europe and Asia, and Macro-Caribbean in the Americas. This leaves aside large uninhabited areas and zones which might have used languages already lost by then. Colin Renfrew (1987, 2007), for his part, outlined four periods of population spread based on technological and climactic factors. In the first period, 100,000 years ago, humans, along with their languages, began to spread out from Africa until they probably reached the habitable areas of the Pacific archipelagoes. At the same time, Johanna Nichols (1992) proposed as a hypothesis that the distribution of languages around the world is correlated with successive settlements of populations which took place in four large waves, originating first in Africa and shifting to Asia in a lateral movement, such that each new wave displaced the previous ones toward the East. Naturally, none of these hypotheses works with exact data of peoples, languages, or places.

In Rome at the end of the eighteenth century and beginning of the nineteenth, the Spanish Jesuit Lorenzo Hervás y Panduro decided to compile the available information about all known languages. To do so, he relied on first-hand information gathered from many Jesuit colleagues who had been missionaries in different parts of the world. That is how Hervás y Panduro came to publish, between 1800 and 1805, the *Catálogo de las lenguas de las naciones conocidas* (*Catalog of the Languages of the Known Nations*). In this catalog, he demonstrated the existence of the family of Indo-European languages 25 years before the German Franz Bopp, considered to be the founder of comparative linguistics, and established, for the first time, the genetic relationship between various Semitic languages, the connection between Basque and Iberian, and the existence of the Malay-Polynesian and Finno-Ugric linguistic families. Alongside this linguistic information, the *Catálogo* included notes on geographic localizations and populations, although with unequal and incomplete data. Thus, about the Guaraní and Pericú peoples, the latter settled in California, he explained the following:

> The Guaraní language is spoken in the thirty populations of the missions called Guaranís (in which there were more than eighty-eight thousand people in 1767, the year when the Jesuits were forced to abandon them) belonging to the dioceses of Buenos Aires and of the Asunción del Paraguay.
> *Hervás y Panduro, 1800–1805: 141*

> Plagues and misfortunes have almost extinguished the Pericú nation which, at the start of this century, consisted of three thousand souls, and at the time of our expulsion from the Spanish domains might have been three hundred. As they all speak Spanish, the Pericú language must already be considered extinct.
> *Hervás y Panduro, 1800–1805: 348*

Closer to our time, dialectology is the linguistic discipline which has established the closest relationships with speakers and their territories. This discipline is interested in the variations shown among languages, within their different levels, and within distinct geographic and social spaces. Dialectal studies are often based on data offered by linguistic atlases: collections of maps which present the varieties of specific linguistic traits. These atlases are developed based on techniques of linguistic geography or geolinguistics, a specialty which should not be confused with the homonymous discipline that is interested in the distribution of languages (Mackey, 1973).

Knowledge accumulated from dialectal studies allows many of the theoretical questions essential to demolinguistics to be addressed, especially how many speakers dominate any particular variety. The same can be said with regard to sociolinguistics, a discipline concerned with the influence of social and contextual factors that affect the use of different profiles of speakers. However, a basic difference between dialectology and sociolinguistics, on the one hand, and demolinguistics, on the other, is that the first treats the social and cultural factors (including population) as attributes of the languages or, at least, as factors that affect them, whereas for demolinguistics, languages are attributes of their populations.

Within each of these linguistic disciplines, there are branches or trends in which attention to languages, their speakers, and territories are expressed in more specific ways. Thus, for example, there is a perceptual dialectology (Preston, 1999, 2011) which is concerned with speakers' opinions of the distance perceived between their own way of speaking and that of other regions located at different distances. This line is associated with what is called perceptual geography, a branch of human geography that analyzes the mental images and perceptions inhabitants of a place have of their own geographic space versus that of others.

Some experts in dialectology and sociolinguistics have taken a more specific interest in demographic questions in a more current sense. In dialectology, Morillo-Velarde Pérez (2003) has practiced a "dialectal demolinguistics" with the goal of calibrating the volume of speakers which use some specific linguistic features, whereas Moreno-Fernández (2009) speaks of "demodialectology" to refer to the demography of the dialectal varieties of any language. As can be imagined, this "demodialectology" (really demography) has nothing to do with the Italian "demodialectology," which is more demological and concerned with the cultures of peoples. As for sociolinguistics, among its many manifestations, one finds what is called "sociology of language," which in turn makes up the field of "linguistic politics and planning," from which questions relating to demolinguistics are addressed, when they're not based directly on demolinguistics. Later chapters will return to these fields in reference to both basic concepts of linguistics and the applications of demolinguistics.

Summary

Demography has received numerous definitions. The majority of these have "population" as a central reference point and allude to its structure and evolving dynamics. Demography's versatility stems from the nature of the phenomena that demographic factors entail: biological, sociocultural, and psychological. These characteristics create important links between demography and sociology, economy, statistics, geography, human ecology, medicine, and genetics.

When the interests of demographic studies are combined with those of linguistic studies, the possibility of speaking of *linguistic demography* or *demolinguistics* arises. The term *demolinguistics* spread during the second half of the twentieth century, starting in the 1960s and '70s. As for linguistics, there has historically been an interest in the relationship between languages, populations, and geography, but this interest had not adopted a demographic perspective until a few decades ago.

Natural languages spread within specific geographies to such an extent that demographic rates or indices affect the populations who speak those languages. Languages, as a human characteristic, have the ability to intervene in demographic processes such as the formation of homes or migrations. At the same time, population dynamics directly influence the configuration of communities and their languages' vitality. Population censuses are the fundamental meeting point in understanding the connection between linguists, demographers, and statisticians.

References

Ballantyne, Paul F. (2002): *Psychology, Society, and Ability Testing (1859–2002): Transformative Alternatives to Mental Darwinism and Interactionism.* York: York University. www.cyberus.ca/~pballan/Toc1.htm. [Retrieved: 01.09.2021]

Billari, Francesco C. (2022): "Demography: fast and slow". *Population and Development Review*, 48: 9–30. https://doi.org/10.1111/padr.12464

Bourgeois-Pichat, Jean (1971): *La démographie.* Paris: Gallimard.

Bronzini, Giovanni Battista (1978): "Demolinguistica e storia della cultura". *Lares*, 44: 503–506.

De Vries, John (1994): "Canada's official language communities: an overview of the current demolinguistic situation". *International Journal of Sociology of Language*, 1994: 37–68.

García Delgado, José Luis, José Antonio Alonso and Juan Carlos Jiménez (2007): *Economía del español: una introducción.* Barcelona: Ariel.

Graunt, John (1662): *Natural and Political Observations.* London.

Hervás y Panduro, Lorenzo (1800–1805): *Catálogo de las lenguas de las naciones conocidas.* Madrid: Administración del Real Arbitrio de Beneficencia.

Kandler, Anne (2009): "Demography and language competition". *Human Biology*, 81: 181–210.

Kertzer, David and Dominique Arel (eds.) (2001): *Census and Identity: the Politics of Race, Ethnicity, and Language in National Censuses.* Cambridge: Cambridge University Press.

Khaldun, Ibn (1377), *The Muqaddima.* Trans. de Franz Rosenthal. https://delong.typepad.com/files/muquaddimah.pdfss

Kirk, Dudley (1972): *Genetic Implications of Demographic Trends*. New York: Macmillan.
Kloss, Heinz and Grant McConnell (eds.) (1974–1984): *Linguistic Composition of the Nations of the World*, vol. 2, *North America*. Québec: Presses de l'Université Laval.
Mackey, William F. (1973): *Three Concepts for Geolinguistics*. Québec: CIRB Publications.
Malthus, Robert (1798): *An Essay on the Principles of Population*. London: J. Johnson.
Moreno-Fernández, Francisco (2009): *La lengua española en su geografía*. Madrid: ArcoLibros.
Moreno-Fernández, Francisco and Jaime Otero Roth (2009): *Atlas de la lengua española en el mundo*. 3rd ed. Barcelona: Ariel.
Morillo-Velarde Pérez, Ramón (2003): "Esbozo de demolingüística dialectal andaluza". In J.L. Girón, F.J. Herrero, S. Iglesias, A. Narbona (eds.), *Estudios ofrecidos al profesor José Jesús de Bustos Tovar*. Vol. I. Madrid: Universidad Complutense, pp. 767–803.
Newell, Colin (1988): *Methods and Models in Demography*. New York: Guilford Press.
Nichols, Johanna (1992): *Linguistic Diversity in Space and Time*. Chicago: University of Chicago Press.
Preston, Dennis R. (1999): *Handbook of Perceptual Dialectology: Volume 1*. Amsterdam: John Benjamins.
Preston, Dennis (2011): "Perceptual dialectology in the 21st Century". In C.A. Anders, M. Hundt and A. Lasch (eds), *Perceptual dialectology: neue Wege der Dialektologie*. Berlin: Mouton–de Gruyter, pp. 1–30.
Pullum, Geoffrey K. (1978): "Language and genocide". *Survival International Review*, 3: 16–17.
Renfrew, Colin (1987): *Archaeology and Language: The Puzzle of Indo-European Origins*. London: Pimlico.
Renfrew, Colin (2007): *Prehistory: The Making of the Human Mind*. London: Weidenfeld & Nicholson.
Reques Velasco, Pedro (2011): *Geodemografía: fundamentos conceptuales y metodológicos*. Santander: Universidad de Cantabria.
Ó Riagáin, Pádraig (2002): "The Consequences of Demographic Trends for Language Learning and Diversity", *Guide for the Development of Language Education Policies in Europe from Linguistic Diversity to Plurilingual Education Reference Study*. Strasbourg: Council of Europe.
Rowland, Donald (2003): *Demographic Methods and Concepts*. Oxford: Oxford University Press.
Ruhlen, Merritt (1994): *The Origin of Language: Tracing the Evolution of the Mother Tongue*. New York: John Wiley & Sons.
Ruiz i San Pascual, Francesc, Rosa Sanz i Ribelles, Jordi Solé i Camardons (2001): *Diccionari de sociolingüística*. Barcelona: Enciclopedia Catalana.
Schweber, Libby (2006): *Disciplining Statistics: Demography and Vital Statistics in France and England, 1830–1885*. Durham: Duke University Press, pp. 35–48.
Siguán Soler, Miguel (1992): *España plurilingüe*. Madrid: Alianza.
Süssmilch, Johann (1741): *Die göttliche Ordnung in den Veränderungen des menschlichen Geschlechts*. Berlin: Spener.
Swadesh, Mauricio (1966): *El lenguaje y la vida humana*. México: FCE.
Toschi, Paolo (1962): *Guida allo studio delle tradizioni popolari*. Turin: Boringhieri.
Wachter, Kenneth (2014): *Essential Demographic Methods*. Cambridge: Harvard University Press.

2
LINGUISTICS FOR DEMOGRAPHERS

Logically, the study of populations in relation to some of their attributes (physical or psychological, individual or societal) requires the knowledge to handle the concepts and dynamics associated with them. Effectively, if "medical demography" exists, it is to be hoped that those who study it would be familiar with the categories and concepts relating to health; if "political demography" exists, one would hope that its scholars would be familiar with political science; if "religious demography" exists, it would be natural for experts in religion and anthropology to be involved; if a "psychiatric demography" exists, it is to be hoped that its scholars know psychiatry. In the same way, if a "linguistic demography" exists, it cannot disregard the conceptualizations and arguments offered by linguistics.

In the case of linguists, if one cannot assume training in demographic matters, the training of demographers in linguistic matters should not be assumed either. With great intellectual honesty, the demographer Anna Cabré states in "Factors demogràfics en l'ús de la llengua: el cas de Catalunya" (1995):

> De les dues parts que té el títol de la meva intervenció, factors demografics i ús de la llengua, jo cree que fóra prudent que em centrés en la primera, és adir, en la referent a demografia, que és del que puc pretendre saber alguna cosa, o almenys del que se suposa que hauria de saberne, mentre que la qüestió de l'ús de la llengua no és directament el meu ambit de treball. D'altra banda, hi ha molts ponents qualificats sobre aquest aspecte que parlaran més endavant. Jo, dones, em centraré en el tema demografic i, en tot cas, haré al·lusions breus a les conseqüencies que té en l'ús de la llengua, segons el meu parer, que no sé si és un parer de demografa o només un parer personal, d'Anna Cabré.

DOI: 10.4324/9781003327349-3

> Of the two components contained in my work's title, demographic factors and the use of language, I think it would be prudent for me to focus on the former; that is to say, on those factors relating to demography which is what I can claim to know something about. At least, demography is what I'm supposed to have deep knowledge of, whereas questions about the use of language are not directly within my field of study. I [...] will focus on demographic issues and, in any event, will make brief allusions to the consequences it has on the use of language. Though I don't know if this is my opinion as a demographer or just a personal opinion of Anna Cabré the individual.
>
> *Cabré, 1995*

Needless to say, it's inevitable that specialists across various disciplines allude to language and its uses when language and languages issues cut across disciplines as seemingly disparate as psychiatry and philosophy; music and geography; neurology and demography. But it's one thing to "allude" to questions of language from a certain perspective and something very different to "know" the concepts that must be handled as units or basic factors of the analysis. In this sense, for the practice of a demography of languages, the approximation to fundamental notions of linguistics proves inescapable.

However, even if linguistics might be defined generically as a "science or scientific study of language," it doesn't present itself as a homogeneous or one-note discipline, but rather as a set of scientific approaches to language. As it concerns a human reality, it is not surprising that language can be approached using different perspectives, different theoretical models, and alternative methodologies. And each of these offers a catalog of concepts and methods which are ultimately not alien to the practice of demolinguistics.

When it comes to understanding linguistic demography, it's prudent to pay heed to the contributions made from general linguistics, the psychology of language, and the sociology of language, as well as from geolinguistics, ecolinguistics, or language policy. In one way or another, all these fields of study of language deal with tasks of linguistic demography. To begin with, in order to quantify the speakers of a language, what is called a "language" and what is called a "speaker" should be clear. In Germany, there would probably be controversy in deciding whether an individual is a speaker of what is popularly understood as standard German because of the possibility that German incorporates dialectal elements; likewise, one could argue about whether a second-generation Hispanic in the United States is a Spanish speaker or not because of the possibility of mixing elements of English and Spanish (let us say "Spanglish"). Likewise, when analyzing the use of a language, it's impossible to ignore where, with whom, and why that language is spoken. Any count of languages and speakers could be confusing or chaotic, if not impossible, if the multiplicity of possible linguistic and social contexts is not considered.

Fundamental Linguistic Concepts

Among the questions that have just been presented, one is fundamental to any demolinguistic analysis. This is determining what should or should not be considered a "language;" that is to say, what attributes must a language possess in order to be one, and what characteristics must a "speaker" have in order to be one? Let us remember that the first censuses interested in "languages spoken" were conceived according to different visions and national interests. The question is so decisive that it must be tackled directly and immediately. Although important nuances will be introduced later, it is convenient to begin with a very general definition of "language."

> Language. N. The system of spoken or written communication used by a particular country, people, community, etc., typically consisting of words used within a regular grammatical and syntactic structure.
>
> *Oxford English Dictionary* (oed.com). *s.v.*

"Speaker," in turn, would simply be the person who speaks the language. In linguistics, however, these definitions are clearly insufficient, as Suzanne Romaine qualifies (1994: 12).

> The very concept of discrete languages is probably a European cultural artefact fostered by processes such as literacy and standardization. Any attempt to count distinct languages will be an artefact of classificatory procedures rather than a reflection of communicative practices.
>
> *Romaine, 1994*

These few lines include two crucial elements for understanding this concept: "standardization" and "communicative practices." In effect, languages are standardized systems, and "standardization" consists of the external endowment of linguistic and social codes that facilitate communication within a community which generally accepts them by consensus. That standardization is imposed in the form of orthographies, grammars, and dictionaries reveals the importance of writing (even if writing is not essential in order for a language to exist as a recognizable reality). "Consensus" implies collective acceptance and awareness; a language exists when the speakers value, believe, and perceive that it exists. In the same way, "communicative practices" are the concrete uses that speakers make of languages in real contexts.

How languages conceive of their own existence is decisive in their social recognition. Popular opinion is usually in opposition to expert opinion on this point. For linguists, reality is made up of "linguistic or communicative practices," in contextualized uses, which share a greater or lesser number of characteristics. When the practices of one group or community of speakers is recognized as common, these come to be categorized or perceived as a variety or as a language, which is the moment when its standardization or normalization can take place. This supposes that any natural linguistic manifestation is an expression of a language, regardless of its social, historic, or geographic consideration. The common perception and consensus about the traits shared by some linguistic practices allow us to speak of "languages" recognizable as such and ready to be labeled as such. Therefore, in linguistics, a language is a reality constructed from the bottom up.

Popular opinion, however, takes for granted the prior and external existence of a reality called *language*, normalized and used in an exemplary way by those who have access to it; that is to say, the "exemplary" speakers (academics, journalists, professors, high-level professionals, etc.). On the other hand, the "non-exemplary speakers" ("normal" speakers) use language in a way that is "normal" and not elevated, from a linguistic and social perspective. When the use of a language is considered to fall outside the "normal," it's because it falls into the categories of "language with mistakes" (that of learners) or "dialect" (speakers of other regions). In this case, language is a reality constructed from the top down (Preston, 1999).

As noted earlier, these differences in conceptions, perceptions, and practices explain how, socially, it is possible to harbor doubts about the categorization (or labeling) of linguistic realities. Thus, for example, doubts arise as to whether the linguistic use of certain Hispanic groups in the United States should be considered a language in its own right or whether it should be ascribed to the construct called Spanish. The same could be said of the Filipino variety called *Chavacano* in relation to Spanish, the variety of English used by Koreans called *Konglish* (*Korean English*), or the kind of relationship the so-called "Frisian languages" maintain among themselves in Germany and the Netherlands; are they the same language or different languages?

These linguistic questions demonstrate the need to establish some basic differences among various concepts used by linguistics which are decisive for demolinguistic analysis. These are the concepts of "standard language," "creole language," and "dialect."

Types of Linguistic Varieties

One way of defining the concepts of "standard language," "creole language," and "dialect" could be through four attributes established by William Stewart in 1962: *standardization, autonomy, historicity,* and *vitality*. *Standardization* consists of having a codification (that is, an orthography, grammar, and dictionaries) which determine correct and incorrect usage in the practice of a linguistic variety. *Autonomy* is an attribute referring to the distinct degree of uniqueness, singularity, or independence of a linguistic variety with respect to other varieties. *Historicity* is perceived in those varieties that have developed over the course of time, which are generally tied to a national or ethnic tradition. *Vitality* has to do with social use and the number of native speakers of a variety. As will be explained, this final attribute has been one of the most controversial, as well as the most decisive, in the study of linguistic communities and their demography.

For the four attributes or criteria outlined above, the following definitions might be proposed:

Language (standard): a variety which has a standardization accepted by the community, autonomy from other varieties, a recognized historicity, and a stable vitality. Examples: English, French, Spanish, Mandarin, Russian, Arabic…

Creole Language / Creole: a variety that doesn't have a standardization (at least, one accepted by the community), nor a clear autonomy with regard to other varieties, nor a recognized historicity, but does have a stable vitality; creoles arise from sociolinguistic contact between two varieties. When this contact is prolonged and stable, it gives rise to native speakers and a community of speakers. Examples: San Andrés–Providencia Creole (Colombia), Annobonese Creole (Equatorial Guinea), French Creole (Venezuela)…

Dialect: a variety which doesn't have a specific standardization, nor a clear autonomy with regard to other varieties, although it might enjoy a recognized historicity and a stable vitality. Examples: Canary Islands dialect (Spanish), Jamaican English, Maghrebi French…

However, the limits of this conceptual distinction immediately blur when one considers:

- The precariousness of our knowledge about the vast majority of the varieties of the world in terms of their linguistic nature and social use.
- The difficulty in establishing or discovering objective limits between close varieties.
- The subjective perception of the varieties, their autonomy and historicity, by their own speakers and by outsiders.
- The diversity of social settings in which some same varieties might develop.

This is because the attributes of autonomy, historicity, and vitality are relevant to the degree to which they are perceived subjectively. Even standardization, externally verifiable, can be valued in different ways in terms of its existence and social incidence, given that there are varieties which have a standardization that is not respected nor appreciated socially. This explains the existence of blurred borders between standardized and creole languages or between languages and dialects.

Effectively, the distinction between standard languages and creoles is not always obvious, and this is true for several reasons. One factor is that many varieties of clearly creole origin have a standardization that allows for their normalized presence in schools or the media, as is the case with Haitian Creole. In this case, such varieties warrant treatment as standard languages (Garvin, 1959). In addition, the autonomy and historicity of some creoles might be even more perceptible or evident than in the many varieties considered to be differentiated languages, as might be the case with Nordic languages: Danish, Norwegian, and Swedish. Nevertheless, the perception of creole languages' autonomy can vary according to their degree of closeness to the European languages that contributed to their creation (bearing the generic name of "acrolects:" French, English, Portuguese, Spanish, Dutch etc.) or according to the distinct phases of post-creolization or de-creolization in which a creole finds itself (Hymes, 1971; Sebba, 1997; Thomason & Kaufman, 1988; Mufwene, 2005; McWhorter, 2018). In any event, all languages, including those with the highest level of standardization, acknowledge the influence of their contacts with other varieties, by which it could be said that all languages in one way or another are somewhat creole.

On the other hand, if standardization is an apparently clear criterion for the identification of a language, the argument founders when one considers that there are many varieties which, despite being standardized with orthography, grammars, and dictionaries, have predominantly oral and not written use. In writing, such varieties gives way to others, especially in public communication, as happens in Belize where Kriol often yields to English in writing and public spaces. What's more, there might be competent speakers who don't know how to write their language, no matter how standardized it is, as is the case of illiterate or semi-illiterate peoples. Likewise, many varieties exist without having their own standardization despite being used by populations of enormous size, as is the case of Wu in China with its nearly 80 million speakers. This latter fact reveals that, with a view to demolinguistic practice, the varieties (languages) analyzed don't necessarily need to be standardized. Keep in mind that a minimum of 45% of the roughly 7,000 languages and dialects that exist in the world don't have any written form (Eberhard, Simons, & Fennig, 2022), which might rise to 90% (UIA, 2021) depending on which sources are used.

Linguistic Distances: Intercomprehension

As they are tied to a large degree to their historicity, when it comes to the autonomy of varieties, there is a very significant factor that led Heinz Kloss (1967) to distinguish between *Abstand* languages, which are linguistically distant and difficult for mutual intelligibility, and A*usbau* languages, differentiated for sociopolitical reasons and not so much for their linguistic distance. The problem lies in adequately establishing or measuring the distances which affect the intercomprehension or intelligibility between varieties. For instance, it's easy to appreciate the distance between languages like Basque and French or between Japanese and Chinese, clearly unintelligible between each other (A*bstand*) because they belong to different linguistic families, but it's not as easy to pinpoint the relative distance that might exist between languages such as Danish, Swedish, and Norwegian, or Bosnian, Serbian, and Croatian (A*usbau*); or even among dialectal varieties of the same language, like Dominican and Puerto Rican Spanish.

The distance, intercomprehension, or intelligibility between languages has been a matter of interest for linguists and non-linguists for decades. Linguist Henri Guiter (1973) tried to quantify the degree of intercomprehension between two linguistic areas according to the number of coinciding traits and proposed a hierarchy based on the coincidences of features located in sets of maps from linguistic atlases. In this way, by analyzing varieties used in two different areas or locales, Guiter established the following criteria:

If the differences are 80% or 90%, they are different languages.
If the differences are between 50 and 80%, they are different dialects.
If the differences are between 30 and 50%, they are different subdialects.
If the differences are between 20 and 30%, we're dealing with different speech.
If the differences are between 15 and 20%, we're dealing with different sub-speech.

Guiter, 1973

The calculation of distances has also been practiced using computer resources. Thus, the initiative *eLinguistics* offers a tool that establishes the proximity between languages based on the comparison of a series of key words and the analysis of their vocalism and consonantism. The result is the measurement of the distance between pairs of languages (a total of 220) expressed with a numerical value between 0 (null distance) and 100 (maximum distance). For example, the distance between Serbian and Croatian has a value of 2.8; between Dutch and German, 18.7; between Spanish and Catalan, 25.5; between English and German, 30.8; and between Chinese and Japanese, 81.5.

A parallel initiative with a lexicostatistical basis is called the "Automated Similarity Judgement Program" (ASJP), which consists of a database that contains lists of 40 words from numerous languages of the world. Comparison between these lists allows for the calculation of a "lexical distance" which can be useful for various tasks, such as classifying linguistic families or investigating the antiquity of the divergences between languages (Wichmann, Holman, & Brown, 2020).

On the other hand, the economics of language has also focused on the distances between languages as a factor that affects various transactions, such as those related to investing in the learning of foreign languages. Thus, the economists Barry Chiswick and Paul Miller (2005) proposed a measurement of linguistic distance based on observations about the quickness with which a second language is acquired in immersion situations. In particular, their study analyzed the acquisition of English by immigrants arriving in the USA and Canada from different linguistic origins. Another proposal was made by Ginsburgh, Melitz, and Toubal (2015), who put forward an econometric analysis of learning foreign languages in 193 countries in which the distance between the language of the learners and the language learned was included as one of five explicative factors. They used the aforementioned ASJP database.

However, it turns out that intercomprehension does not only depend on linguistic factors, but also on processes of a sociolinguistic and psycholinguistic nature. In linguistic distance, not everything is a question of the number of differences, because some might be more significant than others, as many linguistic phenomena do not manifest solely as present or absent, but rather in a variable fashion. Semi-bilingualism consists of learning a language without coming to speak it; that is to say, productive monolingualism and receptive bilingualism (Hockett, 1958). This is without considering other factors such as the affinity between cultures, the psychological nearness between speakers, or the degree of social acceptance or rejection of both individuals and their ways of communicating. As a consequence, distance can function more as perceived reality than as calculated reality, so it is no surprise that doubts arise about the most convenient labeling for each case when it comes to languages and dialects. Suzanne Romaine again comments (1994: 14):

> Situations in which there is widespread agreement as to what constitutes a language arise through the interaction of social, political, psychological, and historical factors and are not due to any inherent properties of the varieties concerned.
>
> *Romaine, 1994*

When demography confronts objects of a linguistic nature, the concepts and arguments mentioned up to this point become unusable. This means it's necessary to determine and present which linguistic reality each analysis alludes to or is dedicated to with the greatest possible clarity. Therefore, demography must not fool itself with the sociopolitical and terminological tricks presented by linguistic diversity. Rather, demography must know which linguistic realities are under consideration at every moment, given the ease of possible confusion among them. As has just been explained, one source of confusion is linguistics itself, though there are others, such as glottonymy (referring to the name of languages or dialects) and psycholinguistic or sociological factors, which will be considered in turn.

Confusion of Languages

With regard to possible confusions for linguistic reasons, it's important to determine the existence of the languages or varieties involved, together with their components and limits. This entails working with entities whose linguistic reality and social presence can be demonstrated with objective criteria. Let us look at an example. The *Ethnologue* catalog (Eberhard, Simons, & Fennig, 2022) has included among the languages used in Spain one called *Quinqui* or *lengua de los mercheros*, but this entity has neither a social use nor does it exist as a language. Its origin, tied to Caló, used by the Gitano people, means that the traits of Quinqui and Caló get confused, but Quinqui doesn't go beyond some slang elements belonging to those who devote themselves to trading in *quincalla* (metal objects of little value). In this way, a demolinguistic study of Quinqui would become a task both impossible to carry out and one lacking in meaning, given that it is not a "language" of Spain or any other territory.

Nevertheless, it's important to clearly establish the limits between varieties. One of the most eloquent examples illustrating the difficulty of establishing these limits is looking at speakers of Hindi, Urdu, or Hindi-Urdu (also Hindustani) in India and Pakistan. From a linguistic perspective, distinguishing between Hindi and Urdu is complicated beyond some dialectal peculiarities, given that the distinction between the two varieties is primarily political and religious: speakers of Urdu are usually Muslims, whereas speakers of Hindi are usually Hindus. On these differences, another of a linguistic nature must be superimposed: writing. In effect, their alphabets comprise a means to make visible from the outside some differences that are blurred from within the languages themselves. Urdu is written in an adaptation of the Persian alphabet, whereas Hindi is written using the Devanagari alphabet. This illustrates that writing systems can lead to demolinguistic confusion if they're exclusively identified with specific languages. Let us consider that the writing system of Wu is the same as that of Mandarin Chinese, but that does not mean that Mandarin and Wu are the same language.

The example from India leads us directly to another source of confusion: the naming of languages or varieties: that is to say, "glottonymy." Just as alphabets can show or intensify the differences between two linguistic varieties, the names of languages themselves can make differences appear, even when they are otherwise non-existent. Examples of this kind of confusion proliferate throughout the world. We've mentioned the case of Hindi and Urdu (sometimes called Hindi-Urdu), but there are similar realities on every continent. For example, the name Brasileiro applied to the language most spoken in Brazil seems strange when it is nothing other than Portuguese. The Spanish language usually receives two names: *español* (Spanish) and *castellano* (Castilian). The use of one or the other depends on various factors, although none is purely linguistic nor affects the reality that these are the same language. In fact, dictionaries usually give *español* and *castellano* as synonyms.

The Catalan language also offers interesting glottonymic aspects, given that Spanish legislation distinguishes Valencian Catalan (although they are historic variants of the same language) along with the Balearic variety. In this case, the glottonymic controversy has come to be so radical that, on occasions, the three names are juxtaposed: *Ethnologue* calls this language *Catalán-Valenciano-Balear,* and one of the best-known dictionaries of these varieties is called precisely the *Diccionari català-valencià-balear* (Alcover & Moll, 2002). Something similar happens with the varieties found in Serbia, Croatia, Bosnia and Herzegovina, Montenegro, and Kosovo, which, despite political desires to demonstrate their differences, including through their alphabets, are usually called Serbo-Croatian or Serbo-Croat. These terms are considered politically incorrect, even if linguistically justified. This glottonymic problem leads to the search for solutions of compromise, which is

TABLE 2.1 Glottonymic distinction of languages.

Kind of criteria	Example
ethnocultural	Urdu (Muslim community) / Hindi (Hindu community)
geographic	Brazilian / Portuguese
political	Serbo-Croatian / names based on nationality (Serbian, Croatian, Bosnian, Montenegrin)

why some language teaching centers offer classes in "Serbo-Croat-Bosnian" as second or foreign languages.

However, the repercussions of glottonyms don't end there, but reach even more sophisticated levels when elevated to specialized fields beyond those of cultural traditions and popular customs. In politics, names given to languages in constitutions, laws, and regulations are crucial, so much so that the issue is often resolved by means of consensus among parties. Political reasons important to nationalist parties led to the term *castellano* being used as the name of the Spanish language in the 1978 Spanish Constitution. Similarly, in 2013, political reasons led to an agreement between the conservative party and the regionalist party in the Spanish autonomous region of Aragón to refer to the varieties close to Catalan spoken in Aragón with the acronym LAPAO (lengua aragonesa propia del área oriental: Aragonese language typical of the eastern area). Likewise, across different specialized areas, including demolinguistics, languages are identified not by their traditional names but by codes under the ISO 639-1 rule: English would be ISO 639-1 en; Spanish ISO 639-1 es; French ISO 639-1 fr; Quechua ISO 630-1 qu, which would include Northern Quechua. Despite the clinical nature of these codes, this apparent terminological objectivity never managed to free itself from the insecurities that the differences between languages and dialects involves.

The aforementioned factors and examples explain with enough eloquence the insurmountable difficulty of undertaking a seemingly simple task which indirectly affects demolinguistics: determining the number of languages in the world. The question "how many languages are spoken in the world?" can't be answered in a direct, clear, and objective way because it depends on how one identifies linguistic systems, the consideration that speakers and their societies give them, and the names which they assign them, among other factors. *Ethnologue*, the best-known source in this regard, clearly explains:

> How many languages are there? This is a difficult question to answer exactly as the distinction between language and dialect is fuzzy and is a matter of politics, geography, history, culture, and linguistics. For example, all varieties of Chinese are considered dialects by Chinese linguists, even though many are mutually unintelligible. The same applies to varieties of Arabic.
>
> *Eberhard, Simons, & Fennig, 2021*

As can be seen, both the manner of perceiving and interpreting linguistic varieties, as well as the way of naming them, can be strongly conditioned by extralinguistic factors, among which one can count religion, politics, ideology, and identity. For this reason, the practice of demolinguistics must value and carefully specify the how and what of the linguistic component in any demographic analysis to be undertaken. Solutions to overcome conceptual or terminological obstacles need not necessarily be those which come from linguistics, given that the goals of a demolinguistic study might respond to considerations of another nature. Whatever the case may be, linguistic arguments must be evaluated from the beginning of any work because an adequate identification of the languages or varieties involved in the analysis is essential.

Geographic Considerations

A relevant question for demolinguistics is establishing where the languages or varieties are spoken when they are the object of demographic study. As is known, demography is interested in populations localized in specific settings and, in those settings, one finds even more linguistic questions at play. This is because the geographic domains in which they are found are decisive for linguistic and social identities: localities, territories, provinces or districts, regions, countries, or sets of countries. Generally, these domains are given to us by administrative or geopolitical criteria. However, when they are correlated with linguistic modalities, the criteria become blurred or confusing, especially with regard to the limits between varieties involved which don't always separate one domain from another in a neat or clean fashion. Furthermore, political borders often don't coincide with linguistic ones.

Borders

Let us look at two examples. In the northeast of Italy, there is a complex situation at the border where Italian is not exactly the main language of reference. Instead, Friulian is a variety tied to the Rhaeto-Romance family, which is also present in Switzerland. In this Italian region along the border with Slovenia, there is a multilingual transition zone of variable width in which Slovenian is also spoken, along with Italian and Friulian. Further north, the Austrian-Italian border separates Friulian from German, even if in some areas German is also spoken, in addition to Friulian, Italian, and Slovenian.

Let us look at a second example. In the popular Western imagination, the Romanian language is clearly associated with one place: Romania. However, the domain of this language goes beyond that single country, and the situation becomes complicated specifically at the border areas. Thus, the Republic of Moldova to the east of Romania declared Romanian its official language after independence in 1991, as Romanian is the mother tongue of two thirds of the population.

Nonetheless, Russian plays an important role in public communication in the new republic, especially in cities, which shows that geographic domains can be very sociolinguistically complex (Ossenkop & Winkelmann, 2018).

These realities, often unknown or ignored, are no impediment to strong convictions in the collective imagination of minority and national groups about the close ties that exist between languages and territories. In some cases, as in indigenous communities located on reservations and protected land, the tie is clearer and more evident, as their territories usually receive "ancestral status"; in other cases, such as regions in which a minority language has historically coexisted with a majority one, the link is more blurred.

Even so, these situations presented as examples reveal a tangled reality which demolinguistic analyses cannot overlook: that borders of languages and their varieties don't necessarily coincide with the borders of countries or regions; nor even with natural borders, although these have been a determining factor over the course of history, as is seen with the Pyrenees or along the borders of the great rivers of Europe. In fact, regarding borders, two basic kinds of languages are distinguished: "border languages" and "cross-border languages" (Chumbow, 1999; Omoniyi, 2010). A border language is spoken along a border, generally a political one, in parallel with another language spoken on the other side of that same border; therefore, the geography of each language is coterminous with its respective country. Cross-border languages, on the other hand, are those whose use crosses an international political border such that their geographic domain is not limited to the geographic territory of one country but extends to the other side of the border. Often, cross-border populations show a historical, cultural, and linguistic affinity, even if they might also make up a single economic or commercial knot, formed by one or various neighboring nuclei.

From another perspective, the crossing of borders that migration entails has brought diversity—and even super-diversity (Vertovec, 2007)—to all kinds of territories, including those which have historically been monolingual. In this way, one can better understand why the idea that one language corresponds to each nation is false, an Enlightenment principle that had strong roots in outdated nationalist ideologies which has prolonged its popular foothold to the present (Heller, 2011). Cultural crossover and diversity enormously complicate the work of demographers of languages.

Communities

Languages are the instrument of communication par excellence in neighborhoods, municipalities, cities, regions, and countries. However, we should not lose sight of the natural association of languages with another more abstract or general concept tied to territory, as well as social life and collective perception (Anderson, 1991). That concept is "community." In effect, languages or varieties are used by communities of speakers, and a demolinguistic analysis can be made of those communities. But what is a community and who is counted as part of it?

Here, once more, it is possible to find diverse interpretations leading us to differentiate between distinct notions; specifically, between "language community," "linguistic community," and "speech community" (Gumperz, 1962; Coseriu, 1981; Gimeno, 1990). "Language community" is understood to be the group of individuals who speak a historic language, both in its past reality and its present, and in any of its modalities and domains. This means that a young contemporary woman from Seville, a Spanish-speaking Filipino man from the early nineteenth century, Isabel Allende, and Miguel de Cervantes all belong to the same language community. As such, this concept is not terribly useful for current demolinguistics, unless one desires to calculate the number of Spanish speakers over time: an interesting exercise of historic demolinguistics.

Closer to current demolinguistic practices are the concepts of "linguistic community" and "speech community." A "linguistic community" is made up of all the individuals who use the same language or the same variety at a specific moment. Following the example from Spanish, all those who could communicate in Spanish at a specific date, whether from the Americas, Africa, Europe, or Asia, would form part of the same linguistic community. It would then be left to specify the degree of knowledge of the language all these speakers of Spanish would need to have in order to be considered speakers. We'll come to that soon.

Finally, "speech community" is defined not just by the knowledge and use of a language or variety, but also by the stable and frequent interaction among its members which creates some unique linguistic profiles that don't necessarily need to coincide in every speech community of the same language. These interactions lead, in turn, to some shared or similar values, attitudes, and rules in relation to the social use of the language. For these reasons, it's common for the limits of speech communities to coincide with those of localities or units of recognizable convenience such as towns or cities, although this does not prevent the existence of communities of a social nature (religious communities, for example) or an inter-local nature (regional communities, for example).

Despite its apparent simplicity, the concept of "speech community" has offered many nuances in its historic journey. Midway through the twentieth century, it was defined simply as a set of people who interacted through a language (Bloomfield, 1933; Hockett, 1958). Later, an important factor was considered: the possibility that communities were either monolingual or bilingual (Gumperz, 1962; Le Page, 1968). This meant recognizing the possible existence of "linguistic groups" within the same community. Finally, it considered not just the use of linguistic elements, but also the existence of a set of shared rules, of a common evaluative behavior, and of a uniformity in the models of variation (Labov, 1972), such that the members of a community are perceived as such by themselves and by outsiders (Bolinger, 1975). This perceptive factor proves fundamental for the recognition of communities, although it entails an obstacle for their delimitation for demolinguistic ends.

On the other hand, dialectal and linguistic studies have contributed interesting evidence in relation to the sociolinguistic profile of speech communities. One example is that communities can be made up of both small clusters of speakers and large collectives. While notable differences might not be discernible within them, most commonly the larger communities include within them a diversity of linguistic groups. The relationship between the relative homogeneity of speakers in areas of modern settlement (such as English in the North American West before the massive arrival of immigrants and the diversity of the English language in areas of longer settlement, for example, on the East Coast of the USA) has also been demonstrated (Tamasi & Antieau, 2015). Likewise, diversity tends to be greater in communities that are more socially complex or have different degrees of integration among the groups that comprise them (Trudgill, 2011). These realities expose the false image of homogeneity, both linguistic as well as sociolinguistic, which is implied by a notion as seemingly simple as "community."

Psychosocial Considerations

In warning of the difficulties demography finds in being applied to speakers of languages or varieties, it has already been anticipated that many of these are due to socio- or psycholinguistic factors. Because, if it is difficult to specify what a "language" is and how to identify one, it is no less difficult to specify who a "speaker" is. Thus, it's often taken for granted that someone is a speaker of a language because it is their "maternal" or "native" language, or because they have it as a "second" or "additional" language. But are these concepts really equivalent? Knowledge of a language can be of different types or levels, and that directly influences the way its speakers are counted.

For demolinguistics, concepts of "mother tongue," "native," "vehicular," "dominant," or "heritage languages" are not indifferent, to mention just some of the qualifications that are usually applied to specify the profile of speakers. In fact, if one wishes to practice good demolinguistics, one should specify what degree of command of the language speakers must have in order to characterize their linguistic profile. Let us consider an example: if one wishes to quantify the world population of English speakers, it's possible to focus exclusively on those considered to be "native speakers" or to also include those who have attained, as a minimum, a fluency equivalent to the B1 level of the Common European Frame of Languages (popularly, basic English). The result would be different in each case, as Braj Kachru (1990, 2017) has shown in his studies of English. Consequently, there are some fundamental concepts in relation to the origin of the acquired language, the level of knowledge attained, and the categories of speakers.

Mother Tongues and Native Speakers

Languages are acquired in many ways. One of these is through the family environment during childhood; another, through the social environment, at different moments of life; finally, another is the result of a process of formalized learning (Krashen, 1982). These different modes of acquisition, together with the diversity of contexts they occur in, allow us to talk of mother tongues or native languages, heritage languages, and learned languages. However, the application of these categories is not simple at all, nor are the possibilities offered by reality exhausted by their use. In fact, linguistic demography shows one of its primary methodological weaknesses in the indiscriminate use of such labels and their manner of application.

The language acquired in the family home is usually called the "mother tongue," "native language," or "birth language," in addition to "initial language" or "first language." These last labels refer simply to the order of individual acquisition, together with "primary language" versus "second language" or "secondary language," "third language," and even "additional language"; that is, a language whose knowledge is added to all the others. The qualifiers "maternal," "native," and "first," however, are not indistinct as far as their reference goes nor in terms of the connotations they evoke.

In principle, "mother tongue" is the most intuitive term, in addition to being the most popular. This refers to the language acquired during earliest childhood and first, such that thought and communication prove most spontaneous in it. The mother tongue will be the one in which a speaker usually counts or calculates, verbally or mentally, even when speaking another language. Moreover, the mother tongue is usually characterized as the language of greatest use and best knowledge by a speaker, and as the one with which they most identify (Skutnabb-Kangas, 1981). However, these final attributes don't define a mother tongue absolutely.

"Native language" could be characterized practically with the same attributes: acquired during childhood and first of all, as well as being the most spontaneous and fluid means of expression. But there are usually other attributes added to the concept of "native" (Davies, 2013): the existence of intuitions as to the acceptability and productivity of the language itself; the ability to write in it creatively; the ability to translate and interpret into it.

These coincidences in characterizing "mother tongue" and "native language" lead us to wonder about the reasons for the preference for one or the other. And, as an answer, there are two lines of argument: the ontological and the epistemological. The ontological line distinguishes between acquisition understood either as a biological and psychological process developed in the most intimate bosom of a family, especially in contact with the "mother" ("mother tongue") or as the result of a primary acquisition process ("native language"). The epistemological line, on the other hand, introduces nuances of convenience or interest at the moment of applying both terms from research. Both lines of argument deserve complementary development.

In the ontological line, exchanging the labels "mother tongue" and "native language" presents no significant difficulties for monolingual speakers and communities. But, when a person knows four, five, or six languages, often it's not so easy, even for speakers themselves, to state which language was acquired as a "mother tongue" and what the exact order of acquisition was, among other reasons because it's possible that speakers can have greater spontaneity and fluency in an acquired language in another phase of their lives. Here, labels like "dominant language," "language of habitual use," and "principal language" gain greater meaning. In many cases, both the brain and the first interactions of a multilingual speaker are regarded as an opaque box that encloses intertwined variables that are difficult to decipher, which facilitates the preference for the term "native language."

Along the epistemological line, research can place emphasis upon one aspect or another of acquisition according to each discipline's convenience or needs. For ethnolinguistics, ecolinguistics, or the study of minority languages, for example, mother tongue is tied to community life and emphasizes the importance of the process of socialization in the acquisition of the first language. The maternal language is interpreted, then, as the first linguistic instrument that the person manages in the community with which they identify. Thus, there is talk, especially in francophone linguistics, of the mother tongue group (*groupe de langue maternelle*, GLM) (Weinreich, 1968), understanding the mother tongue as an attribute of a community and making it the equivalent of a "vernacular language." This conception is promoted by political and cultural organizations, such as the Organisation Internationale de la Francophonie (OIF) (Ouane, 1995) or UNESCO. However, in linguistics applied to the teaching of languages or in the study of the acquisition of second languages (ASL), the terms "first language" or "L1" and "second language" or "L2," among others, are considered to be much clearer and more reasonable than "mother tongue," precisely because of the difficulty of accessing the internal and external variables that condition acquisition in plurilingual individuals or those belonging to socioculturally complex communities.

On the other hand, statistics institutes usually propose their own definitions in terms of the objectives of the census instruments being used. Thus, Statistics Canada understands "mother tongue" as not just the language that is spoken but also that which is understood, having been acquired in childhood, even though it may no longer be spoken (Termote, 2003). This entails referring to the mother tongue in terms of the past and not necessarily the present. What's more, in Canadian censuses, knowledge of language is understood as the ability to understand a language well enough to maintain a conversation. In contrast, the censuses of the United States and the United Kingdom give preference to the concept of "language spoken in the home" without going into detail about how it was acquired. However, this operational decision has not escaped criticism of the label, nor has it sidestepped its linguistic and social weaknesses (Blommaert, 2017; Espinoza, 2019).

With regard to the operational line, the use of "native language" can be understood as that which is acquired in childhood, in interaction with the family, in the bosom of a community, or through schooling (Swann, Deumert, Lillis, & Mesthrie, 2004), granting a broader space to a diversity of possibilities of acquisition and a greater weight to the result of the process. That result entails centering the focus on the speakers and not so much on the languages, as well as granting greater importance to the ability to interact or the possibility of being considered members of an idiomatic community. Consider that "native" is an adjective that can be applied to both the language and the speaker, whereas "mother" / "maternal" can only be applied directly to the language.

From this applied perspective, demolinguistic studies use "native skills cluster" to refer to the set of speakers of a language formed by individuals whose linguistic or communicative ability resembles or is equivalent to that of its native speakers (Moreno-Fernández, 2014). In 1985, Thomas Paikeday published a work with a self-explanatory title: *The Native Speaker is Dead!* However, the concept of "native fluency,' which has just been outlined, proves much more flexible. Therefore, if the notion of "native" was ever dead, it could now be considered to be "reanimated" or "reembodied."

Obviously, decisions made in censuses and studies about the knowledge of languages don't escape from subjectivity in the gathering and interpretation of data but they suppose a more direct and practical approach to reality. Inconveniences actually arise when, in approaching a demolinguistic task, one doesn't explain with sufficient detail the decisions these factors imply in relation to the terms "mother tongue" or "native language," accompanied not infrequently by other labels: "primary language," "habitual language," "dominant language," "vehicular language," etc. This conceptual and terminological diversity also greatly complicates the demolinguistic comparison of geographic areas or different moments in time.

Heritage Languages and Learned Languages

The acquisition of language within the family does not always result in the speaker's dominant or primary language. The social and cultural environment in which the process develops also has an appreciable impact, both in children who acquire the language and in their parents or caretakers. In relation to the language of the family or part of the family, when the acquired language is not the vehicular or predominant language (but instead a minority language in the social environment where the family lives), the phenomenon of "heritage languages" or "inherited languages" appears. In reality, this is not a special kind of language but a way of acquiring and using a mother tongue or native language in which the abilities of oral interaction coincide with those of native speakers, but the skills of written interaction don't develop, or they do so later in school contexts. In this way, the heritage language becomes an instrument of family communication, a mark of origin or of cultural identity which coexists with the acquisition of the majority or vehicular language in the social environment in which it is developed.

The best-known example of heritage languages is that of the languages of immigrant groups in the United States: these speakers acquire Spanish, Chinese, Korean, Italian, Russian, or Greek in the family home, whereas English is acquired in the public and social environment. Naturally, the examples of heritage languages multiply in other regions of the world: Turkish in Germany, Maghreb Arabic in Spain, Tagalog in Hong Kong… A special case is that of indigenous or first nations languages when their speakers move to areas of a majority language (for example, when they emigrate to large cities). Strictly speaking, these languages could be treated as heritage languages in their new contexts, but there is resistance in this regard when the original languages and the majority languages are both considered to belong to the same country, as can be seen in the consideration they receive in legislation (Gallant, 2020). However, the case of plurilingual speakers in multilingual countries is even more complicated (for example, in India or the Philippines), when they are considered heritage speakers of a single standard language taught for political or cultural reasons (Arabic in the Philippines; Hindi in India) (Polinsky & Kagan, 2007).

Traditionally, the category of heritage language speakers has not been the object of demolinguistic investigation. To a large degree, this is because the concept has not been integrated into the linguistic panorama until recently (Valdés, 2001). But it's also due to certain obstacles in research that are difficult to surmount: if a speaker orally inherits a (minority) language in the environment of another (majority) language, it's complicated to ascertain to what degree they can maintain that inheritance, if in fact they do. Just as it is complicated to access the black box of the learning brain, it's also difficult to introduce oneself into the intimacy of each home to know how the speakers there resolve the interplay of multilingual exchanges. As with everything, some studies have ventured to calculate the number of heritage speakers in a community, relying on deduction based on indirect information: the existence of educational instruments of support for maintaining the heritage language, the presence of community initiatives to promote the minority identity, or close knowledge of the environment in which the heritage language is used (Loureda Lamas, Moreno-Fernández, Álvarez Mella, Scheffler, 2020).

Much easier to count are the speakers who acquire a second or third language, or an additional language, through guided learning from education centers, whether public or private, in a process of immersion in a group created for that purpose or through immersion within a real community. Language learned in this way is generally called a "foreign language," although in the majority of cases it does not cease to be a second, third, or additional language. In this case, demolinguistics must turn to statistics to find out the number of students of each language at each level offered in each center, and calculate how many people learn and speak the language to varying degrees. Likewise, it's possible to find out how many speakers of these languages graduate each year from these kinds of courses and with what level of knowledge. In many cases, the centers themselves have this information; in other cases, one can turn to the data of people who have taken exams or language certification tests organized by different institutions: *Trinity College London, Cambridge University, Educational Testing Services* (for English), *Instituto Cervantes* (for Spanish), *Institut Français* (for French), *Goethe Institut* (for German), and *Università per Stranieri di Perugia* (for Italian), among others.

When demolinguistics takes an interest in the speakers of a language in the broadest sense (that is, those who have acquired it via any of the methods presented here), the concept of a "community of potential users" of a language emerges. With its methodological implications, the conceptual contrast between a "mother tongue group" (*groupe de langue maternelle* or GLM) and a "linguistic community of potential users" (LCPU) is evident, because acquisition becomes separated from use and identity from functionality. These differences are fundamental when undertaking a demolinguistic analysis.

Knowledge of Languages

From the typology of languages and the modes of acquisition commented on in earlier sections, one can deduce that one of the most difficult hurdles to overcome for researchers of any discipline is to verify speakers' levels of knowledge of languages, especially if they are plurilingual. In this regard, it's worth remembering the conceptual difference established by the Common European Framework of Reference for Language (CEFR) between multilingualism and plurilingualism:

> *Multilingualism* is the knowledge of a number of languages, or the co-existence of different languages in a given society. It may be attained by simply diversifying the languages on offer in a particular school or educational system.
>
> *Plurilingualism* is a personal or individual fact. The plurilingual approach emphasizes the fact that as an individual person's experience of language in its cultural contexts expands, from the language of the home to that of society at large, the individual [...] builds up a communicative competence to which all knowledge and experience of language contributes and in which languages interrelate and interact.
>
> Council of Europe, 2001

This information is fundamental for approaching censuses in an effective fashion if one does not wish to arrive at muddled statistics. The only way to avoid confusion is by adequately explaining the concepts handled and giving a detailed description of the linguistic and population realities that constitute the object of analysis.

As for linguistic knowledge, an important first consideration affects the age and moment when a person begins to speak a language. In the case of children, it is considered that they begin to speak the native language when they are around one or two years old, even if in many cases they don't until they are three or four years old in normal conditions. This reality, together with the fact that the abilities of social interaction don't develop until much later, means demolinguistics does not generally consider minors under five years of age for analysis, as they are confined to a category of "child language." Such a methodological decision coincides with the under-representation of children under five that is usual in population censuses, even if this circumstance is being corrected in some censuses, such as in the United States.

Moving on to other issues, if demolinguistics is interested in the populations that speak specific languages or varieties, it cannot ignore that speakers might know them to different degrees and use them with different levels of ability or fluency. At the same time, that fluency might be unequal in each of the basic abilities: speaking, understanding, reading, and writing (Kaplan, 2010). We've already mentioned that heritage speakers are not usually skilled in written interaction (reading and writing) unless they receive specific education in it, which, if it comes, is usually late and via schooling. Of course, in those languages which lack a written form, the primary ability adheres to orality.

In general, knowledge of a language is measured externally, keeping in mind the levels established in the international systems of language instruction. The Council of Europe (2001), for example, through its CEFR establishes three levels for the organization of language learning (A, B, and C). The three fundamental levels are "basic speaker," "independent speaker," and "proficient speaker." Each of these levels is further divided into two sub-levels (Council of Europe 2001).

Basic speaker (A): the person is able to communicate in very everyday situations, with commonly used expressions, and using basic vocabulary and grammar.

Independent speaker (B): the person can interact with native speakers with a sufficient degree of fluency and naturalness, such that communication is held without effort by all participants.

Proficient speaker (C): the person has an advanced level of competence appropriate for more complex work and study tasks.

The Council of Europe considers that level C or proficient speaker is not equivalent to that of a native speaker, but the reality is that people who acquire and surpass this level show a command of the language equivalent to that of native speakers, and can even perform tasks in the language that many native speakers wouldn't be able to handle. As such, the speakers of additional languages, but who have high levels of competence in them, could be considered to be speakers with fluency equivalent to that of native speakers. Native fluency (or its equivalent) is shown in many ways, among which "fluency" and "correctness" are especially notable. The latter term is defined as adapting to standards and conventions when performing language skills. Fluency is the ability to process and produce language with coherence and speed resembling that of a native speaker. In general, fluency is correlated with the process of acquisition in addition to the frequency of use of the language itself (Grosjean, 2010: 20).

Among heritage speakers, the degree of fluency depends on the need to communicate in the heritage language but, above all, on the quality and quantity of linguistic input received during childhood. That is why fluency is usually greater not in the heritage language but in the majority language of their environment, which is the one most needed for daily communication outside of the family. On the contrary, in speakers of a second or additional language, fluency is usually greater in their mother tongue than in the learned language (Montrul, 2015). This does not mean that there aren't also heritage speakers with native fluency in their familial minority language.

Regarding the knowledge of languages, another fundamental factor must be kept in mind: the concept of "competence," which can alternate with that of "proficiency" (Silva-Corvalán, 2014). Competence can be defined as the set of individual knowledge, skills, and abilities which are drawn upon in the personal and social use of a language. From this perspective, it is supposed that a native speaker has a native competence for the development of their communicative activity at all levels. However, the expansion of multilingualism, the diversity of sociolinguistic environments, and the multiple modes and degrees of language acquisition mean this doesn't always lead to a competence equivalent to that of a native speaker. When this happens in heritage speakers, Silvia Montrul (2015) refers to the existence of an "incomplete competence," a concept that poses serious problems from a sociolinguistic perspective: the competence of a heritage speaker is not in itself complete nor incomplete, but adequate to certain conditions and needs which manifest in variable and dynamic ways.

In a parallel although clearly differentiated line are the demolinguistic studies that propose the notion of "limited competence" (Moreno-Fernández & Otero Roth, 2006), to refer to the ability to speak a language when linguistically limited by not enjoying all the resources available with native competence, or when sociolinguistically and/or stylistically limited, or when its use is restricted to certain kinds of interactions or communicative situations. From this perspective, one could consider speakers with limited competence to include those heritage speakers who have reduced or almost abandoned the use of their family language, students of a language who have not attained a level of competence, immigrants in the process of linguistic integration, or the speakers of a creole language whose social presence is limited, socially or stylistically, normally by the concurrence of one or more majority languages. In this regard, the fact that a language or variation can be considered to be maternal, as is the case with heritage or creole languages, is not incompatible with its possible linguistic, sociolinguistic, or stylistic limitations.

To a large degree, the scant attention paid to speakers of heritage languages and learned languages in the field of linguistic demographics is due to the difficulty of establishing with sufficient objectivity the level of knowledge of these languages. These are epistemological reasons. But they are not the only ones: there are also ideological reasons. In the field of acquisition and language learning, there is a clear conceptual predominance, almost an idealization, of the figure of the "native speaker." Holliday (2006) has spoken of *"native-speakerism"* to refer to the importance usually given to being native or, specifically, to native professionals for teaching languages. This idea is also very widespread in other fields, including demolinguistics, where native speakers are considered central to the effects of investigation, and non-natives as peripheral, even though they're far from non-existent. In fact, the native language or mother tongue and its speakers have been the primary concerns for all kinds of ethnographic, anthropological, political, and demolinguistic studies, which has led to the marginalization of other speaker profiles, such as bilinguals, heritage, and learners. Likewise, the mother or native language is still considered an essential factor to determine the origin of refugees (Cambier-Langeveld, 2010) or to justify processes of linguistic revitalization (Doerr, 2009), without considering that multilingualism and super-diversity (Blommaert, 2010), with all their sociolinguistic implications, enormously complicate the identification of languages, varieties, and speakers. This complication grows larger when the coexistence of languages in a person is not understood as the presence of two parallel competences, but as a single complex and "translanguaging" multilingual competence (García & Wei, 2013).

Finally, in relation to the knowledge and command of languages, there is one aspect halfway between psychology and sociolinguistics, passing through pedagogy, that deserves special attention. Basil Bernstein (1971) proposed a theory that correlates children's control of linguistic and communicative means (tied to their intellectual development) with the main contexts of socialization: family, school, community. Called "deficit theory," this idea refers to the level of knowledge or command of language. It distinguishes two forms of linguistic expression or codes: the "restricted code" and the "elaborated code." The restricted code predominates in the working classes or strata, and the elaborated code in the middle classes. The codes refer to styles of interaction, processes of cognition, and different ways of interpreting social structure. For Bernstein, all speakers of any social class have access to a restricted code, but only some groups have access to the elaborated code; for these latter cases, the restricted code is reserved for certain situations, normally family communication. As such, deficit theory is concerned with the children of economically deprived families and neighborhoods whose knowledge and use of language is clearly deficient or in "deficit" compared to that of the middle classes.

Theoretically, the children of the working classes have access to more limited linguistic resources and cognitive instruments, which can be a barrier in education and lead to failure at school, given that habitual use is made of an elaborated code there. This code, less formally predictable than the restricted, opens the possibility of individuation, in being oriented toward the person, whereas the restricted is more oriented toward the position of the individual within a group. The characteristics of each code are acquired within a specific cultural and linguistic environment and are transmitted from one generation to another, perpetuating certain linguistic, cognitive, and social patterns, as the works of Pierre Bourdieu (1984) later explained.

Bilingual Speakers

The diversity of acquisition styles has as a natural consequence for the diversity of kinds of speakers susceptible to demolinguistic analysis. One fundamental type is monolingual speakers of a language acquired as a native language or mother tongue and used as the vehicular or principal language. However, this is not the most common profile of speaker in the world; rather, bilinguals are much more common and, increasingly, multilinguals. As experts have explained (Grosjean, 2010), bilinguals need not have acquired their languages in childhood, speak their languages at home, or have lived in communities with two languages.

Generally, bilingual speakers are people who know and are able to use two languages equally; this is what is usually called "balanced bilingualism" (Wei, 2000), defined as the equivalent command of two languages. Beyond the question of determining who is a balanced bilingual and to what degree in each language, it proves rather complicated simply to determine who bilingual speakers are, due either to the differences in mode of acquisition of each language, the level of command acquired in each of them with different communicative aims, or the degree of personal and sociocultural identification of each speaker with each of their languages.

Therefore, if a demographer decides to analyze bilingual populations, they cannot take for granted that bilingualism will present in a homogeneous fashion. In fact, the diversity of bilingualism has allowed for the construction of different categories, (with their corresponding labels) for speakers of different profiles. Strictly speaking, it would be possible to proceed with the distinction of different profiles. Here are some of the categories involved in the field of bilingualism from a psycholinguistic perspective.

Categories of Bilingual Speakers on a Psychological Basis

Active bilinguals: those who have fundamental skills (understanding, speaking) in two languages.

Passive bilinguals / receptive bilinguals: those who can understand a language without actively being able to produce it.

Balanced bilinguals: those who have a high competence in two languages which they use with similar ease and efficiency; bilinguals in their most developed degree.

Subordinate bilinguals: those who have a dominant language and a subordinate language, such that the units of the subordinate language are interpreted from the equivalent units of the dominant language.

Secondary speakers: those who know and speak a language as a second language or L2.

Semi-bilingual speakers: those who can understand a language without coming to speak it.

Translingual speakers: those who don't use or consider their two or more languages as separate or independent competences.

The way in which bilingualism manifests in these noted categories is strongly related to the vitality of the languages within a community, which leads us directly to concepts and considerations of a social, ideological, and political nature.

Social and Ethnic Considerations

Until now, we've offered notions and arguments about what is spoken and who is doing the speaking. Now is the moment to tackle questions that directly affect the social or community use of languages: how many speak a language, with whom, and why is it spoken. In effect, if bilingualism is a quality of people in a psycholinguistic dimension ("individual bilingualism"), it is also a characteristic of communities in their social dimension ("social bilingualism" or "multilingualism"). Bilingualism, then, must be understood as a transversal and multidimensional concept.

A bilingual community is one in which two languages are spoken; when more languages are of social use, one says that that the community is multilingual. The sum of languages and varieties that have a social presence within a community and which, in one way or another, are available for its members, is called a "linguistic repertoire" or "verbal repertoire," although these terms can also be applied to the set of varieties that an individual uses or which are used in a socially significant context (Ruiz, Sanz, & Solé, 2001).

From a community perspective, all populations of a certain magnitude have *de facto* speakers of two or more languages, but that doesn't make them bilingual or multilingual communities. A report about Barcelona (Spain) (Linguapax, 2019) reveals that more than 300 languages are spoken in the Catalan city by the more than 300,000 foreigners or immigrants who live there, but that doesn't turn Barcelona into a "hectolingual" city. Languages require a public and conventional use in order to be considered an identifying part of communities. When bilingualism is attained through acquisition in a family setting or through intergenerational transmission, one speaks of "natural bilingualism;" when a second language is introduced in a social setting in which it has a greater demographic or cultural weight, one speaks of "environmental bilingualism" (Badia i Margarit, 1964).

Domains of Language Use

The social presence of two or more languages within a community does not imply, on the other hand, that all are used with the same goals or by the same speakers. There are different contexts or circles in which each language might be preferred or be the majority language of communication; that is to say, the use of each language can be suitable and more common depending on the speakers and their relationships, on the areas of communication, or the subjects being dealt with. These fields are called "domains" in the Sociology of Language (Fishman, 1965), a concept that should not be confused with geographic territory. Thus, a domain is defined as an area of linguistic use and social and functional significance, often institutionalized. Joshua Fishman (1972) proposed the distinction of five domains of use of language as an analytical tool: family, friendship, education, religion, and work (commerce, services...), based on domains suggested by Schmidt-Rohr (1932). Out of all of these, family has the greatest relevance for demolinguistics, through the category of "language spoken at home," which is included on national censuses like those of the United States and Germany.

The characterization of the domains as institutionalized contexts or environments has led to the use of a catalog of domains somewhat different from that initially proposed by Fishman. The domain of education (school) is rather well characterized and proves useful for demolinguistics when it works with students or language learners. However, within the domain of work relationships, it's possible to distinguish other areas, precisely because of their institutionalized nature; specifically, we could speak of the "workplace" and "administration" and, within this latter area, "civil administration" and "justice." Thus, family relationships, emotional relationships, and friendships are domains of private use, whereas school, work, religious celebrations, administration, and justice are domains of public use. It's worth adding to all of these the means of social communication, which is less significant for demolinguistics. The domains of school, work, administration, and justice usually answer to sociolinguistic guidelines in which "social status" is of great importance, whereas in the domains of the family and neighborhood, the concept of "solidarity" is more important in communication.

Even though home and school are the domains of greatest importance in demographic terms, additional domains listed here can also be relevant, and in one way or another, all of them have been used as demographic indicators. The indicator "language spoken at home" is defined in different ways according to each census and used with different goals. The *US Census Bureau* considers it to be a basic indicator of linguistic use, with the goal, in theory, of knowing the linguistic skills of the population in order to supply information regarding elections, safety, and public health. In particular, it seeks to know if English is or is not the only language of a household. In the case of Canada, "language used at home" is interpreted as the one which is most frequently spoken and accepts a declaration of using various languages, just as it accepts the possibility that a person might have various mother tongues. However, in studies carried out by Spain's Center for Sociological Research (Centro de Estudios Sociológicos de España), more factors are considered in order to know the private use of languages, distinguishing the language spoken with one's father, one's mother, one's partner, one's children, or one's friends (Siguán, 1994).

As for public use, the domains considered vary from one survey to another. Béland (1999) analyzed the public use of French in Québec (Canada), distinguishing the following domains: shopping centers, small businesses, banks, professional associations, non-professional associations, schools, health centers, hospitals, private clinics, and government services (in writing and in verbal communication). These settings and domains allow for "linguistic groups" to be identified within a community, as well as quantifying them and analyzing them with different social or political aims. The larger a presence a language has in these public domains, the greater its "vitality." In parallel, the vitality of a language is greater when more speakers use it as a second language (Calvet & Calvet, 2012).

Diglossia

Closely related to the concepts of "domain" and "vitality" is that of "diglossia." Diglossia exists within a community when a language or variety that is considered to be familiar, popular, or "low" (B) is used alongside another language variety that is socially superimposed over the first (A). This superimposed variety (usually of higher prestige) would be a very divergent variety with regard to the first and highly codified (often grammatically more complex). It would be the vehicle of a considerable part of the written literature, whether from an earlier period or even belonging to another linguistic community which is learned primarily through regulated teaching, and is used in oral or written forms with different social aims (Ferguson, 1959; Fishman, 1972; Fasold, 1984). In principle, diglossia appears as a relatively stable linguistic situation, but in reality, it is a dynamic situation, given that the B language can reach public domains and come to compete with the A language. This happens in Paraguay with the use of Guaraní with regard to Spanish, and in Catalonia and Galicia with the use of Catalan and Galician, again with regard to Spanish. Joshua Fishman (1991) speaks in these cases of processes of "reversal," generally promoted from linguistic planning and politics.

The differences in functions and prestige among languages and varieties is likewise evident in the concept of the "linguistic market," as conceived by David Sankoff and Suzanne Laberge (1978), on the one hand, and by Pierre Bourdieu (1984), on the other. The concept is based on the idea that linguistic conduct is determined by the relationship of the speakers with the means of production. A market reflects conduct correlated with the socioeconomic activities of the individuals, such that the speakers who undertake certain professions tend to make a normative use of language, whereas those who undertake other professions don't do so, or don't need to do so, even though both share similar socioeconomic profiles. Think, for example, of the need that teachers or media announcers have to mold themselves to a prestigious linguistic model. Speakers, consequently, hold different places in the market, depending on the need they have to make a prestigious use of language. For Bourdieu, language acts as an instrument of access to the market, such that those who use it in accordance with the model of prestige have open access, whereas those who use languages or varieties which are not promoted by the power groups don't enjoy such access.

Linguistic Attitudes

Prestige is a factor that deeply affects "linguistic attitudes." The study of attitudes, moreover, is one of the aspects on which demolinguistics usually focuses because the use of languages, their coexistence, maintenance, and possible loss depend on these. Attitudes are a fundamental component of linguistic opinion, understood as the vision of the identity and geographic and social positioning of languages (Preston, 2010). These attitudes are formed by the action of three components that can be the object of study and measurement: cognitive (the speaker's internal beliefs), affective (emotions caused by the languages or their uses), and conative (reactions to the languages or their uses).

The analysis of linguistic opinion entails paying attention to the cognitive states and processes that guide what people say, as well as those states and processes that guide conscious and unconscious reactions to languages or their uses. Speakers perceive external linguistic stimuli at the same time as they internally conceptualize their linguistic opinions. These concepts and perceptions are created in individuals and communities regarding all kinds of linguistic realities: linguistic identity, the presence of foreign words, linguistic correctness or incorrectness, dialect usage, coexistence of languages, etc.

Generally, the perception of diversity and linguistic variation answers to a process of categorization based on discriminatory learning acquired through schooling and progressive contact between speakers (Moreno-Fernández, 2016). Languages and varieties can be perceived as more central or peripheral according to their cultural, political, and economic prestige, as well as their history, which leads to the existence of languages and varieties that are more or less prestigious, or more or less accepted in specific domains and contexts. The opinions and attitudes of speakers are so important that these are included among the decisive factors when it comes to evaluating the possibility that a language might be maintained or displaced, or disappear.

Minority Languages

The distribution of domains and contexts within a bilingual or multilingual community reflects the space that each language holds within the "linguistic market" and the dynamic each one generates within these areas, forming a linguistic ecology of societies; that is to say, they form a set of hierarchic relationships whose configuration controls many aspects of the very evolution of the languages (Fill & Mülhäusler, 2001; Bastardas, 2003). The linguistic ecology or ecolinguistic perspective comes to coincide with the sociology of language in the distinction between majority and minority languages (Ferguson, 1966) whose relationships experience processes of "minoritization," "displacement," or "substitution" (Mackey, 1973; Breton 1975, 1976). In parallel, it is possible to find processes of "majoritization," "normalization," or "language maintenance."

Among the concepts that have just been mentioned, "minority language" proves fundamental and can be defined from different perspectives. Erik Allardt (1984) lists four basic criteria common to all linguistic minorities: (1) self-categorization; (2) common descent; (3) distinctive linguistic, cultural, or historic traits related to language; and (4) social organization which places the group in a minority position. For his part, Charles Ferguson (1966) characterized minority languages with a quantitative criterion as those used by less than 25% of a population. In its *European Charter for Regional or Minority Languages* (1992), the Council of Europe characterizes them as those which are historically present in a territory in which they are less used than other languages and are not considered official languages. From a perspective of defense of rights, minority languages are considered to be undervalued and marginalized within their communities, and there is often a conflicting relationship with the majority languages because of the expansive, demographic, and cultural nature these usually have.

However, minority languages should not be understood in such absolute or historic terms, given that the creation of new minorities is always possible, as happens in the context of migration. In other words, the minority nature of a language is relative, as these two examples illustrate: firstly, the European Union has no majority language, and thus all the languages spoken within it can be considered minority ones (Extra, 2010); secondly, a language like Catalan, generally considered a minority language, has very widespread use within Catalan society, and its total number of speakers is greater than that of other languages which are considered to be majority ones in their respective territories, such as Finnish or Icelandic.

Among the minority languages of the world, those called indigenous or native languages are the ones that best represent this category. They are often languages of minority ethnic groups that are frequently marginal within national politics and who, therefore, usually demand recognition of their identity (Moreno-Fernández, 2020). The conflict can be appreciated even in the very labeling of these groups and languages, which usually shifts between "indigenous languages" and "native languages." In Spanish, "lenguas indígenas" is a term tolerated in North and Central America, for example, while "lenguas originarias" is the preferred label in the Southern Cone. To avoid using terms that minority ethnic groups might consider demeaning, including "patrimonial language," "ethnic language," and "language in danger of extinction," the Rama people of Nicaragua proposed the term "treasure language" ("lengua tesoro"), which clearly expresses the value granted to these languages and the desire to preserve them (Grinevald & Pivot, 2013).

However, minority languages should not be confused, at least conceptually, with "minoritized languages." Minoritized languages show a weakening of their social presence in a community due to the express action of the speakers of the majority or dominant languages. Despite the fact that minority languages are also frequently minoritized languages, minoritized languages are not always minority ones, as can be observed in numerous contexts in the United States in which Spanish is a minoritized language without being a minority language from an international perspective.

The processes of minoritization usually lead to linguistic "shift," "replacement," or "substitution." Language shift is a process which entails the abandonment of the use of a language in certain contexts to the benefit of another, generally majority, language. This situation places languages in a vulnerable position by which they come to be "threatened languages" or "languages in danger (of extinction)." In these situations, the attitude of "language loyalty" usually flourishes or is strengthened among a language's speakers (García, Peltz, & Schiffman, 2006), an attitude which has its counterpoint in "language disloyalty" which can be adopted by speakers of both minority and majority languages.

Language Loyalty. Language loyalty denotes the mental state in which language (like nationality), in its quality as an intact entity and in counterpoint to other languages, holds an elevated position on the value scale, a position which needs to be "defended."

Weinreich, 1953

Language Disloyalty. The state, attitude, or feeling of a monolingual who rejects their own language or its use in the desire to move closer to the feelings and attitudes of those who are loyal to their language, especially this last one.

Salvador, 1983

"Language loyalty" can be understood either as a desire to continue using a language (in contexts of minoritization) or as the active transmission of the language to the next generation. Within encounters between social groups and different languages (primarily in the context of bilingualism or diglossia), language loyalty becomes more relevant when situations of replacement of one language with another arise, but speakers choose to maintain their local, traditional, or linguistic identity. For its part, "language disloyalty" is an attitude characterized by the abandonment of the family language, either because it's considered to be of low prestige, through social pressure (exercised by a majority language), or because with that language, although it is a majority one, the speaker can't satisfy the discursive demands of their immediate environment. This situation could provoke the displacement of the family language.

As mentioned, language shift is a process by which a community abandons one language to the benefit of another; that is, shift or substitution is a process through which a community collectively decides to stop using the language or languages it has traditionally used and to move to using a new language. For example, Caló, the variety of Romani used on the Iberian Peninsula, which is of interest for knowledge about the Gitano population. Even if the existence of this variety has been documented in Spain for centuries, its survival in the present as a vehicular language in communication among Gitanos is not so certain. *Ethnologue* attributes a population of 60,000 speakers to Caló, but its vehicular use, beyond the discontinuous use of lexical or phraseological forms, is weak or non-existent. In fact, many Caló speakers have learned it recently or have learned the language alongside Romani (the more international variety) in a desire to reinforce or vindicate their identity. The current use of Caló does not usually forgo its reliance on other languages like Spanish or Portuguese. In these conditions, the demolinguistic analysis of Caló involves enormous complexity because the sociolinguistic reality is difficult to grasp. When languages face a definitive process of substitution, they are considered to be "dying languages" until their possible extinction.

In contrast to replacement, shift, or substitution, there are cases of maintenance and expansion. "Language maintenance" is a process through which a community has decided to actively and collectively continue using their traditional language or languages, especially in a situation in which their replacement might have occurred. The maintenance of a minority language can be reinforced by the will of the speakers of a majority language when they decide to become "new speakers" of the minority language.

On the other hand, societies can promote the expansion of their languages through the incorporation of new international speakers, as the United Kingdom, France, or Spain do, with regard to English, French, or Spanish. In this sense, the position adopted by third parties is an important factor in the competition to acquire new speakers. A worthy example: French was the vehicular language in the negotiation of important agreements during the twentieth century, such as the Treaty of Versailles (1919); however, since World War II, French has seen its international presence decline precisely because of the actions of other countries, which have wound up leaning toward an international use of English. Although on occasions they can be connected, the concept of "maintenance" should not be confused with that of "expansion," among other reasons because the factors that initially facilitate the expansion of a language don't necessarily tend to coincide with those that favor its continuity (Lieberson, 1982).

The situations described within these social and ethnic considerations lead us to present new kinds of speakers to be kept under consideration in demolinguistic analysis:

Quasi-speakers / semi-speakers: those who have knowledge of a threatened or dying language and maintain some of its uses or expressions without being able to speak it fluently.

Neo-speakers / new speakers: those who actively decide to substitute the use of their initial language for that of a minoritized language, generally learned outside the family environment, whether to express themselves exclusively in this language or to use it in specific contexts or situations (Frías, 2006; Ramallo, Amorrortu, & Puigdevall, 2019).

Semilingual speakers: those who make precarious use of at least one of the two languages of a community, generally in contexts of language teaching / learning.

Pseudo-speakers: those who in a context of bilingualism are counted as full speakers of a language without really being so.

This last kind of speaker did not arise from linguistics but was instead derived from analyses, both demographic and in other fields, which have not considered many of the concepts explained in this text. Therefore, they have not managed to offer an adequate tally of the speakers within a community.

Language Vitality

Among the attributes that William Stewart (1962) used to classify linguistic varieties, "vitality" is one of the most significant and controversial. At that time, vitality was associated with social use and the number of native speakers of a variety, which allowed for an easy association with demography.

In effect, language vitality concerns language's functionality in the different contexts of interaction within a community (Comajoan-Colomé & Coronel-Molina, 2021), but it also deals with the volume of its community of native speakers and with the recognition these speakers grant their own language. Therefore, it's a complex attribute defined by both objective and subjective factors (Viladot, 1995) and which, regarding minority languages, is usually analyzed in relation to the presence of another (generally majority) language in the same communicative space. The basis of the study of the factors that affect language vitality comes from an initiative proposed by Joshua Fishman in 1991 to measure the degree of intergenerational transmission of a language which resulted years later in the Expanded Graded Intergenerational Disruption Scale (EGIDS) of several levels of vitality given shape in the Sustainable Use Model for Language Development (SUM Model) (Lewis & Simons, 2010).

TABLE 2.2 Levels of vitality according to the SUM Model.

Level	Vitality
0	International
1	National
2	Regional
3	Trade
4	Educational
5	Written
6a	Vigorous
6b	Threatened
7	Shifting
8a	Moribund
8b	Dormant
9	Extinct

Source: Lewis & Simons (2010).

According to this model, the sustainability of a language depends on certain specific conditions of vitality and on the actions undertaken to improve them. The five basic conditions that determine language vitality are: functions, acquisition, motivation, environment, and differentiation. These conditions will be discussed again later (in chapter 5). Based on these, the levels of vitality established are as follows:

One way of deciding where to place each language with regard to these characteristics is to refer to the decision tree that Lewis and Simons proposed in 2010. This procedure for identifying the EGIDS grade is based on two basic questions. The first is the function of the language, which basically allows the vehicular function to be distinguished from the function in the home. In the first case, the level of official use is taken into account: International (0), National (1), Regional (2), and Non-Official or Trade (3). In the second case–use at home–it is essential to know whether the parents transmit the language to their children. If they do, the degree of the scale will be determined by the literacy status achieved: Institutional (4), Incipient with writing (5), or None (6). When parents do not pass the language to subsequent generations, it is crucial to know which is the youngest generation with proficient speakers to determine the degree of transmission on the scale.

To produce this scale, both Fishman's original scale and the degrees of vitality established by UNESCO were considered (Brenzinger et al., 2003).

The levels of vitality, from both EGIDS and UNESCO, are determined simply by identifying the level or degree at which each language is located. Demography proves especially significant for language vitality, given that the "numeric force" of a population is a fundamental asset of ethnic groups. The number of speakers of a language is a tool for legitimization when demanding and conceding institutional

Linguistics for Demographers 55

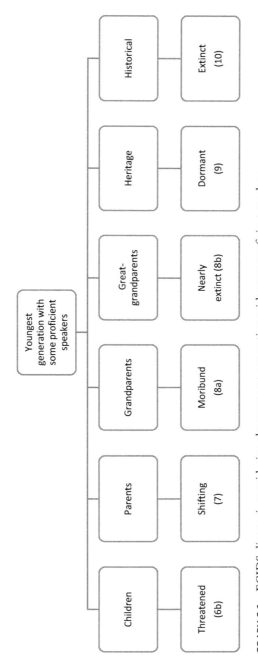

GRAPH 2.1 EGIDS diagnosis considering the youngest generation with some proficient speakers.

Source: Based on Lewis & Simons (2010).

TABLE 2.3 Degrees of vitality of languages according to UNESCO.

Degree of vitality	Use of the language and speakers
5 *not in danger:*	the language is used by all age groups, even children;
4 *vulnerable:*	the language is used by some children in all areas, and by all children in restricted areas;
3 *clearly in danger:*	the language is used primarily by the parental generation and older;
2 *seriously in danger:*	the language is used primarily by the generation of grandparents and older;
1 *in critical situation:*	the language is used by very few speakers, primarily from the generation of the great-grandparents;
0 *extinct:*	no speakers remain.

Source: Brenzinger et al. (2003).

support with the goal of making its development within a multilingual framework possible. As can be supposed, demographic variables (birth and death rates, age distributions, mixed marriages, or migratory models) decisively affect the absolute number of speakers of a language and its territorial distribution.

Summary

Linguistics offers fundamental concepts for the development of a demography of language. Given that languages are attributes of populations and that the individuals who make up these populations are its speakers, it is necessary to clearly determine what is understood by "language" and by "speaker" from psychological, social, cultural, and of course linguistic perspectives. Linguistics, in addition to highlighting the difficulties in defining and identifying languages, demands that those variations which are not equivalent to languages in and of themselves are not to be considered of equal value.

From a psycho-sociolinguistic perspective, the model in which languages are identified and named proves decisive, given that the indiscriminate use of labels can blur demographic analysis. It is not the same to speak of a "mother tongue" as it is to speak of a "native language," "first language," or "dominant language." In the same fashion, the reality of second languages should be distinguished from the reality of inherited languages. This gives rise to a typology of speakers, with bilinguals holding special prominence, as they prove very relevant for demolinguistics.

Among the concepts of interest for demolinguistics, "community" is worthy of special consideration, given that the limits of communities serve as a reference for the demarcation of populations. When various languages coexist within a community, the coexistence can take shape as "diglossia," in which the languages involved fulfill different social functions in different "areas" of use. Likewise, it's important for demolinguistics to know the dynamics of minority and minoritized languages, as their vitality depends on qualitative and quantitative factors. Linguistic demography has devoted important efforts to studying the situation of minority languages, although its fundamental methodological instruments are valid for the analysis of any other kinds of languages.

References

Alcover, Antoni M. and Frances de Borja Moll (2002): *Diccionari català-valencià-balear*. Barcelona: Instituto d'Estudis Catalans. Online version: https://dcvb.iec.cat/.
Allardt, Erik (1984): "What constitutes a language minority?". *Journal of Multilingual and Multicultural Development*, 5: 195–205.
Anderson, Benedict (1991): *Imagined Communities*. Rev. edition. London: Verso.
Badia Margarit, Antoni (1964): *Llengua i cultura als països catalans*. Barcelona: Edicions 62.
Bastardas, Albert (2003): "Ecodinámica sociolingüística: comparaciones y analogías entre la diversidad lingüística y la diversidad biológica". *Revista de Llengua i Dret*, 39: 119–148.
Béland, Paul (1999): *Le français, langue d'usage public au Québec en 1997*. Québec: Conseil de la Langue Française.
Bernstein, Basil (1971): *Class, Codes and Control*. London: Routledge.
Blommaert, Jan (2010): *The Sociolinguistics of Globalization*. Cambridge: Cambridge University Press.
Blommaert, Jan (2017): "'Home language': some questions". *Tilburg Papers in Culture Studies*, 183.
Bloomfield, Leonard (1933): *Language*. London: Allen-Unwin.
Bolinger, Dwight (1975): *Aspects of Language*. New York: Harcourt Brace Jovanovich.
Bourdieu, Pierre (1984): "Capital et marché linguistiques". *Linguistische Berichte*, 90: 3–24.
Brenzinger, Matthias, Tjeerd de Graaf, Arienne Dwyer, Colette Grinevald, Michael Krauss, Osahito Miyaoka, Nicholas Olster, Osamu Sakiyama, María Villalón, Akira Yamamoto, and Ofelia Zepeda (2003): *Language Vitality and Endangerment: UNESCO Ad Hoc Expert Group Meeting on Endangered Languages*. Paris: UNESCO.
Breton, Roland (1975): "La place de la géographie des langues". *Annales de Géographie*, 465: 513–525.
Breton, Roland (1976): *Géographie des langues*. Paris: PUF.
Cabré, Anna (1995): "Factors demogràfics en l'ús de la llengua: el cas de Catalunya". *Actes del Simposi de Demolingüística. III Trobada de Sociolingüistes Catalans*. Barcelona: Generalitat de Catalunya, pp. 9–13.
Calvet, Alain and Louis-Jean Calvet (2012): *Baromètre Calvet des langues du monde*. Paris: Ministère de la Culture.
Cambier-Langeveld, Tina (2010): "The role of linguists and native speakers in language analysis for the determination of speaker origin". *International Journal of Speech, Language & the Law*, 17: 67–93.
Chiswick, Barry and Paul Miller (2005): *Linguistic Distance: A Quantitative Measure of the Distance Between English and Other Languages*. Bonn: IZA. DP No. 1246.
Chumbow, Beban Sammy (1999): "Transborder languages of Africa". *Social Dynamics*, 25: 51–69.
Comajoan-Colomé, Llorenç and Serafín M. Coronel-Molina (2021): "What does language revitalisation in the twenty-first century look like? New trends and frameworks". *Journal of Multilingual and Multicultural Development*, 42: 897–904.

Coseriu, Eugenio (1981): *Lecciones de lingüística general*. Madrid: Gredos.
Council of Europe (2001): *Common European Framework of Reference for Languages*: *Learning, Teaching, Assessment*. Strasbourg: Council of Europe.
Davies, Alan (2013): *Native Speakers and Native Users: Loss and Gain*. Cambridge: Cambridge University Press.
Doerr, Neriko (ed.) (2009): *The Native Speaker Concept: Ethnographic Investigations of Native Speaker Effects*. Berlin: Walter de Gruyter.
Eberhard, David, Gary Simons, and Charles D. Fennig (eds.) (2022): *Ethnologue: Languages of the World*, 245th ed. Dallas: SIL International. Online version: http://www.ethnologue.com.
Espinoza Alvarado, Marco (2019): "El 'nativohablantismo' en la investigación sociolingüística de las lenguas indígenas". *Trabalhos de. Linguistica Aplicada*, 58: 795–825.
Extra, Guus (2010): "Mapping Linguistic Diversity in Multicultural Contexts: Demolinguistic Perspectives". In J. Fishman and O. Garcia (eds.), *Handbook of Language and Ethnic Identity*, 2nd ed. Oxford: Oxford University Press. pp: 107–122.
Fasold, Ralph (1984): *The Sociolinguistics of Society*. Oxford: Blackwell.
Ferguson, Charles (1959): "Diglossia". *Word*, 15: 325–340.
Ferguson, Charles (1966): "National Sociolinguistic Profile Formulas". In W. Bright (ed.), *Sociolinguistics: Proceedings of the UCLA Sociolinguistics Conference, 1964*. The Hague: Mouton, pp. 309–315.
Fill, Alwin and Peter Mühlhäusler (eds.) (2001): *The Ecolinguistic Reader: Language, Ecology and Environment*. London: Continuum.
Fishman, Joshua (1965): "Who speaks what language to whom and when?". *La Linguistique*, 1: 67–88.
Fishman, Joshua A. (1972): *Language in Sociocultural Change*. Ed. Anwar Dil. California: Stanford University Press.
Fishman, Joshua (1991): *Reversing Language Shift*. Clevedon: Multilingual Matters.
Frías Conde, X. (2006). "A normalización lingüística na Romania: A normalización da lingua e normalización dos falantes (o caso dos neofalantes)". *Ianua. Revista Philologica Romanica*, 6: 49–68.
Gallant, David J. (2020): "Indigenous Languages in Canada". In *The Canadian Encyclopedia*. Online: www.thecanadianencyclopedia.ca/en/article/aboriginal-people-languages.
García, Ofelia and Li Wei (2013): *Translanguaging: Language, Bilingualism and Education*. Basingstoke: Palgrave.
García, Ofelia, Rakhmiel Peltz, and Harold Schiffman (eds.) (2006): *Language Loyalty, Continuity and Change: Joshua A. Fishman's Contributions to International Sociolinguistics*. Clevedon: Multilingual Matters.
Garvin, Paul (1959): "The standard language problem: concepts and methods". *Anthropological Linguistics*, 1: 28–31.
Gimeno, Francisco (1990): *Dialectología y sociolingüística españolas*. Alicante: Universitat d'Alacant.
Ginsburgh, Victor, Jacques Melitz, and Farid Toubal (2015): "Foreign language learning: an econometric analysis". *Working Papers*, 2015-13, CEPII research center.
Grinevald, Colette and Bénédicte Pivot (2013): "On the Revitalization of a 'Treasure Language': The Rama Language Project of Nicaragua". In M. Jones and S. Ogilvie (eds.), *Keeping Languages Alive: Documentation, Pedagogy and Revitalization*. Cambridge: Cambridge University Press, pp. 181–197.
Grosjean, François (2010): *Bilingual: Life and Reality*. Cambridge: Harvard University Press.

Guiter, Henri (1973): "Atlas et frontières linguistiques". In *Les dialectos romans de France à la lumière des atlas regionaux*. Paris: CNRS, pp. 61–109.
Gumperz, John J. (1962): "Types of linguistic communities". *Anthropological Linguistics*, 4: 28–40.
Heller, Monica (2011): *Paths to Postnationalism: A Critical Ethnography of Language and Identity*. Oxford: Oxford University Press.
Hockett, Charles (1958): *A Course in Modern Linguistics*. New York: Macmillan.
Holliday, Adrian (2006): "Native-speakerism". *ELT Journal*, 60: 385–387.
Hymes, Dell H. (ed.) (1971): *Pidginization and Creolization of Languages*. Cambridge: Cambridge University Press.
Kachru, Braj (1990): *The Alchemy of English: The Spread, Functions, and Models of Non-native Englishes*. Urbana / Chicago: University of Illinois Press.
Kachru, Braj (2017): *World Englishes and Culture Wars*. Cambridge: Cambridge University Press.
Kaplan, Robert (ed.) (2010): *The Oxford Handbook of Applied Linguistics*. 2nd ed. Oxford: Oxford University Press.
Kloss, Heinz (1967): "'Abstand' languages and 'Ausbau languages'". *Anthropological Linguistics*, 9: 29–41.
Krashen, Stephen D. (1982): *Principles and Practice in Second Language Acquisition*. Oxford: Pergamon.
Labov, William (1972): *Sociolinguistic Patterns*. Philadelphia: University of Pennsylvania Press.
Le Page, Robert B. (1968): "Problems of description in multilingual communities". *Transactions of the Philological Society*, 67: 189–212.
Lewis, M. Paul and Gary F. Simons (2010): "Assessing endangerment: expanding Fishman's GIDS". *Revue Roumaine de Linguistique*, 55:103–120.
Lieberson, Stanley (1982): "Forces Affecting Language Spread: Some Basic Propositions". In R.L. Cooper (ed.), *Language Spread: Studies in Diffusion and Social Change*. Bloomington: Indiana University Press, pp. 37–62.
Linguapax (2019): *Diversitat lingüística i cultural: un patrimoni comú de valor inestimable*. Barcelona: Linguapax International.
Loureda Lamas, Óscar, Francisco Moreno-Fernández, Héctor Álvarez Mella, David Scheffler (2020): *Demolingüística del español en Alemania*. Madrid: Instituto Cervantes.
Mackey, William F. (1973): *Three Concepts for Geolinguistics*. Québec: CIRB Publications.
McWhorter, John H. (2018): *The Creole Debate*. Cambridge: Cambridge University Press.
Montrul, Silvina (2015): *The Acquisition of Heritage Languages*. Cambridge: Cambridge University Press.
Moreno-Fernández, Francisco (2014): "Fundamentos de demografía lingüística: a propósito de la lengua española". *Revista Internacional de Lingüística Iberoamericana*, 12: 19–38.
Moreno-Fernández, Francisco (2016): *A Framework for Cognitive Sociolinguistics*. London: Routledge.
Moreno-Fernández, Francisco (2020): *La lengua y el sueño de la identidad*. Rome: Aracne.
Moreno-Fernández, Francisco and Jaime Otero Roth (2006): *Demografía de la lengua española*. Madrid: Instituto Complutense de Estudios Internacionales.
Mufwene, Salikoko (2005): *Créoles, écologie sociale, évolution linguistique*. Paris: L'Harmattan.
Omoniyi, Tope (2010): "Borders". In J. Fishman and O. García (eds.), *Handbook of Language and Ethnic Identity: Disciplinary and Regional Perspectives*, Vol 1, Oxford: Oxford University Press, pp. 123–134.
Ossenkop, Christina and Otto Winkelmann (eds.) (2018): *Manuel des frontières linguistiques dans la Romania*. Berlin: DeGruyter.

Ouane, Adama (ed.) (1995): *Vers une culture multilingue de l'éducation*. Hamburg: Institut de l'UNESCO pour l'Éducation.
Paikeday, Thomas (1985). *The Native Speaker is Dead!*. Toronto: Paikeday Publishing.
Polinsky, Maria and Olga Kagan (2007): "Heritage languages: in the 'wild' and in the classroom". *Language and Linguistic Compass*, 1: 368–395.
Preston, Dennis (1999): *Handbook of Perceptual Dialectology: Volume 1*. Amsterdam / Philadelphia: John Benjamins.
Preston, Dennis (2010): "Perceptual Dialectology in the 21st Century". In C.A. Anders, M. Hundt and A. Lasch (eds.), *Perceptual Dialectology. Neue Wege der Dialektologie*. Berlin: Mouton–de Gruyter, pp. 1–30.
Ramallo, Fernando, Estíbaliz Amorrortu, and Maite Puigdevall (eds.) (2019): *Neohablantes de lenguas minorizadas en el Estado Español*. Madrid: Iberoamericana Vervuet.
Romaine, Suzanne (1994): *Language in Society: An Introduction to Sociolinguistics*. Oxford: Oxford University Press.
Ruiz i San Pascual, Francesc, Rosa Sanz i Ribelles, Jordi Solé i Camardons (2001): *Diccionari de Sociolingüística*. Barcelona: Enciclopedia Catalana.
Salvador, Gregorio (1983): "Sobre la deslealtad lingüística". *Lingüística Española Actual*, 5: 173–178.
Sankoff, David and Suzanne Laberge (1978): "The Linguistic Market and the Statistical Explanation of Variability". In D. Sankoff (ed.), *Linguistic Variation: Models and Methods*. New York: Academic Press, pp. 239–250.
Schimdt-Rohr, Georg (1932). *Die Sprache als Bildnerin der Völker*. Jena: Eugen Diederichs.
Sebba, Mark (1997): *Contact Languages: Pidgins and Creoles*. New York: Palgrave.
Siguán Soler, Miguel (ed.) (1994): *Conocimiento y usos de las lenguas de España*. Madrid: Centro de Investigaciones Sociológicas.
Silva-Corvalán, Carmen (2014): *Bilingual Language Acquisition: Spanish and English in the First Six Years*. Cambridge: Cambridge University Press.
Skutnabb-Kangas, Tove (1981): *Tvåspråkighet*. Lund: Liber Läromedel.
Stewart, William (1962): "Outline of Linguistic Typology for Describing Multilingualism". In F.A. Rice (ed.), *Study of the Role of Second Languages in Asia, Africa, and Latin America*. Washington: Center for Applied Linguistics, pp. 15–25.
Swann, Joan, Ana Deumert, Theresa Lillis, and Rajend Mesthrie (2004): *A Dictionary of Sociolinguistics*. Edinburgh: University of Edinburgh Press.
Tamasi, Susan and Lamont Antieau (2015): *Language and Linguistic Diversity in the US: An Introduction*. London: Routledge.
Termote, Marc (2003): "La dynamique démolinguistique du Québec et de ses régions". In C. Le Bourdais and V. Piché (eds.) *La démographie québécoise*. Montréal: Presse Universitaire de Montréal, pp. 264–299.
Thomason, Sarah Grey and Terrence Kaufman (1988): *Language Contact, Creolization, and Genetic Linguistics*. Berkeley: University of California Press.
Trudgill, Peter (2011): *Sociolinguistic Typology: Social Determinants of Linguistic Complexity*. Oxford: Oxford University Press.
Union of International Associations (UIA) (2021): *The Encyclopedia of World Problems and Human Potential*. http://encyclopedia.uia.org/en/problem/149536 Online resource.
Valdés, Guadalupe (2001): "Heritage Language Students: Profiles and Possibilities". In J.K. Peyton, D.A: Ranard, and S. McGinnis (eds.), *Heritage Languages in America: Preserving a National Resource*. Washington: Center for Applied Linguistics, pp. 37–77.
Vertovec, Steven (2007): "Super-diversity and its implications". *Ethnic and Racial Studies*, 30: 1024–1054.

Viladot, M. Àngels (1995): "Les dades demogràfiques en el concepte de vitalitat lingüística". In *Actes del Simposi de Demolingüística. III Trobada de Sociolingüistes Catalans*. Barcelona: Generalitat de Catalunya, pp. 20–33.

Wei, Li (ed.) (2000): *The Bilingualism Reader*. London: Routledge.

Weinreich, Uriel (1953): *Languages in Contact*. New York: Linguistic Circle of New York.

Weinreich, Uriel (1968): "Unilinguisme et multilinguisme". In A. Martinet (ed.), *Le langage*. Paris: La Pléyade, pp. 647–684.

Wichmann, Søren, Eric Holman, and Cecil Brown (eds.) (2020), *The ASJP Database*. Version 19. https://asjp.clld.org/ Online resource.

3
DEMOGRAPHY FOR LINGUISTS

Demography reveals a broad range of specialized concepts that must be understood in order to be utilized in the study of languages and speakers (Preston, Heuveline, & Guillot, 2000). Many of these concepts have their origin in commonly used words or expressions (*fecundity, mortality, birth, home, generation, cohort…*); nonetheless, within the demographic specialty, they take on technical meanings. This double use of demographic terminology (the popular and the technical) frequently gives rise to confusion in references and meanings. Thus, a notion as apparently simple and popular as "family" encompasses a large variety of references from a specialized perspective, and this requires the use of further qualifiers to avoid ambiguities: *nuclear family, monoparental family, homoparental family, adoptive family…* At the same time, the dissemination of demographic knowledge has made some terms (morbidity, generational replacement) pass from the technical realm into ordinary language, sometimes provoking erroneous interpretations. As a result of all this, organizations interested in demography and its application (the United Nations, census offices, national statistics institutes, etc.) usually establish specialized glossaries that help to interpret the demographic reality in an adequate and accurate fashion. These are some of the most consulted glossaries:

United Nations. *Demopædia. Multilingual Demographic Dictionary.* 2013
United Nations. *Glossary of Demographic Terms.* 2022
United States Census Bureau. *Glossary.* United States. 2022
Max Planck Institute for Demographic Research, *Glossary of Demographic Terms.* Germany. 2022
Instituto Nacional de Estadística. *Glosario de conceptos.* Spain. 2022

DOI: 10.4324/9781003327349-4

Demography is characterized by studying populations based on their characteristics, structures, and internal dynamics. Therefore, populations (with their components, distribution, and changes) are the center of gravity of the entire demographic framework. In general, populations are described based on certain fundamental demographic factors which can be personal or individual as well as social or collective:

a. From the individual's perspective, personal factors can be identified together with individual vital statistics and concepts. Unquestionably, "vital statistics" form the vertebra of demography in all its manifestations. These statistics are, fundamentally, births and deaths, which lead to essential abstract concepts such as "natality," "fecundity," "reproduction," "longevity," and "mortality." The most relevant personal factors for demography are "age," "sex," and "educational level;" as for the relationship between the individual and their territory or living area, demography is interested in attributes such as being "native," "resident," or "migrant" (immigrant or emigrant) or others like being a "national" or "foreigner," according to the political entity of origin. In any event, individual factors can also be interpreted from a social perspective.
b. Social factors are essential for demography, given that the dynamics and development of populations depend on their influence. The very concept of population implies a social dimension that presupposes the existence of a determined size, density, and distribution. Nonetheless, the fundamental factors for demography, from a social perspective, revolve around the basic notions of "family," "residence," and "area." Of these, the most significant is unquestionably "family," given that other cardinal demographic concepts are associated with it, such as "matrimony" and "generation."

The aim of this chapter is to present the fundamental concepts required in the practice of demography and demolinguistics. These pages will present a demography oriented towards interests related to languages and their varieties. In this way and as much as possible, demographic concepts will be exemplified by taking real linguistic situations as points of reference. The intention is to limit our conceptual deployment to those aspects that have to do with languages, their speakers, and their communities. In any case, it is very relevant to remember that the reference to speakers and communities evidences the relationship, which the more quantitative and coldly statistical factors establish, with more qualitative and human factors, reflecting the realities of people in their contexts (Nemeth, 2004).

Population

In one way or another, most resources and ideas handled in demography affect the "population" and its changes, distribution, and composition. Therefore, the central concept of demography is undoubtedly "population" (Ryder, 1964). Let us recall that the prefix *demo*–"people"–makes up part of the discipline's name. However, the term *population* has different meanings, which should be adequately differentiated. On the one hand, one speaks of *population* to refer to any set of people or living beings who share a characteristic. This being the case, it is possible to speak of the population of people residing on the coast of a province, the population of people with brown hair, or the population of people who speak a specific language within a country. This meaning is used across very different disciplines such as sociology, anthropology, or sociolinguistics.

On the other hand, a population can also be conceived of as the set of individuals who make up a universe or collective about which observations are made, such as the population residing in Germany in the year 2020, the population of political refugees coming from western Asia, or the Spanish-speaking population in the United States. This interpretation belongs more to statistics and would be equivalent to the notion of "universe." In any event, this concept of population refers to aggregate characteristics of the population of a specific place or area. This entails that demography manages descriptions that affect a community, not necessarily a single individual, and that the concept of population includes all the components of that community, not just a part of it.

When demographers speak of populations, their primary reference is a set of people, normally linked to an administrative, political, or geographic entity during a set period of time, with a specific volume and a defined internal structure. The latter are properly demographic characteristics. In short, a population is a set of people who live at a certain moment and in a certain place. On the other hand, demography is interested in populations as collectives with continuity over time which obey the vital dynamics of the individuals who comprise them. The first of these aforementioned meanings refers to a population conceived as stock; that is, as a quantifiable reality at a specific moment; the second meaning refers to the population as a "reproduction system," which is understood as dynamic and evolving; that is, as a set of processes which give rise to dynamism, variety, and evolution within the population. As a synonym for population, one could also use "herd," even if its use is restricted to certain specialties such as epidemiology wherein one speaks of "herd immunity," "group immunity," or "collective immunity."

If one draws a parallel with the concept of "community" handled by linguistics, it could be said that a "speech community" would be made up by a population; that is, by a set of people who, in this case, are speakers of certain specific language(s) or variety(ies) tied to a specific geographic entity at a certain moment and who engage in stable and frequent interaction. If communities or groups are understood not as a stock of speakers but instead as a reproduction system, one can talk of speaker populations that make up "linguistic communities" with their own varieties and changes. In establishing a correlation between "population" and "linguistic community," it is possible to see that the limits of the latter can be appreciated more clearly in the field of demography than in linguistics, given that populations are usually ascribed to specific administrative entities or geographies, whereas linguistic communities offer boundaries that are more blurred and unstable.

From a demographic perspective, it's important to distinguish between the notions of "population" and "settlement" and between those terms and "population system." A "settlement" consists of the settling or installation of a group of individuals in a defined geographic space. A "population system," on the other hand, is understood as the organization and evolution belonging to a population, such that a system can be identified beyond the disappearance of the members who comprise it. This concept has served as the basis for both demographic theories with a biological or Darwinian basis and those with a social foundation, including those of nationalist ideologies. Biologists maintain that the basis of populations' evolution is biological; that is, it is marked by individual biological events such as births and deaths. Social theories interpret populations as always being concerned with social factors, including migrations, internal mobility, and the differentiated evolution of the groups that comprise them; for nationalists, collective identities exist beyond those of the individuals who comprise the collectives. In this fashion, when speech communities are localized in specific geographic spaces, they make up settlements, which can have, for example, the form of urban or rural centers whose internal dynamics would be of interest for social theories more than biological ones. From a nationalist perspective, populations who are speakers of a language would be defined by their collective identity which would make them permanent in time and situate them closer to the concept of a "language community."

Within a general population, when a group of people shares one or more common characteristics, one can speak of a "subpopulation." Those characteristics can be quite varied: people over 65 years of age, having an Asian background, residents in certain neighborhoods, belonging to this or that generation, or being of foreign origin and not having become naturalized... Thus, when one identifies speakers of two or more languages within a speech community, one speaks of the existence of "linguistic groups," each of them referred to as a subpopulation with speakers of each of the languages.

Composition of the Population

Populations have an internal composition based on basic factors such as age, sex, civil status, religion, educational level, profession, socioeconomic status, race, or ethnicity. These are the most common factors in the demographic analysis of national populations and of Western societies. Each of these factors can serve to identify subpopulations which, in turn, can have a heterogeneous internal composition. The fact that such diversity is possible does not preclude populations with scant internal complexity from existing.

Knowledge of the factors that comprise and condition populations is essential for the application of demography with social, political, economic, or cultural aims. Likewise, these factors can be correlated with linguistic components (languages, dialects, varieties...) whose manifestation and dynamics depend to a large degree upon them.

Age

Age is a factor that affects each person in particular and which is expressed by the number of years already lived. The "age" factor conditions individuals in multiple vital aspects, such as their school or university education, their period of fertility, or their social rights and obligations: the right to vote, license to drive, social or military service, retirement, and civil and criminal liability, among other areas. From the linguistic point of view, age also conditions aspects as important as the period of acquisition of the first language, the period of communicative socialization, or the processes of linguistic deterioration which are very tied to cognitive deterioration.

Despite its obvious relevance for every person individually, age is a factor with strong social implications. Some of these are reflected in the life stages which have just been outlined; others have a direct impact within demography. When the common characteristic of people who make up a subpopulation is having lived through a specific experience or event during the same time frame, one speaks specifically of "cohort"; for example, the cohort of those born in 2000. When the event experienced is "birth" in the same time period, a cohort is equivalent to a "generation." While it's certain that there are no natural limits that establish absolute categories of individuals in terms of time, demography introduces ranges according to the specific goals of its studies. Therefore, the set of people born at a certain moment or period within a population is given the name of either cohort or generation when the moment corresponds to birth. Cohorts can reflect specific periods of the life cycle as well as groups within a determined subpopulation: for example, that of students who begin a degree or educational cycle on a specific date.

In a cohort, the time period considered presupposes certain effects are similar or identical upon the members that comprise it. This entails a process of socialization similar in all its components, with all its consequences, and certain analogous cultural, socioeconomic, or historical experiences. This is the reason that generational cohorts are given specific denominations: *baby boomers, millennials, Generation Z, pandemials...* In this way, from a sociolinguistic perspective, generations clearly marked by certain events have existed; for example, the school-aged Filipino population who received their education completely in English after 1901 because of the de-hispanization ordered by the US after the war with Spain.

In demography, people's ages are usually considered either for specific years or in five-year periods, although segmentation by age can be flexible and organized into "periods" or "synthetic or hypothetical cohorts." When segmented by age, the "mode" (most repeated value) and the "median" (value under which 50% of the population finds itself) are usually measurements of reference in demography. However, subdividing populations by five-year age groups has meant that information about the use of languages doesn't include minors under the age of five, as happened until 2020 in the US census. This leads to a disconnect in relation to the real process of linguistic acquisition which begins to become evident at two or three years of age and doesn't need to be limited to a single language. Therefore, there is a lapse of two or three years in which the information about the knowledge and use of languages by children is nebulous. On the other hand, from a social perspective, there are differences between the languages spoken by some generations and others, generally in contexts of immigration in which the first generation, in situations of heteroglossia, usually don't have fluency in the language of the host community, but the second generation does, with a high probability that the third or fourth generation no longer knows the language of their family's origin.

Sex or Gender

Sex, as a biological factor, characterizes people in a particular way, even if one cannot overlook its social, economic, and of course demographic dimensions. The social dimension of sex is clearly appreciated when it is considered not as a strictly biological fact, but as a construct related to social traditions, roles, and functions. Demography, as well as linguistics, habitually works with the categories "man" and "woman," although studies are incorporating a category of "other" or "gender diverse" which reflects the emergence and increased visibility of a more diversified social reality.

In general, societies display a distribution of the sexes that shows a certain percentage equilibrium between the two majority groups with a slight advantage for women, despite proportions varying according to age. Specifically, more men are usually born than women, but there is a balance in proportions from the 20s and 30s, which becomes unbalanced once more, this time in favor of a majority of women among people older than 80. In any event, the composition by sex of a population, with a very small percentage of people of diverse identity, tends to be balanced, save for in some specific populations. For example, Mount Athos is an autonomous state under Greek sovereignty in which some 2,000 monks live, all men, scattered among 20 or so Orthodox monasteries. The territory is called the Monastic State of the Holy Mountain and no females of any species are allowed there, apart from female cats and hens (Nikolic, 2020). A more recent case is that of the community called *SuperShe* on an island in the Baltic Sea which only women are allowed to visit to rest and distance themselves from social pressures: it's a business which only admits female clients, generally of high social status, where the whole staff is also made up of women. These kinds of communities, nonetheless, can be deemed exceptional.

The social nature of sex or gender is clearly appreciated when it is correlated with different social realities. Thus, historically and traditionally, women have held roles tied to childrearing and family life which are also related to playing a key role in the generational transmission of culture and language: consider the term *mother tongues*. In more modern Western societies, women have increasingly been employed more often than men in administrative roles, in offices or service industries, with salary conditions inferior to those of men. In migratory contexts, specialization in work roles by sex also often occurs; for example, in the first decades of the twenty-first century in Europe, many migrant women, especially those of older ages, devoted themselves to taking care of the sick or the dependent, whereas men found work in construction, transportation, or agriculture. This work reality determines their position within the linguistic market, even ignoring any previously acquired academic education. In general, the processes of discrimination against women regarding the knowledge and use of languages have been a fertile field of investigation which links sociology and anthropology with linguistics or sociolinguistics, among other disciplines (Holmes & Meyerhoff, 2003).

Race, Ethnicity, and Religion

The concepts of "race," "ethnicity," and "religion" refer to complex realities that often intersect or overlap. Notable difficulties are entailed in both defining them and identifying them in an adequate (or at least reasonable) fashion and, consequently, in analyzing them. These realities often appear to be linked to the linguistic diversity of a territory or community and are especially associated with the knowledge and use of minority languages.

Race, ethnicity, and religion are notions used in demography to identify or classify population groups characterized by racial, cultural, historic, geographic, or even sociopolitical traits. As a point of departure, race is associated with biological differences between populations; ethnic group (or ethnicity) is associated with the cultures, nations, or peoples of origin of a population (Guibernau & Rex, 1997); and religion, logically, marks differences between groups who adhere to different belief systems. The apparent simplicity of these characteristics breaks down when one tries to be precise as to what their components are or identify specific individuals of each of the supposed races, ethnicities, or religions recognized within a society.

Despite its biological nature, race is more of a social construct than pure genetics. Thus, while in Brazil race is identified by phenotypes, such that two siblings with different phenotypes can be considered to be of different races, in the United States it is identified by bloodlines; as a result, a person with a white phenotype could be considered Black if they have an ancestor of that race. Ethnicity, for its part, offers some blurred boundaries for the identification of its members, given that history, culture, or ancestry are not absolute values; thus, racial phenotypes are often resorted to in order to identify members of one ethnicity or another.

As for religion, there are well-defined confessional groups, but one cannot overlook that these are personal beliefs, not always confessed or accompanied by external practices. The identification of a citizen of Germany as a Turk is often tied to the practice of the Muslim religion and to a darker skin color, but these correlations don't always exist, needless to say. Race and religion are factors that live in the origin of deep social divides and complex processes of discrimination. Thus, racialization is a process experienced by very different kinds of varieties and expressions that are associated with specific racial or ethnic characteristics which become a prototype of speaking a language poorly (Rosa, 2019). Thus, the Spanish of bilingual people of the Andes can racialize them and burden them with a lack of prestige for incorporating transferences from the Quechua or Aymara languages (Zavala & Back, 2020); likewise, the English of Hispanics in the US can racialize them to the degree that they become the subject of mockery by native English speakers (Hill, 1993; Alim, Reyes, & Kroskrity, 2020).

The difficulties in identifying races, ethnicities, and religions can logically be noted in the practice of demography. For this reason, analysis becomes complex, if not impossible. But this complexity also affects the individuals themselves who might have doubts about their racial, ethnic, or religious identity (or even deny them) and therefore encounter internal conflicts when they attempt to answer questions about their identity. Martin Guardado (2019) has presented identity visually as a system of concentric layers in which the identification with a specific ethnic origin usually predominates within a national allegiance, pan-ethnic identity, or cosmopolitanism. In this way, a young North American from a Mayan

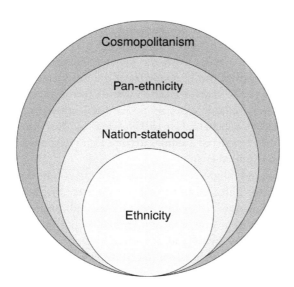

FIGURE 3.1 Concentric levels of identity.
Source: Guardado (2019).

family who comes from Mexico could identify as Mayan, as American, as Latino, or as a citizen of the world, without encountering any contradictions.

Therefore, this system of superimposed notions can make it difficult to place races, ethnicities, and religions in the disciplines or entities that categorize them with different goals, be these scientific, such as demographic ones, or administrative or functional, as in the case of censuses. Alain Blum (2004: 134) clarifies the following with regard to ethnicity, understood as the distinctive character of an ethnic group:

> Ethnicity cannot be established by criteria such as origin, whether defined by birthplace or ancestry, given that this results from a combination of multiple criteria, which likewise have to do with origin: place of residence, social networks, migratory history, etc.
>
> *Blum, 2004*

Given these difficulties, demolinguistics has proposed some basic criteria for the definition and identification of individuals and communities, criteria which prove especially useful when the societies are multicultural ones. For Extra and Gorter (2001), these basic criteria are "nationality," "birth country," "self-identification," and "language spoken at home," and can be applied both to individuals and to social groups, communities, countries, or other kinds of territories. The same Extra and Gorter (2001) proposed characterizing the countries of the European Union with regard to ethnicity, language, and religion. According to these criteria, Austria would be characterized as a country by its language (German is the majority) and by its religion (Catholicism is the majority); Spain would be characterized as a country only by language (Spanish is the majority), whereas Ireland would be identified by ethnicity, language, and religion. Extra and Gorter (2008) have developed a chart with the general identification criteria used in censuses and statistics from the 27 countries of the European Union.

Of course, this kind of characterization doesn't factor in certain aspects which are essential to other methodologies, so no hard reflection is necessary to find its weak points, whether conceptual or methodological. Nonetheless, it should be understood that it is considered a simple attempt to understand a tangled reality in the pursuit of some applied goals.

Race, ethnicity, and religion are all factors that can also be interpreted through a socioeconomic lens. Thus, it can be said that these factors, beyond their specific characterization, function in many societies as indicators of socioeconomic differences that can lead to situations of marginality or sociocultural disparaging. Examples exist in many fields and are often related to language. As is well reflected in censuses, the case of Black (racial issue) and Hispanic (ethnicity issue) populations in the United States is paradigmatic, given that the poverty indexes among these population groups are up to three times higher than that of non-Hispanic white populations, and their income levels are also usually 70% lower

TABLE 3.1 Identification of ethnicity, language, and religion in 27 EU countries.

EU country	Ethnicity/Ethnic nationality	Language	Religion
Austria	-	+	+
Belgium	-	-	-
Bulgaria	★	★	★
Cyprus	+	+	+
Czech Republic	+	+	+
Denmark	-	-	-
Estonia	+	+	+
Finland	-	+	+
France	-	-	-
Germany	-	-	+
Greece	-	-	-
Hungary	★	★	★
Ireland	+	+	+
Italy	-	-	-
Latvia	+	+	-
Lithuania	+	+	+
Luxembourg	-	-	-
Malta	-	+	-
Netherlands	-	-	-
Poland	+	+	-
Portugal	-	-	★
Romania	+	+	+
Slovakia	+	+	+
Slovenia	★	+	★
Spain	-	+	-
Sweden	-	-	-
United Kingdom	+	+	★

★ Voluntary/optional question
Source: Extra & Gorter (2008: 19).

than the latter (Creamer, 2020). Furthermore, the lower education level of both groups, on average, had repercussions of more complicated access to jobs and salaries at the highest levels. It's no coincidence, then, that the "Black or African American Vernacular English" used among the African American population is considered by many to be an impoverished variety (Labov, 2012) or that the Hispanic population is associated with a poorly viewed ethnicity and characterized by a retention of Spanish that supposedly interferes with their knowledge of English (Rosa, 2019). This last belief is very firmly rooted in the United States, despite being clearly refuted by data: the 2020 census revealed that the Hispanic population with a good command of English has increased from 59% to 70% in just ten years. With regard to socioeconomic factors, knowing the evolution of these population groups (that is, their growth index) proves of great interest for social, economic, and political planning, given their impact on public and private events in American society.

On the other hand, while race, ethnicity, and religion can be interpreted socioeconomically, they can also be viewed from an eminently cultural and, of course, linguistic perspective. These factors usually establish close ties with other data, such as country of birth or origin of ancestry, which proves essential for knowing the cultural and linguistic profile of the members of a population, as they can be indicators of preferences in the consumption of food or clothing, in the purchase of cultural products of different kinds (books, newspapers, audiovisual media...), or in participation in cultural, religious, sports, or other groups.

In the case of immigrant groups, association with regional homes, friendship circles, volunteer and social action groups, or educational and recreational organizations usually plays a decisive role in the processes of integration and socialization within the host community. These organizations often have a linguistic dimension, given that they bring together people of a similar profile, which can foster, for example, processes for the maintenance of heritage languages (Guardado, 2019). Speakers of minority languages or varieties find in these socialization spaces an environment for communication and for the reinforcement or vindication of their racial, ethnic, or religious identity. Examples of this can be found in Black churches in the United States or Gitano churches in Spain.

Education Level

Demography also pays attention to the level of education or degree of training or instruction that members of communities hold. This individual factor clearly affects the linguistic repertoire, as well as the knowledge and use of one or more languages (either vernacular or of other origins) within a population.

The education levels that characterize individuals are established by the political authorities for the society in each area or territory. This is not an obstacle to using categories based either on general levels or on the number of years of schooling. As for general education levels, although UNESCO proposes an International Standard Classification of Education (ISCED. v. Ch. 5), institutes for statistics usually distinguish the following categories:

1. Illiterate because of physical or mental causes.
2. Illiterate for other reasons.
3. Without schooling.
4. Primary school or equivalent.
5. General secondary education.
6. Professional education.
7. University studies or equivalent.

Within each category, one can distinguish subcategories which, in general, are called cycles. As for the years of schooling, education is usually distributed as follows: preschool; schooling from 6–12 years; schooling from 12–18 years; and the university period, generally between 18 and 25, even if the formative period can extend up to 35. Of course, each community or country distributes their educational periods and ages according to their own organizational criteria. Moreover, each society distinguishes and organizes regulated education (official and / or obligatory) and non-regulated education (unofficial and voluntary).

As can be easily deduced, people's educational level is closely tied to work and, unquestionably, to socioeconomic factors. Educational level conditions access to the labor market, as well as employment and job mobility. The correlation between level of studies, employment, and income levels is usually direct and establishes various correlations with other individual factors, such as sex and age, according to societies and their evolutionary periods.

The incidence of education level on languages known and used by individuals is more than evident, as shown by Bourdieu's (1984) theories about control of the linguistic market and sociolinguistic studies about mastering more prestigious varieties in order to access certain social spaces, an ability usually acquired through schooling (Labov, 2001; Moreno-Fernández, 2009a). Likewise, educational periods determine at what age access to a second, third, or fourth language is offered, and what degree of fluency students can attain. In parallel, private educational offerings can complete or complement individual linguistic training. To understand how this happens, a detailed analysis of education systems is necessary.

Civil Status

Generally, a person's civil status refers to their condition in terms of their birth, nationality, family, or marriage. These conditions are usually reflected in the civil register of each administrative entity (country, state, province, etc.) and affect people's rights and obligations. Of the possible civil statuses, only the one that affects marriage between individuals will now be considered. It is true that the existence or lack of a marriage does not (either in itself or directly) affect the knowledge or use of languages, but the information provided by administrative registers in this matter can be quite revealing for sociolinguistic purposes.

In general, civil registers, as well as censuses and other demographic instruments, contain information about people who have never married, those who are married, and those who have ceased to be married, in order to pass on to other states: separation, divorce, or widowhood. These registers do not of course reflect the state of those people who have not registered or formalized their relationship; that is, those who have not given their marriage a formal status or who have not made formal notice of their separation. Likewise, there is no direct correlation between registered marriages with their possible descendants, and the number of members who cohabit in the home.

As far as registered marriages go, it is of special interest for demography to know the origins of conjugal partners. And here is where the concepts of "endogamy" and "exogamy" arise. If a marriage is strictly endogamic, it can be understood as one between members with a common ancestry. For anthropology and sociology, endogamy exists when the union takes places between individuals of like or similar condition, whereas exogamy happens when the marriage joins two people belonging to different groups or categories (race, social class…). From this perspective, a society can be endogamic and exogamic at the same time: exogamic as far as the family is concerned and endogamic with regard to race, for example (Lévi-Strauss, 1981). This latter case was very evident in Nazi Germany and Apartheid South Africa, but it is also possible to find in many other societies. At the same time, a distinction is made between homogamy (marriage between individuals of the same class, profession, or education) and hypergamy / hypogamy (marriage between individuals of a higher or lower social group) (Rodríguez-García, 2002).

Demography often takes note of the frequency of marriages (the number that take place within a generation), as well as the calendar (median age of first marriage), and calculates the "nuptiality indexes" of a specific community or group. In general, it considers first marriages, although not exclusively. This kind of accounting clearly reveals the existence of a correlation between marriage and sociocultural factors. Thus, the median age of access to marriage is clearly lower in communities of Africa than in communities of Europe; within Europe, the median is lower in the Mediterranean countries than the Nordic ones, and lower in rural areas than urban ones. Likewise, differences exist in the dynamics of the marriage markets. A "marriage market" is the theoretical meeting place for people who are willing to legally constitute a couple, and there are communities in which those meeting places are socioculturally restricted.

With regard to languages and their speakers, a distinction is usually made between "exogamic marriages" (between members of different linguistic communities) and "endogamic marriages" (between members of the same linguistic community). In the first case, one also can speak of "mixed marriages." As can be easily understood, these unions of whatever kind don't necessarily need to be formalized, but their registration alone allows for a systematic demographic analysis. The greater indexes of marriages of one kind or another can be conditioned by sociocultural factors, often associated with race, ethnicity, and religion.

The linguistic outcomes of mixed unions can be diverse, according to the social conditions that produce them. Colonial Hispanic America distinguished more than 50 kinds of "castes" which were seen as products of the union of people of different racial configurations: white man with indigenous woman, mestizo; indigenous man with Black woman, zambo; mestizo man with indigenous woman, cholo… (León, 1924; Alvar, 1998). The union between individuals of the same race or caste favored the maintenance of their habitual means of communication, whereas the mixing of races favored the language of the member tied to the social group of greater prestige and socioeconomic weight. In current communities, mixed marriages can favor bilingualism (or even plurilingualism), the maintenance of a minority language, or, on the contrary, its replacement by the social presence of the predominant language.

Employment and Socioeconomic Status

The factors mentioned up until now have clear socioeconomic implications. Nonetheless, specifically socioeconomic factors also affect people in terms of their employment situation, their employment type, and their means of obtaining resources.

In demography, the most often used measurements to determine wealth and poverty (that is to say, individuals' socioeconomic levels) are "per capita income" and "median income." "Per capita income," also called "per capita gross domestic product" or "income per capita" is defined as the average income per person in a specific group, community, or territory; and the "median income" is defined as the average income per household or family within a specific group, community, or territory. This income can include amounts received regularly as payment for work, from public funds, from pensions funds, or payments in kind. Per capita income is an indicator of wellbeing tied to values of wealth and poverty. It's generally determined by an external reference which is the minimum income level necessary to achieve a certain quality of life in a country in accordance with its characteristics and habits.

Income level is determined to a large degree by individuals' work situations, which are in turn affected by employment. There are many different classifications of employment correlated with socioeconomic status. One of the best known is by Erikson and Goldthorpe (1992), which served to establish a framework of classes with hierarchized employment as follows:

TABLE 3.2 Class scheme.

I. Higher-grade professionals, administrators, and officials; managers in large industrial establishments; large proprietors
II. Lower-grade professionals, administrators, and officials; higher-grade technicians; managers in small businesses and industrial establishments; supervisors of non-manual employees
IIIa. Higher-grade non-manual routine employees (administration and commerce)
IIIb. Lower-grade non-manual routine employees (sales and services)
IVa. Small proprietors, artisans, etc. with employees
IVb. Small proprietors, artisans, etc. without employees
IVc. Farmers and smallholders; other self-employed workers in primary production
V. Lower-grade technicians; manual worker supervisors
VI. Skilled manual workers
VIIa. Semi-skilled and unskilled manual workers (not in agriculture, etc.)
VIIb. Farm workers and other workers in primary production

Source: Erikson & Goldthorpe (1992).

This typology of occupations is constructed upon the basis of the training or education acquired and correlated with income levels; this contributes to determining the socioeconomic status of individuals and social classes. As such, the better an education one has, the better one's job and income level. Likewise, the occupational situation of members of a society corresponds with the social dimension of the factors involved which allow for individuals to be grouped into sectors, social classes, or scales of socioeconomic statuses. Therefore, they are social variables that are more than purely demographic, but which have effects upon demography by influencing mortality, fertility, family configuration, or migration.

On the other hand, occupations can be identified by the productive or economic sector they are tied to. Economic sectors are divided into the primary sector (activities for the extraction of resources from the natural environment), the secondary sector (activities for the transformation of raw materials), and the tertiary sector (service activities). Within the latter, one can identify activities related to intellectual work and the knowledge economy (the quaternary sector), as well as activities of creation, interpretation, and organization of data and projects (quinary sector). However, specific productive sectors are often managed independently, separated from the three main ones: the agricultural sector, the industrial sector, and the livestock sector.

It's also worth mentioning that the scope of socioeconomic status within a society, in addition to being measured through complex indices and scales, as Erikson and Goldthorpe (1992) did, can give rise to occupational prestige indices. Among these indices, one of the best known is the National Opinion Research Center (NORC) index, which, through a system of surveys, established the prestige of numerous occupations in the United States (Reiss *et al.*, 1961). This prestige index reflected both the correlation between employment, income, and education, and the level of inequality reached by a society.

With this same goal, the Human Development Index (HDI) was created. The HDI, calculated by the United Nations Development Program (UNDP) since 1990, summarizes the opportunities for progress in the respective countries through indicators that go beyond mere gross domestic product, incorporating indices such as life expectancy at birth (health), expectancy and average years of schooling (education), and gross domestic product per capita in relation to purchasing power (economy) (UNDP, 2020). The HDI reveals the growth potential of each country and its general living conditions if inequality did not exist. This composite index was developed and applied as a result of the influential works of Amartya Sen (1987), which also served as the basis for the construction of other indices, such as the Multidimensional Poverty Index (MPI) or inequality indexes, including gender (Sen 1976, 1981, 1992). Sen's analytical proposals have had a great impact upon all social sciences.

In short, socioeconomic status is a variable that makes it possible to determine behavioral patterns and service needs based on a society's components. But it's also a variable that affects languages and their varieties. Levels of literacy, reading and entertainment habits, access to knowledge of other languages, with or without stays abroad, or the acquisition of broader or more specialized linguistic registers may all depend on socioeconomic status. Socioeconomic status ultimately determines the existence or nonexistence of what is known in sociolinguistics as the "linguistic deficit" (Bernstein, 1971).

Population Distribution

Demography pays special attention to the distribution of populations. So much so that any information about the characteristics of a population and its components always refers to a specific place, group, space, or territory. When speaking of "population distribution," reference is made to the places where the population is located (for example, rural or urban areas, small or large cities, metropolitan and non-metropolitan areas, etc.), to its surface area or size, and the density of the concentrated population. In general, developed nations show patterns of increasing population concentration in their largest urban centers. These distributions can be conditioned by geographic, physical, or socioeconomic factors, and at the same time be subject to redistribution processes caused by mortality, fertility, and migration.

In general, demography, like demolinguistics, is applied to countries, subnational organizations (municipalities, administrative regions, districts, provinces, autonomous communities), or supranational or transnational organizations (for example. the European Union). However, nothing prevents their application to groups derived from any of the factors presented here: age groups, groups by sex or gender, groups with specific educational levels.

A population's territorial distribution is fundamental with regard to language. In this respect, the entities that are usually considered for demolinguistic analysis can be very diverse. Of course, countries are a recurring reference, but so are cities, regions, districts, states, or provinces. Information on this distribution is usually included in the categories "place of residence," "address," or "postal district," alongside "country, region, or place of origin or provenance." Censuses and registers of these entities may include, directly or indirectly, information of interest regarding languages. Likewise, data referring to specific social groups can be useful for learning about linguistic or dialectal aspects: for example, the languages studied by the school population, knowledge of languages according to occupations, or the level of use of a particular language among members of a generation. In this way, it is evident that demolinguistics can be interested in both the geographic distribution and the social distribution of populations.

Household and Family

Demography pays special attention to the configuration of one of the core organizations of societies: the home. However, "home" is a complex concept, intimately linked to notions of "family" and "marriage" and, therefore, must be treated with caution and precision. Home has great social relevance because it is usually the breeding ground for some similar behaviors among its members. Likewise, its importance is decisive for people's linguistic dimension, given that the acquisition of language and the first experiences of social life usually take place in the home. In fact, people who do not live in households usually live in collective residences (military barracks, monasteries, prisons) in which there is no intergenerational linguistic transmission.

With regard to "residence," it's important to note the differences between the notions of "family" and "home." The former is built on biological or parental bases so that demographers do not speak of "single-member families." Households, on the other hand, are formed for reasons of coexistence, and as such a household may include individuals not related by biology or kinship, and there can even be households made up of a single person. Likewise, households are usually formed in "dwellings" built in "areas" of different kinds: "urban" (cities), "functional urban," "conurban," "rural," "municipal," "provincial" or "departmental," "regional" (of different sociopolitical profiles), or "national."

Thus, "home" and "family" can be understood as synonyms only when they refer to a group of people related to one another who also live together. But, in turn, the kinds of familial relationships can be very diverse. It has been already observed that the notion of family requires, within demography, precision that indicates what kind of configuration is involved in each case: "nuclear family," "extended or complex family," "single-parent family," "same-sex family," "foster family," or "adoptive family." Within families, the person who is the main economic breadwinner usually has the status of "head of the family," in terms of both income and ownership of the home or residence. Regardless of its type, the family or, if one prefers, the "family home" is a key factor for generational replacement, hence the trend called "familism," which defends the need to constantly develop programs to support and defend the institution of the family (Popenoe, 1988; Garzón 1998).

On the other hand, the configuration of households and families is not static but subject to demographic changes. In Western societies, for example, there has been evidence of a trend toward a reduction in the size of households and in the number of households made up of married couples, while non-family households are gradually increasing. All of this also affects the processes of linguistic transmission although, for demolinguistics, the concept of "language spoken at home" continues to be fundamental and the subject of specific treatment in censuses.

Demographic Changes

Changes in a population (or subpopulation) are the consequence of three primary demographic processes: births, deaths, and migrations. Naturally, these events have repercussions for all the characteristics associated with the populations that experience them, including the knowledge and use of languages. A population change occurs depending on the number of births, deaths, and migrations at the beginning and the end of a set interval of time. When the population at the end is greater than at the beginning, one speaks of "demographic growth;" the difference between the number of people who are born and those who die indicates the "natural growth" of a population. Therefore, these processes of change have to do with the fertility, mortality, and migratory processes of populations.

Fertility

In principle, fertility is a faculty that relates essentially to individuals. It is a biological process, derived from the sexual behavior of people which gives rise to the birth of children. However, demography interprets it as the reproductive behavior of populations and defines it as the number of children a generation produces over the course of their reproductive life, if it were not affected by mortality. The concept usually refers to the reproductive capacity of the female population, although it's also possible to apply it to male fertility. In general, even if conditioned by multiple factors, childbearing years usually begin between 10 and 15 and last until the age of 45–50.

At this point, it's important to introduce a new concept (fecundity) and establish a clear distinction from the first (fertility). In English, "fecundity" is understood as the biological capacity to conceive and have children. Therefore, on the one hand, one has the number of children that one has (fertility) and, on the other, the ability to conceive and have them (fecundity). The need to clearly distinguish between the two concepts is not only due to the fact that they refer to different but related notions, but also because, in other languages, including Spanish, the meanings of fecundity and fertility are reversed. Given the influence of English on international research, meanings can become confused, and their English meanings may end up being dominant.

The social effects of fertility also reach the realm of languages. When a population receives young immigrants who speak a language different from the usual language in the host community, it is foreseeable that the linguistic group of the immigrants will have a proportionally greater growth than that of the total population. This is because fertility is higher among women in their 20s, whereas it's lower at later ages or when the final childbearing years are approaching. Demography has likewise shown that fecundity is usually higher among populations or subpopulations with lower purchasing power. This reality explains why the Hispanic population of the United States, most of whom speak Spanish and generally have fewer economic resources, has demonstrated a greater fertility during the final decades of the twentieth century and the first ones of the twenty-first century, to the point that, in some states, the Hispanic population has come to outnumber the non-Hispanic white population (Krogstad, Passel, & Noe-Bustamante, 2021).

Mortality

Like fertility, mortality is a quality experienced by individuals but which, referring to a specific period or a specific cause, also affects populations. In short, mortality refers to the incidence of deaths within a population, although it is often specified as the survival probability within a population during a given period.

The mortality of a population is sensitive to the socioeconomic conditions of groups and individuals, as evidenced by its greater incidence among those with scarcer economic resources. In fact, one way of measuring the level of a community's or any population's economic development is to know the incidence of "infant mortality;" that is, the deaths of those children under one year old. Mortality also directly affects other demographic concepts, such as "life expectancy," "demographic growth," or "natural growth." Life expectancy at birth refers to the frequency with which people die at each age; that is to say, in different generations. This is the same as knowing the average number of years that people born in a specific period can or usually live. The "natural growth" of a population reflects the balance between the number of people who are born and those who die. When migratory movements are added to births and deaths, one knows the overall "demographic growth" of a population.

As both an individual and collective factor of populations, demographic mortality also affects languages. A language does not survive without a population of speakers. Therefore, one part of linguistics has been directly interested in the death of languages linked to the extinction of communities or population groups (Hagège, 2000; Nettle & Romaine, 2000; Crystal, 2000). There are even records of "last speakers"; among the best-known cases are those of Dolly Pentreath, the last native speaker of Cornish (1777) in the British Isles; Tuone Udaina, last speaker of Dalmatian (1898) in Mediterranean Europe; Mary Joachina Yee, last speaker of the Barbareño language (1965) in North America; Big Bill Neidjie, the last speaker of Gaadujiu (2002) in Australia; and Cristina Calderón, the last speaker of Yamana (2022) in Chile, to mention cases from a few continents (Harrison, 2010).

However, it's not necessary for an entire community or ethnic group to disappear for a language to become extinct; it's enough that it stops being spoken by part of a population. Experts are at work on languages in danger of extinction, as well as on the processes of shift and abandonment of languages, and the findings are reflected in inventories such as those carried out by *Ethnologue* or UNESCO. At the same time, there are displacement processes that lead languages to disappear, not in an absolute way, but within a specific community or group. Often, these cases are the effect of the coexistence of languages within a territory or community. This coexistence may have originated between neighboring territories or between populations overlapping as a consequence of colonization or migration.

Migrations

Migrations entail singularly striking population changes with particular characteristics versus other factors of change. Numerous definitions of the phenomenon of migration have been given; for P. Neal Ritchey (1976), for example, migration is simply the change of residence that implies a movement between communities. The *Glossary of Migration* (IOM, 2019) offers a broader definition:

> The movement of persons away from their place of usual residence, either across an international border or within a State.
>
> IOM, 2019

Other definitions focus more on social aspects; for example, Mangalam and Schwarzweller (1968) interpret migration as the movement from one social system to another in which the migrant must change friendships and social and economic relationships. At the same time, other definitions are limited to specific circumstances, such as the one offered by the United States Census Bureau when referring to a change of residence when the origin and destination are in different counties.

This diversity of definitions reveals that migration is a complex reality that involves movements that can be interpreted on very different scales. Thus, migrations can be characterized by their direction ("north-south migration," "rural-urban migration," "urban-rural," "rural-rural," "urban-urban"…), by the entity of the regions of origin and destination ("international migration," "internal migration"), by their duration ("temporary migration," "permanent migration") or by the way in which they happen, in relation to legislation ("clandestine migration," "irregular migration") or in relation to the means available ("spontaneous migration," "encouraged migration," "unprotected migration"). Similarly, migrations can be characterized by the causes of movement ("economic migration," "forced migration," "political migration"…) or by the individual profiles of the people moving ("child migration," "youth migration," "female migration"…).

All these migratory possibilities have led to the development of a complicated network of specific concepts and terms. As for people, the terms "migrants," "immigrants" (who have arrived in a country), or "emigrants" (who have left a country) are used; although more precise characterizations can also be made: "exiles," "refugees," "clandestine migrants," "irregular migrants," "documented" or "undocumented" (without papers), or "unaccompanied migrants." As for places, "countries of origin" are distinguished from "host countries" or "destination countries." And these concepts can receive more specific definitions depending on the circumstances of each country or each migration process. For example, the "Immigration and Colonization Law" enacted in Argentina in 1876 clearly defined an *immigrant* as:

> every foreign laborer, artisan, industrialist, farmer, or teacher who, being under sixty years of age and accrediting his morality and aptitudes, arrives in the republic to settle there, on steam or sailing ships, paying second–or third-class passage, or having the trip paid for by the Nation, the provinces, or private companies, protectors of immigration and colonization.
>
> *Immigration and Colonization Law N°. 817. Argentina. 1876*

The Instituto Nacional de Estadística (INE) of Spain defines an immigrant as follows:

> An "immigrant" is a person [...] who was born abroad, is over 15 years of age and has lived in Spain (or intends to do so) for 1 year or more. (The case of Spaniards by birth born outside of Spain who are under two years old when they arrive in Spain are excluded.)
>
> *INE, 2022*

With all its conceptual and terminological baggage, migration is an essential part of demographic analysis, as it also is of demolinguistics. Demography distinguishes "gross" or "total migration," referring to the sum of movements in and out of a place, from "net migration," referring to the difference between movements in and out. The glossary of the International Organization for Migration (IOM) (2011) offers these definitions:

> Total Migration. The sum of the entries or arrivals of immigrants, and of exits, or departures of emigrants, yields the total volume of migration, and is termed total migration, as distinct from net migration, or the migration balance, resulting from the difference between arrivals and departures.

> Net Migration. Difference between the number of persons entering the territory of a State and the number of persons who leave the territory in the same period. Also called "migratory balance." This balance is called net immigration when arrivals exceed departures, and net emigration when departures exceed arrivals.
>
> *IOM, 2011*

Therefore, analysis of migrations requires determining when and where a displacement has taken place. For this reason, it's important not to confuse migration with other types of continuous or short-distance movements, such as daily transfers to work (commuting) or movements within the same area of residence. Regarding the subjects of migrations, demography specifies, for example, whether the movements occur with greater intensity and frequency among adults or youth, among those with precarious or solid socioeconomic conditions, or among people from countries with certain social, political, or economic situations.

The importance of all these variables is enormous for a population, given that, if the birth or mortality rates show their effects over the medium and long term, migrations do so in very short periods of time, with repercussions (or even immediate impacts) for multiple areas of the host community; for example, in the demand for supplies, the need for services of all kinds, such as education, or the provision of labor in neglected sectors. Among these consequences, there are also those of a demographic nature, given that the arrival of certain groups of immigrants can drag in new groups for various reasons, such as family reunification or the ease of integration into the host community thanks to the support of migrants who arrived earlier.

Migrations are usually the result of the intersection of a long series of social, economic, political, legal, or cultural factors. In general, when migration occurs for economic reasons, immigrants may have an average income that is much lower than the average of the destination society. In 2020, the household income of the migrant population in Spain was 46% lower than the average income of Spaniards. This situation causes the immigrant population of foreign origin to concentrate at the lowest levels of the economic structures.

Along with migratory processes and the people involved, it's also necessary to consider other aspects of great significance for demolinguistics. Among these are the administrative status of migrants and the phenomenon of descent, especially when it comes to permanent migrations. Regarding the first, demography considers for its analysis the nationality of migrants who can maintain their nationality of origin, acquiring local documentation that generally evidences their status as a foreign immigrant, or they can be naturalized, keeping or losing their nationality of origin, according to a country's legislation. Therefore, registries and censuses can make counts of unnaturalized foreigners (distinguishing nationalities of origin) and of naturalized foreigners; likewise, there are registers of nationals of a country residing abroad whose data are of great interest for demolinguistic analysis.

The descendants of immigrants deserve special treatment for their involvement in multiple areas, including linguistic ones. On the one hand, the nature of this offspring must be assessed; on the other, it develops over successive generations. With regard to the first, the nationality of the children of immigrants depends to a large extent on the legislation of each country, even if it's also usually strongly conditioned by being married (or not) to a person with the nationality of the host country. When neither of the parents are nationals of the host country, the offspring frequently acquires their parents' nationality, although exceptions are usually contemplated; for example, if the parents are stateless or in the case of adoption prior to the age of 18. As has been pointed out, if one of the parents is a national of the country of residence, the children usually acquire that nationality through the principle of *jus sanguinis*.

TABLE 3.3 Generations of immigrants.

First generation: People who migrated as adults (over 18)
Generation 1.25: People who migrated as teens (13–17 years)
Generation 1.5: People who migrated as children (6–12 years)
Generation 1.75: People who migrated as infants (0–5 years)
Second generation: People born in the host country with both migrant parents
Generation 2.25: People born in the host country with one migrant parent
Third generation: People born in the host country to parents born in the host country, with one or more migrant grandparents
Fourth generation: People whose parents and grandparents were born in the host country

Source: Bolzman, Bernardi, & Le Goff (2017).

As for successive generations descending from immigrants, a first relevant trait for demographic analysis is the way in which they self-identify. The immigrants who have arrived in the host country are called the first generation; second-generation immigrants will be the offspring of the first generation, third-generation immigrants the offspring of the second, and so on, although it is not very common for analyses to go beyond the fourth generation, given that, by this point, integration is considered complete. Indeed, there are studies, for example, of fourth-generation Hispanics or Asians in the United States, but they are not the most abundant (Bolzman, Bernardi, & Le Goff, 2017).

The linguistic analysis of the aforementioned generations has led to the introduction of three interesting concepts. One, already mentioned, is that of "heritage speakers," a label that corresponds to those of second or later generations. A second concept is that of the "1.5 generation" to refer to the offspring of first-generation immigrants arriving in the host country during their childhood. The concept was introduced from studies on Asians in the United States to characterize those children who, having arrived with their parents, grew up in the host country without being socially categorized clearly as members of either the first generation or the second (Ryu, 1991). Later, other generational nuances have been defined (Waters, 2014; Bolzman, Bernardi, & Le Goff, 2017). In those specific generations, the phenomenon of heritage languages is especially complex and interesting.

The third concept worthy of mention in this regard is the idea of "third culture kids" (Guardado, 2019). This label is applied to individuals who have spent a significant period of time in two or more ethnic or cultural environments and, as such, combine characteristics of both in the form of a "third culture" (Fail, Thompson, & Walker, 2004).

Successive generations of immigrants may undergo a process of integration or assimilation in which language takes on a unique value. Integration is a process of adjustment between an immigrant population and a host or resident population which makes possible the intersubjective construction of the social reality of

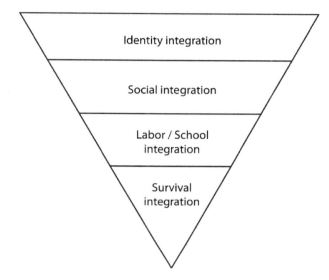

FIGURE 3.2 Pyramid of the integration process.
Source: Moreno-Fernández (2009b).

both populations and leads them to share values, whether they be those of the resident population or of the immigrant population. Integration is a bidirectional process, one of continuous reproduction and renewal, through which residents and immigrants organize their activity within a host community. The integration of immigrants can be divided into several levels (or phases, if they take place successively): survival integration, labor or school integration, social integration, and identity integration (Moreno-Fernández, 2009b).

As for (socio)linguistic integration, the factors involved are also varied and complex, including phenomena such as diglossia, reduction, and substitution. The linguistic origin (languages and varieties) of the migrants plays a notable role in this, which is why we speak of "alloglot" migrants (who speak a language other than that of the residents) or "homoglot" migrants (who share the same language with the residents). These situations make it possible to distinguish "native speakers" from "foreign speakers," with the implicit difficulty that foreignness is not a linguistic quality. Hence the disputes about the use of the labels "second language" and "foreign language" and the fact that a language brought by immigrants but long settled in a territory should not be treated as "foreign."

But other factors also influence integration, in addition to the length of residence: the languages handled and taught in the educational system, the way in which socialization takes place in the new community, or the idiomatic and dialectal repertoire of the host community. In fact, there is a scale of the linguistic complexity of the host country or area whose components could be combined with a scale of linguistic affinity between the language of the migrants and that of residents, giving rise to various kinds of combinations:

1. Monolingual community with a single variety.
2. Monolingual community with several varieties.
3. Bilingual community with little social relevance for a second language.
4. Bilingual community with social relevance for a second language.

When the host community is bilingual, the preference by immigrants for one language or another will be determined by factors such as the prestige of each language, the distribution of the public and private domains of the resident languages, prior knowledge of the resident languages by the immigrants, or the affinity of the immigrants' language with each of the resident languages. Faced with situations that favor multilingualism and the maintenance of immigrant languages, monolingual contexts can lead to the progressive loss by immigrants of their language, even within the migrant community and, in a more advanced phase, within the families that comprise it.

From Facts to Theories

Finally, it's worth mentioning that information obtained from the concepts, facts, indicators, or projections of demography allows for the elaboration of comprehensive theories with the ability to interpret or predict major demographic events. From a general perspective, theories have been formulated that explain human evolution in terms similar to those of other living beings ("biologist theories") and theories that highlight the influence of culture and education on birth rates and, therefore, on demographic growth ("cultural demographic theories"). Among the latter, one of the most famous is the Malthusian theory, which maintains that the growth of the world population is geometric, whereas the growth of natural resources is arithmetic, and as such humanity is condemned to a progressive impoverishment that can lead to its complete disappearance (Malthus, 1798).

Another theory of great relevance during the past century has been "demographic transition," which explains the passage from a situation of high birth and mortality rates, especially in the preindustrial age, to a period of low mortality and birth rates. From here, the "theory of productive revolution" has been formulated, according to which a paradigm shift is taking place in which high survival rates guarantee the maintenance of the population, as well as an optimal intergenerational proportion.

In one way or another, these theoretical proposals contribute to understanding various trends in the processes of language death in minority, marginal, or marginalized communities, or diffusion of the linguistic varieties typical of the most vigorous population groups.

Later, in the 1980s and '90s, Dirk Van de Kaa (1987) and Ron Lesthaeghe (1991) formulated their theory of "second demographic transition," based mainly on the transformations in family dynamics which take place in Europe: later marriages, increase in divorces, postponement of fertility, families without children. This transition, like the first, was largely due to the improvement in people's quality of life and the changes in norms and attitudes that resulted from that.

Likewise, the theoretical contributions of demographers such as Ronald Lee (2003, 2016) and John Caldwell (1982) are worth mentioning. They related demographic transition and vital statistics, especially aging and mortality, with intergenerational changes; for example, the way of making financial transfers. The demography of households and families has been a growing line in demography since the 1970s (Caldwell *et al.*, 2006; Lee & Mason, 2010; Yépez-Martínez, 2013) which deserves to be explored in more detail in sociolinguistics and demolinguistics.

Summary

The notions presented in this chapter are commonly handled in demographic descriptions and explanations and allow for the conceptual map of the specialty to be drawn. Demography works fundamentally with populations and, because languages are spoken by individuals grouped in populations, any analysis of these results in a better understanding of the social life of languages. Demography, therefore, has enormous significance for the study of languages and their varieties within society.

Demographic studies are interested in populations and their composition, distribution, and changes. The composition of populations is determined by factors such as age, gender, race, ethnicity, religion, educational level, and employment. Although they materialize in individuals, each of these factors offers a social dimension which inevitably reveals implications of a socioeconomic nature. Likewise, each of these factors can be correlated with linguistic aspects, such that the confluence of the study of languages and societies leads to a better understanding of the vitality of languages and their varieties.

With regard to the distribution of populations, it's obvious that this is also reflected in the distribution of languages. This can be geographical, of course, but it is also social, even on the household level. As for the changes experienced by populations (the true nucleus of demographic analysis), it's evident that birth and death rates of human groups have repercussions for the vitality of languages. Likewise, migrations determine movements of groups of speakers and give rise to social conditions that affect processes as decisive as intergenerational transmission, the formation of bilingual communities, or linguistic substitutions.

References

Alim, Samy, Angela Reyes, and Paul V. Kroskrity (eds.) (2020): *The Oxford Handbook of Language and Race*. Oxford: Oxford University Press.

Alvar López, Manuel (1998): *Las castas coloniales en un cuadro de la Real Academia Española*. Madrid: Espasa-Calpe.

Bernstein, Basil (1971): *Class, Codes and Control*. London: Routledge.
Blum, Alain (2001): "Resistance to Identity Categorization in France". In D. Kertzer and D. Arel (eds.), *Census and Identity*. Cambridge: Cambridge University Press, pp. 121–147
Bolzman, Claudio, Laura Bernardi, and Jean-Marie Le Goff (eds.) (2017): *Situating Children of Migrants across Borders and Origins: A Methodological Overview*. Dordrecht: Springer.
Bourdieu, Pierre (1984): "Capital et marché linguistiques". *Linguistische Berichte*, 90: 3–24.
Caldwell, John (1982): *Theory of Fertility Decline*. London: Academic Press.
Caldwell, John C., Bruce K. Caldwell, Pat Caldwell, Peter McDonald, and Thomas Schindlmayr (2006): *Demographic Transition Theory*. Dordrecht: Springer.
Creamer, John (2020): *Inequalities Persist Despite Decline in Poverty for All Major Race and Hispanic Origin Groups*. Washington: United States Census Bureau.
Crystal, David (2000): *Language Death*. Cambridge: Cambridge University Press.
Erikson, Robert and John Goldthorpe (1992): *The Constant Flux: Class Mobility in Industrial Societies*. Oxford: Clarendon Press.
Extra, Guus and Durk Gorter (eds.) (2001): *The Other Languages of Europe*. Clevedon: Multilingual Matters.
Extra, Guus and Durk Gorter (eds.) (2008): *Multilingual Europe: Facts and Policies*. Berlin: De Gruyter.
Fail, Helen, Jeff Thompson, and George Walker (2004): "Belonging, identity and third culture kids: life histories of former international school students". *Journal of Research in International Education*, 3: 319–338.
Garzón, Adela (1998): "Familismo y creencias políticas". *Psicología Política*, 17: 101–128.
Guardado, Martin (2019): *Discourse, Ideology and Heritage Language Socialization: Micro and Macro Perspectives*. Berlin: De Gruyter-Mouton.
Guibernau, Montserrat and John Rex (eds.) (1997): *The Ethnicity Reader: Nationalism, Multiculturalism and Migration*. Oxford: Polity Press.
Hagège, Claude (2000): *Halte à la mort des langues*. Paris: Odile Jacob.
Harrison, K. David (2010): *The Last Speakers: The Quest to Save the World's Most Endangered Languages*. Washington: National Geographic.
Hill, Jane (1993): "Hasta la vista, baby: Anglo Spanish in the American southwest". *Critique of Anthropology*, 13: 145–176.
Holmes, Janet and Miriam Meyerhoff (eds.) (2003): *The Handbook of Language and Gender*. Oxford: Blackwell.
Instituto Nacional de Estadística (2022): *Glosario de conceptos*. www.ine.es/DEFIne/?L=0 Online resource.
IOM (2011): *Glossary on Migration*. Geneva: IOM / UN Migration.
Krogstad, Jens, Jeffrey Passel, and Luis Noe-Bustamente (2021): *Key Facts about U.S. Latinos for National Hispanic Heritage Month*. Washington: Pew Research Center.
Labov, William (2001): *Principles of Linguistic Change: Social Factors*. Malden: Blackwell.
Labov, William (2012): *Dialect Diversity in America: The Politics of Language Change*. Charlottesville: University of Virginia Press.
Lee, Ronald (2003): "Demographic change, welfare, and intergenerational transfers: a global overview". *Genus*, 59: 43–70.
Lee, Ronald (2016): "Macroeconomics, Aging, and Growth". In J. Piggott and A. Woodland (eds.), *Handbook of the Economics of Population Aging*. Amsterdam: Elsevier, pp. 59–118.
Lee, Ronald and Andrew Mason (2010): "Fertility, human capital, and economic growth over the demographic transition". *European Journal of Population*, 26: 159–182.

León, Nicolás (1924): *Las castas del México colonial o Nueva España*. México: Museo Nacional de Arqueología, Historia y Etnografía.
Lesthaeghe, Ron (1991): "The second demographic transition in western countries: an interpretation". *IPD Working Papers*.
Lévi-Strauss, Claude (1981): *Las estructuras elementales del parentesco*. Buenos Aires: Paidós.
Malthus, Robert (1798): *An Essay on the Principles of Population*. London: J. Johnson.
Mangalam, Joseph J. and Harry Schwarzweller (1968): "General theory in the study of migration: current needs and difficulties". *International Migration Review*, 3: 3–18.
Max Planck Institute for Demographic Research (2022): *Glossary of Demographic Terms*. www.demogr.mpg.de/en/about_us_6113/what_is_demography_6674/glossary_of _demographic_terms_6982/ Online resource.
Moreno-Fernández, Francisco (2009a): *Principios de sociolingüística y sociología del lenguaje*. 4th ed. Barcelona: Ariel.
Moreno-Fernández, Francisco (2009b): "Integración sociolingüística en contextos de inmigración: marco epistemológico para su estudio en España". *Lengua y migración / Language & Migration*, 1: 121–156.
Nemeth, Christopher (2004): *Human Factors Methods for Design: Making Systems Human-Centered*. Boca Ratón: CRC Press.
Nettle, Daniel and Suzanne Romaine (2000): *Vanishing Languages: The Extinction of the World's Languages*. Oxford: Oxford University Press.
Nikolic, Zoran (2020): *Atlas de fronteras insólitas*. Barcelona: Planeta.
Popenoe, David (1988): *Disturbing the Nest: Family Change and Decline in Modern Societies*. New York: Aldine de Gruyter.
Preston, Samuel, Patrick Heuveline, and Michel Guillot (2000): *Demography: Measuring and Modeling Population Processes*. Oxford: Wiley.
Reiss, Jr., Albert J., Otis Dudley Duncan, Paul K. Hatt, and Cecil C. North (1961): *Occupations and Social Status*. New York: Free Press of Glencoe.
Ritchey, P. Neal (1976): "Explanations of migration". *Annual Review of Sociology*, 2: 363–404.
Rodríguez García, Dan (2002): *Endogamia, exogamia y relaciones interétnicas*. Barcelona: Universitat Autònoma de Barcelona.
Rosa, Jonathan (2019): *Looking Like a Language, Sounding Like a Race: Raciolinguistic Ideologies and the Learning of Latinidad*. New York: Oxford University Press.
Ryder, Norman B. (1964): "Notes on the concept of a population". *American Journal of Sociology*, 69: 447–463.
Ryu, Charles (1991): "Generation 1.5". In J.F.J. Lee (ed.), *Asian American Experiences in the Unites States: Oral Histories of First to Fourth Generation Americans from China, the Philippines, Japan, India, the Pacific Islands, Vietnam and Cambodia*. Jefferson: McFarland, pp. 50–54.
Sen, Amartya (1976): "Poverty: an ordinal approach to measurement". *Econometrica*, 44: 219–313.
Sen, Amartya (1981): *Poverty and Famines: An Essay on Entitlements and Deprivation*. Oxford: Clarendon Press.
Sen, Amartya (1987): *The Standard of Living*. Cambridge: Cambridge University Press.
Sen, Amartya (1992): *Inequality Reexamined*. Cambridge: Harvard University Press.
United Nations (2013): *Demopædia: Multilingual Demographic Dictionary*. www.demopaedia. org/ Online resource.
United Nations (2022) *Glossary of Demographic Terms*. https://population.un.org/wpp/Glo ssaryOfDemographicTerms/ Online resource.

United Nations Development Program (UNDP) (2020): *Human Development Report 2020*. New York: UNDP.
United States Census Bureau. (2022): *Glossary*. www.census.gov/programs-surveys/geography/about/glossary.html Online resource.
Van de Kaa, Dirk (1987): "Europe's second demographic transition". *Population Bulletin*, 42: 1–59.
Waters, Mary D. (2014): "Defining difference: the role of immigrant generation and race in American and British immigration studies". *Ethnic and Racial Studies*, 37: 10–26.
Yépez-Martínez, Brenda (2013): "La demografía de la familia y los hogares". *Cuadernos del CENDES*, 83: 121–133.
Zavala, Virginia and Michele Back (2020): "Discourse and Racialization". In A. De Fina and A. Georgakopoulou (eds.), *The Cambridge Handbook of Discourse Studies*. Cambridge: Cambridge University Press, pp. 527–546.

4
DEMOLINGUISTIC DATA AND SOURCES

Demolinguistic research encounters many theoretical, methodological, and technical difficulties. In addition, its development requires study closely related to reality in terms of sociopolitical or ethnic contexts, as well as in terms of the idiomatic repertories of populations and the dynamics of social use of languages and varieties. This epistemological complexity and the diversity of possible communities to be studied, together with the involvement of different disciplines, requires the handling of very diverse but complementary sources and data, as well as constant verifications throughout the research process so that the analyses and conclusions are sufficiently clear and reliable.

This chapter aims to explain the basic components of demolinguistic methodology and the ways in which they manifest in different types of communities and for different purposes. To address questions of demolinguistic research and confront the conceptual challenges these present, it is essential to have information about populations and their linguistic characteristics, for both individuals and the subgroups that comprise populations. This information takes the form of data coming from various sources.

Data

The data used by demolinguistics comes from each of the linguistic and demographic factors relevant for analysis. Therefore, these data correspond to the number of speakers (within their different typologies), the number of learners (within their different levels), the number of births and deaths among the members of the linguistic groups, the makeup of homes and families, the number and profile of the members of all kinds of groups or associations, and the

DOI: 10.4324/9781003327349-5

number of immigrants and emigrants of each linguistic group with regard to some communities of origin and destination, among other possibilities.

As can be easily deduced, these data are not all of the same nature; as such, it proves especially complicated to establish a simple and fixed typology. Some basic distinctions will be proposed that will aid in finding corresponding sources and later in approaching demolinguistic analysis.

A basic first distinction separates the data that have a direct relationship with languages or varieties (their knowledge and use) from those whose relationship with them is inferential, rather than direct. The following kinds of data belong to the first group: number of speakers of a language in a community, language spoken in the home, language spoken with parents / partners / children / grandparents / friends / colleagues, language spoken in different domains (private and public), and the number of students of a language in an educational center, among others. In contrast, data such as the following would have an inferential relationship with language: components of mixed marriages, number of migrants from a specific origin, descendants of persons with certain ethnic or racial origins, members of a specific cultural association or social group, members of a specific religious congregation, number of naturalized or non-naturalized persons in a community, and the number of foreign residents in a country, among others. From these kinds of information, "inferential" data can be obtained.

These data may be "exact" in some cases and "approximate" in others when they cannot be directly verified in each of their units. Likewise, the data can be "direct" or "original" when they correspond to an actual observation or census taken by researchers, or they can be "indirect" when the data have been obtained through samplings or statistical analysis, although the data labeled "inferential" can also be considered indirect. On the other hand, data can be "primary" if their collection is made by the researchers themselves, or "secondary" or "second-hand" if there is not a direct relationship between those who gather the data and those who carry out their analysis with purposes that don't necessarily need to coincide.

Finally, demography often works with a distinction between "raw," "corrected," and "refined" data. "Raw" data are those that are handled in their original form, without later modification, adjustment, or aggregation/disaggregation. "Corrected" data are those that are mathematically modified to adjust them to patterns, models, or formats, or data that are the consequence of a revision of the original data to correct possible errors. "Refined" data are those that are mathematically or formally suitable for inclusion in an argumentation or in the demonstration of a hypothesis. In demography, it's important not to confuse raw data with "gross rate" or "crude rate," which refer to the rate or the average of a demographic fact within the whole of a population.

Direct data about the knowledge and use of languages are also enriched by information or linguistic data that can be considered to be indirect that help one to better understand and interpret the former. This is how information related to media broadcast in a specific language or the presence of one or more languages in mass media or on social media can be understood. One can similarly understand the number of bilingual education programs offered to a community for its literacy, the number of texts, literary or not, translated from or into a language, the volume of web pages created in a language by a community, and the nature and specificity of the linguistic legislation that may exist in a country. Another kind of data that could be added to this is called "attitudinal," because it refers to attitudes toward languages among the members of a specific population or linguistic group, given the importance of this factor for the processes of maintenance, displacement, or substitution of languages, especially minority ones.

Regarding the manner of collecting data of demolinguistic interest, the procedures do not stray far from those common in other disciplines, especially when dealing with quantification-oriented data: observation, discussion or focus groups, questionnaires, and interviews. It is possible to use all of these when dealing with demolinguistic analysis and factors (Newell, 1988).

Sources

Data collection is a basic, delicate, and complex task: basic because all demolinguistic analysis must be built upon data; delicate because biases and errors can occur that must be avoided as much as possible; and complex because there is no single way of carrying out data analysis. Most data collected for demolinguistic purposes do not have a specifically linguistic origin; instead, they're derived from administrative actions and procedures, at local, national, or international level. This means that the data collection of interest to demolinguistics does not (in many cases) follow a process designed, executed, or controlled by demolinguists.

Demolinguistic data basically come from collecting demographic information from specific sources. There are, unquestionably, data and sources that are properly demolinguistic, but these are proportionally scarce, as well as irregular in time and form. This reality, however, situates us before a first fundamental difference: that of identifying, on the one hand, those sources which are demolinguistic properly speaking and, on the other, those which are demographic, ethnological, economic, political, or sociological. This basic distinction is subordinated to another, more general one, referring to the process of collecting demographic information in general, and to the sources associated with each case. According to this last aspect, the collection of dynamic information is distinguished from the collection of static information. Dynamic information is provided by statistical registers; static information is provided by censuses and surveys.

In principle, it is possible therefore to distinguish between two general sources (demographic and demolinguistic) and two classes of information (dynamic and static) that refer to three specific sources (registers, censuses, and surveys). This simple classification can be expanded with other categories, such as distinguishing primary, secondary, and tertiary sources of information. "Primary sources" or

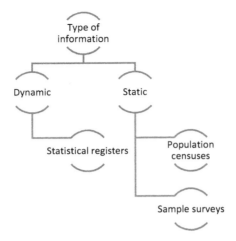

GRAPH 4.1 Sources and types of information.

"direct sources" are understood to be those that provide original information which has not been previously modified, interpreted, or evaluated. These sources can be found either in print or digital format. Direct sources in demolinguistics are those that offer first-hand information about, for example, the number of speakers of a language in a given territory.

"Secondary sources" or "indirect sources" are those that offer modified or interpreted primary information for a purpose different from that of the investigation being undertaken. These sources, also printed or digital, are useful when access to primary sources is lacking either because they don't exist, due to a lack of resources, or for other reasons; secondary sources are a good means of confirming data or analysis, or expanding the information offered by primary sources. In the demolinguistic field, indirect sources are considered to be those that do not provide first-hand data on the number of speakers of a language in a given territory, but which allow that information to be deduced based on other kinds of (primary) data, such as ethnicity, race, schooling, or nationality (Moreno-Fernández, 2014: 24–25). Finally, "tertiary sources" are those that offer information about the content and localization of primary or secondary sources. As an example, it could be said that censuses are primary sources, the reports and data provided by other researchers are secondary sources, and bibliographic catalogs or internet links are tertiary sources.

These classifications are very important when conducting research because they help both the researchers and readers to interpret and evaluate the quality of the analyses and results. In any case, the preeminence of three principal sources for demographic, and consequently demolinguistic, analysis is highlighted: registers, censuses, and surveys. Registers and censuses are created by administrative authorities of a territory and are essential sources for demographic analysis. Both registers and censuses can address different aspects of populations and allow one to know their composition, distribution, and dynamics, generally to plan the provision of essential services. Surveys, on the other hand, can be carried out either by administrative authorities or by other kinds of entities or even private initiatives, generally in order to know a reality or investigate it. Interviews and focus groups can be considered complementary modalities of surveys, properly speaking

Administrative Registers

There are many different types of registers referring to different aspects of populations and their components: civil registers, commercial registers, land registers… In general, these are entities with administrative purposes, not purely demographic ones, although demographic information, including demolinguistic information, can be derived or deduced from them. Since the Middle Ages, a good part of the registers of demographic content have been organized and kept by the religious or ecclesiastic authorities of a nation, especially through parish records. But since the nineteenth century, after the French Revolution and through the Napoleonic Code, this responsibility has been taken over by civil authorities. Today, most developed countries have public registration services.

Among the many registers that exist, "civil registers" are notable for their relevance for demographic purposes. Civil registries are public service administrative entities, often linked to ministries of justice, to which the names and surnames, births, adoptions, marriages, divorces, deaths, and naturalizations, among other facts, are reported by the citizens themselves or the entities that offer them direct services. Civil registries are often also called "civil registration and identification," "registry," "acts of civil state / status," "population registration," or "register office"; and in other languages "registro dello statto civile" (Italian), "registre de l'état civil"(French), and "registro civil e identificación" or "registro nacional de las personas" (Spanish).

Complementary to the civil register, as well as to the main censuses, are the records kept by the municipal census or its equivalent. These are registers prepared by town councils where data that affects their municipalities are collected: births, deaths, migratory movements, and changes of residence. The information in these registers is updated continuously which allows one to track the evolution of the population almost in real time. This information is sent by municipalities to national statistics institutes to be collected and aggregated into more general statistics. Broadly speaking, the source data are reliable, although it is possible that errors exist, usually due to a lack of answers, their possible falsification, or a lack of understanding or procedural knowledge on the part of those registered.

Also of great importance for demography are "migratory registers," often run by countries' ministries or departments of the interior. In this case, immigrant individuals register at the border or formally report their arrival in a country.

These registers are of great administrative value because they allow the authorities to control the migrant population, as well as to issue the necessary documentation so that this population can function normally in the host country (certificates, ID cards, travel documents...). In many cases, this registration is also carried out in the consulates maintained in the host country as a service to the citizens of the country of origin. Depending on the area of study, in addition to the immigrant population, the presence of a refugee population might be of interest; these data are handled by the United Nations Refugee Agency (UNHCR), which regularly publishes news and reports. For demolinguistic study, the migrant and refugee registries are essential because they allow one to know the number of people who, due to their origin, can supposedly speak one or more specific languages.

The primary characteristic of the registries that record dates of demographic validity is their dynamism and their practically continuous nature. These services, however, are costly to establish and maintain, due to the demands posed by the evolution of the population. For this reason, countries with fewer public resources do not usually offer this service with sufficient guarantees. Such shortcomings are aggravated when there is no participation or obligation for citizens to account for their own vital circumstances. In fact, there are many countries or periods in which the registrations of births and deaths are carried out long after the moment these occur or where they are simply not done; throughout the world, it has been estimated that up to 25% of vital events are not subject to accurate, timely, or continuous registration. All this leads to information being incomplete and outdated. Where resources allow, registration processes are carried out through computers.

One of the most significant documents for demographic research are the *Vital Statistic Yearbooks*, produced from the work of administrative registries. These reports cover an annual period and present or summarize updated information about births, marriages, civil unions, deaths, or other events that have taken place in a country. Vital statistics come from administrative registries when they are continuous and mandatory and are usually subjected to statistical treatment for their interpretation.

Generally, statistical institutes receive information on vital events in the form of databases, and they are in charge of the aggregation, treatment, and dissemination of this information, for example through the annual directory. However, the development of computer resources of all kinds makes it possible to directly consult demographic data in an open and permanent way, without having to wait for the publication of the corresponding annual directory in order to access the information. This technological development is likewise impacting the carrying out and publication of censuses.

Censuses

As is the case with registers, there are also different kinds of censuses which collect information about people or groups, among many other aspects of individuals, their communities, and activities. There are economic, electoral, agricultural, livestock, and forestry censuses, etc.; likewise, there are language censuses.

In general, information about languages and their speakers is obtained from what is normally known as "population censuses" or "population and housing censuses." Some of these censuses collect specific data about the knowledge and use of the languages of a territory, especially those called "indigenous community censuses" or "native community censuses" (INEGI, 2020; INEC, 2006; INEI, 2018). Most censuses, however, do not do so, although the population data they contain often allow the linguistic reality to be inferred or deduced.

Population censuses are the most important primary source of demographic data: they show a snapshot of a given population and describe it in quantitative terms. This information is highly relevant for government purposes and for the economic and social planning of a community. The collection of population data is carried out upon the universe being studied at a specific moment. The fundamental characteristics of a population census are the following:

1. The census is carried out using a well-defined territory from a political-administrative perspective, with the help of the necessary cartographic instruments.
2. Normally, population censuses are carried out at the national state level, with the collaboration of regional or local administrative entities, and through specialized agencies, such as national statistics institutes or census offices.
3. The data are collected through questionnaires that are filled out by census agents with the information provided personally by the individuals being registered. These questionnaires can be single or multiple and can be more or less detailed depending on the aspects that the census is attempting to record.
4. The data collected must be simultaneous; that is, they must be collected during a predetermined period or moment, within a limit called the "census moment," which marks, for example, that people have been counted as born or deceased within that period.
5. The information must reference all the individuals that comprise a population without omissions or duplications, given that a census implies the enumeration of everyone who belongs to a community with their corresponding characteristics.
6. In traditional censuses, the collection of information is carried out periodically and regularly, usually at ten-year intervals.

As far as the procedure for data collection is concerned, it's worth distinguishing between *"de facto* censuses," which include data from individuals present at a given time and place, whether or not they are permanent residents, and *"de jure* censuses," which include data about all persons residing in a given place, even if they are absent at the moment when the census data collection takes place. When the entities responsible for the census launch surveys about population samples in

TABLE 4.1 Dates and types of censuses in Ibero-America by country and decade in the 2000s and 2010s.

Country	Census date 2000s	Census date 2010s	Census type 2000s	Census type 2010s
Argentina	17/11/2001	27/10/2010	de facto	de facto
Bolivia	05/09/2001	21/11/2012	de facto	de facto
Brazil	01/08/2000	01/08/2010	de jure	de jure
Chile	24/04/2002	19/04/2017	de facto	de facto
Colombia	22/05/2005	02/01/2018	de jure	de jure
Costa Rica	28/06/2000	30/05/2011	de jure	de jure
Cuba	07/09/2002	15/09/2012	de jure	de jure
Ecuador	25/11/2001	28/11/2010	de facto	de facto
El Salvador	12/05/2007	...	de jure	...
Guatemala	24/11/2002	23/07/2018	de jure	de jure
Haiti	12/01/2003	...	de jure	...
Honduras	28/07/2001	10/08/2013	de jure	de jure
México	14/02/2000	12/06/2010	de jure	de jure
Nicaragua	28/05/2005	...	de jure	...
Panamá	14/05/2000	16/05/2010	de facto	de facto
Paraguay	28/08/2002	15/10/2012	de facto	de jure
Perú	21/10/2007	22/10/2017	de facto	de facto
Dominican Republic	18/10/2002	01/12/2010	de jure	de jure
Uruguay	01/06/2004	01/09/2011	de jure	de jure
Venezuela	01/10/2001	01/09/2011	de jure	de jure

Source: CEPAL (2021).

successive years (for example, to determine the evolution of a series of population indicators), one speaks of a "continuous census." On the other hand, a distinction is also made between "censuses," which are carried out across the entirety of a population, and "sample surveys," which are based on a sample of the population with different levels of representation.

Census agencies often coordinate and combine the tasks aimed at collecting data about the population and those regarding housing data. Therefore, "population and housing censuses" abound. These censuses make it possible to obtain information about people (sex, age, education, employment, nationality, and immigration status), about households (size, composition, and characteristics), or about dwellings (dimensions, number of rooms, tenancy, ownership...). Therefore, it's a complicated task that demands the ability to manage reliable "pre-census" information from administrative registries and carry out extensive and exhaustive fieldwork. Included in the information regarding households, there is usually reference to the languages spoken in the home, especially in those countries where migratory mobility is most intense.

With regard specifically to content related to languages, their knowledge, and use among a given population, there are many questions that are of interest from a methodological point of view which affect what to ask and how to ask it at the moment of conducting a census. The decisions made in this regard condition the nature of the answers to such a degree that they can lead to contrary or contradictory information. Given that questions of method regarding language are also raised in the preparation of specific surveys, these aspects will be addressed in the section dealing with the surveys themselves.

Census methodology has a long tradition and widespread international implementation. However, this methodology is in a process of transformation which must evolve from a demography based on censuses to one based on registers. The close relationship that exists between administrative registries of vital events and statistics institutes has already been mentioned, as well as the existence of "continuous censuses" based on samples and surveys. It is precisely thanks to these realities that census methodology is undergoing a worldwide transformation.

This initiative has been under way since the 1990s when Scandinavian countries announced their intention to replace traditional censuses with cross-operations of continuous registers of populations and specific surveys. This methodological change currently implies the abandonment of census fieldwork and the incorporation of techniques based on big data. As Rocío Treviño Maruri and Andreu Domingo (2020) explain, these changes allow, on the one hand, access to population information without having to wait a decade, and on the other, improved reliability of the data by incorporating digital media and data mining, avoiding the biases derived from the lack of reliability of some annotations or the absence of responses. One could also add cost reduction to these reasons and, taken together, they are leading to a transformation of public statistics.

Nonetheless, as can be seen on the map, the methodological transformation of censuses is not taking place in a synchronized fashion throughout the world. Along with the countries that follow a traditional methodology, with a single questionnaire (A) or with a long and short questionnaire (B), there are countries that combine registry data with the enumeration of individuals (combined A) and others that combine registers with surveys (combined B). For the moment, those who base their methodology solely on registers or on continuous censuses are in the minority.

Finally, it is interesting to note the importance of censuses of indigenous or native communities for knowledge about their linguistic situations. However, these censuses are not always precise or explanatory. It is true that ethnic origin is an indicator of the linguistic uses of a population, given that ethnicity, culture, and language tend, in fact, to amalgamate, but it is no less true that such amalgamation is not without errors regarding language and is frequently reflected from the subjective evaluation of those involved. It is common for individuals to be asked about their self-identification with the ethnic group they supposedly belong to or which their ancestors belonged to. But, even in the latter case, the notion of ethnic group can be a vague one, especially when the ancestors encompass a diversity of ethnic origins (Morning, 2008; Busch, 2016).

100 Demolinguistic Data and Sources

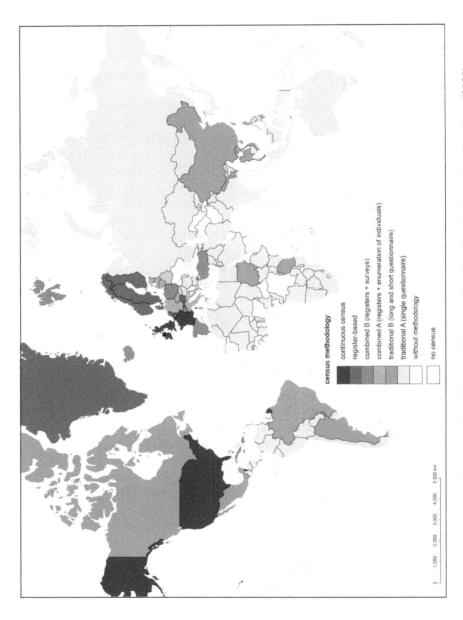

MAP 4.1 Population census methodology in the 2010s. Re-elaboration based on Treviño Maruri & Domingo (2020).

Surveys

A survey is a procedure for obtaining data and information about populations used by various entities: from statistics institutes and government-run census offices to transnational, international, national, or regional organizations with very different profiles, as well as research centers and non-governmental organizations.

Demographic surveys can be "prospective" or "retrospective." The first are usually carried out through repeated surveys over time to discover the evolution of some specific demographic facts; the latter are applied once in search of information about events that took place during a specific past time. Likewise, surveys can refer to very different content domains. In Mexico, for example, some 20 surveys are carried out about households (income and expenses, job and employment, consumer confidence, energy consumption…) and an equal number concerning establishments (business opinion, services, transportation, technological research and development, information, and communication technologies, etc.).

At this point, it is important to jump ahead to explain the difference between a "survey" and a "questionnaire." The "survey" is a process of inquiry and investigation aimed at knowing or verifying specific information through a series of standardized questions that are posed to a representative sample of a population. The "questionnaire" is the document that collects the relevant answers to such questions about a matter planned in advance. As such, survey campaigns are usually carried out with the help of questionnaires, although they are not the only procedure that uses them. Censuses can also use questionnaires, and hence the methodological aspects that affect the content have many points in common with surveys of a population for demographic purposes. Questionnaires, in turn, can be of two kinds: closed (reactive method with options provided) and open (reactive method that involves subjects providing their own free-form information). Despite their seeming simplicity or automatism, questionnaires of whatever kind are able to reveal the respondents' worldview (Bartmiński, 2012: 35), as well as the subjective perceptions of the speakers about many aspects of the social life of languages.

In conducting surveys, the form and content of the questionnaires are as essential as the selection of respondents. Generally, surveys are carried out using a sample of individuals, not on entire populations. This means that the survey offers representative information of a population based on data collected from a part or "sample" of that population. Thus, the data collected through a survey must be representative and generalizable with regard to the overall population.

To be carried out correctly, surveys need to complete some tasks beforehand and others subsequently. The previous tasks, or those of "prenumbering," have to do principally with the construction of the samples and the elaboration of the questionnaires; the first involves an adequate knowledge of the universe and its composition; the second requires an adequate knowledge of the content to be addressed. The subsequent tasks, or those of "postnumbering," have to do with the evaluation of the survey process, with quality checking the data, and with its projection upon the whole of the analyzed population. There are different ways to carry out this evaluation: comparing the observed data with some expected values, comparing the data collected from one population with those coming from other populations, crossing the demographic variables, repeating the data collection process if necessary, or correcting errors that have been detected. Many of these tasks are handled in the data analysis phase, even if it is advisable for the data to undergo the highest possible purification before starting the analysis.

The forms that surveys can take are quite varied, depending on the interests of the promoting entities. They can be continuous (with an established periodicity: annual, monthly, etc.) or occasional and special; they can be general or specialized, depending on the demographic aspects being sought. Among specialized surveys are those dedicated to demolinguistic issues: that is, to the collection of data about languages, their speakers, knowledge, and use. The possibility of working on samples of different compositions also exists: random sampling, stratified or quota sampling, cluster sampling, or systematic sampling (random sampling of the first component and selection by fixed or systematic intervals of the subsequent elements) (Cochran, 1991). Likewise, the size of samples can vary depending on several factors, among which the diversity in the internal composition of the population is notable.

The construction of survey content in the form of questionnaires can give rise to "content errors" if the wording is inadequate; the sampling process, for its part, can give rise to "coverage errors" when an inadequate number of people are chosen, or they have the wrong profile. Content errors don't only occur in the pre-survey stage but can also arise during a survey itself if the questionnaires are not applied in a way that suits the understanding and expression of the respondents. Language itself can be a barrier to adequately understanding a questionnaire. That's why, in some cases, there are attempts to adapt the language of the questionnaire to that of the people being censused or surveyed, as is the case with the United States census, which is offered in 59 languages in addition to English, or with the census of India, which in 2021 was offered in 16 languages. Coverage errors, aside from deficiencies in the sample, can occur in the selection of individuals if some are duplicated or omitted in a given area. In addition, the possibility of a simple error or misunderstanding at the moment of entering data must also be considered.

The content of a questionnaire and the way it is presented are crucial aspects of conducting surveys. To a large extent, the conceptual difficulties related to linguistic questions acquire materiality in the construction of census questionnaires or those for specialized surveys. Hence the importance of the chapter about linguistic concepts and terms that this book includes. There are numerous works that address the study of linguistic issues, such as the vitality of Mapudungun in Chile (Lagos, 2006), the languages of South Africa (Kehl, 2011), or the So language in Thailand (Tehan & Markowski, 2017). Let's look at some examples of surveys and censuses in which specific attention is paid to languages.

Switzerland has a *Survey on Language, Religion and Culture* (LRCS) which is part of the survey program of the Federal Population Census and has been carried out by the Federal Statistical Office (FSO, 2016) every five years since 2014. The survey is done by sampling and consists of a computer-assisted telephone interview (CATI) followed by a written questionnaire in print or online. The respondents are those who form part of the permanently resident population aged 15 or older, who live in private households, and can answer in German, French, or Italian. In case one does not have sufficient linguistic knowledge of one of these languages, the first part (CATI) can be completed with the help of a third person (proxy interview). In the survey carried out in 2019, 13,417 people (51% women and 49% men) took part, of which 76% were Swiss citizens and 24% foreign residents in Switzerland. In this case, the content of the survey referred specifically to languages in the following way:

- Main and known languages(s).
- Language(s) spoken at home.
- Main language(s) spoken in / by the adult relationships.
- Language(s) spoken in childhood.
- Language(s) learned or desired.
- Language(s) used in the family and with friends outside the home (frequency).
- Language(s) used to read, to watch television, to listen to the radio, to browse and interact on the internet (frequency).
- Language(s) used at work (frequency).

In this case, the concepts handled are those of "main language" and "language spoken or used at home," which are generally given as options that can be chosen and presented in writing (closed structure); for example, German (or Swiss German), French (or Swiss French Patois), Italian (or Grisons or Ticino Italian dialects), Rhaeto-Romance, Serbo-Croatian, Albanian, Portuguese, Spanish, and English, among others. The mere preparation of the list, as well as establishing the names of the languages and varieties included, entails a highly relevant demolinguistic exercise. In this regard, the information provided by Alexandre Duchêne, Philippe N. Humbert, and Renata Coray (2018) on the process that led to the decision on how to ask the question and the kind of linguistic information that was being sought in the Swiss survey is especially illustrative.

As can be seen from the successive corrections, the editors of the questionnaire were fully aware of what was involved in choosing one term over another, not to mention the specific phrasing. The 2014 version is what ultimately forms part of the LRCS.

Another example is provided by the Third Census of Native Communities of Peru (INEI, 2018). This is a *de facto* census, given that the population studied was made up of all the people who were found in the dwelling at the "moment of the census" (midnight on the day of the census) regardless of their habitual place

November 2011 "Catalogue"	August 2012 First draft of the questionnaire	February 2013 Second draft (pilot survey)	September 2013 Third draft (after the pilot)	February 2014 Final version
	'To begin with, could you tell me what your main language is, namely the language or the dialect in which you think and that you know best?'	'To begin with, could you indicate what your main language is, namely the language ~~or the dialect in which you~~ ~~think and~~ that you know best? If you think you have more than one main language, indicate them all.'	'To begin with, can you indicate what your main language is or what your main languages are, namely the language or the languages that you know best? ~~If you think~~ ~~that you have~~ ~~more than one~~ ~~main language,~~ ~~indicate them~~ ~~all.~~'	'To begin with, can you indicate what your main language is ~~or what~~ ~~your main~~ ~~languages are,~~ namely the language or the languages that you know best?'

FIGURE 4.1 Evolution of the discussions regarding the wording of the question about main languages in the Swiss surveys.

Source: Duchêne, Humbert, & Coray (2018).

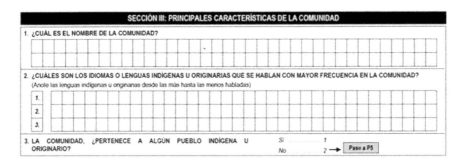

FIGURE 4.2 Fragment referring to languages from the questionnaire used in the Third Census of Native Communities of Peru (INEI, 2018).

of residence. In total, the census included 108 questions divided into sections, of which Section III ("Main characteristics of the community") is particularly interesting because it collects information about the name of the community, the indigenous languages spoken with greatest frequency, and the indigenous or native peoples its members belong to. Information was also collected about the settlements that make up the community.

Demolinguistic Data and Sources **105**

For the purposes of the census, Peru's indigenous or native peoples are defined as those who descend from populations that inhabited the country at the time of colonization and who conserve their own social, economic, cultural, and political institutions, or part of these, and who at the same time self-identify as such. In the definition, great value is placed on self-recognition or self-ascription, while ignoring the possible contacts, fusions, or developments of these peoples after colonization.

On the other hand, the census understands as indigenous or native all those languages of Peru that were present prior to the spread of the Castilian or Spanish language and which are preserved and used within the national territory. The specific question about languages asks simply whether they are spoken without going into detail about the process of acquisition or their social implantation. Among other reasons, this information is gathered in order to identify the country's monolingual and multilingual areas so as to facilitate the implementation of programs for the bilingual education of this population, respecting the right of expression in their own language according to their traditions.

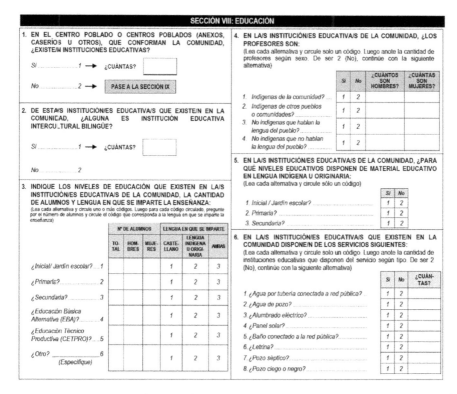

FIGURE 4.3 Section on education from the questionnaire used in the Third Census of Native Communities of Peru (INEI, 2018).

In fact, in the section of the census dedicated to education, languages are also alluded to in asking about the bilingual or monolingual nature of the community's educational centers and about the teachers' knowledge of languages. The linguistic information, however, is gathered with little nuance concerning the social presence of the languages and of their knowledge and use in specific domains.

In general, very unequal treatment can be found from one country to another among censuses and surveys that deal with languages, probably due to both the differences in idiomatic and sociolinguistic realities and the political or social interests for which the information is gathered by the responsible agencies. The statistical services of the United Nations are aware that censuses usually collect three kinds of data: mother tongue, language of habitual use, and proficiency in one or more languages. However, questions about the use of languages take many different forms (main language, commonly used language, best-spoken language, language spoken at home, language spoken fluently) and sometimes ignore the ability to use different languages in different situations.

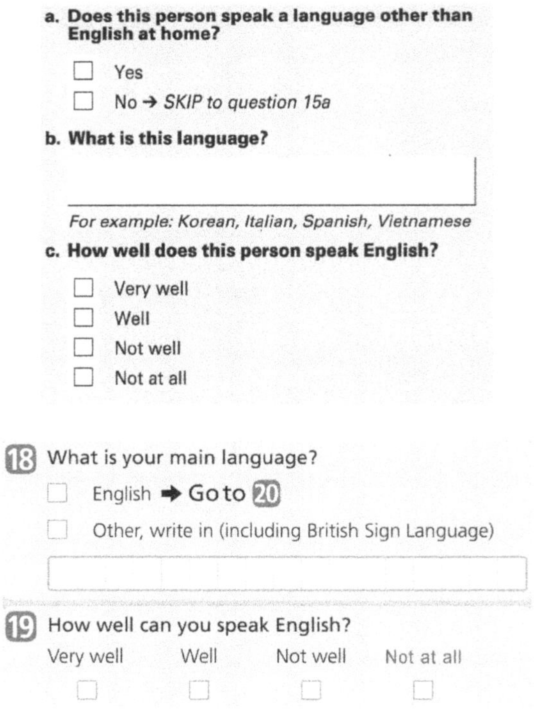

a. **Does this person speak a language other than English at home?**
   ☐ Yes
   ☐ No → SKIP to question 15a

b. **What is this language?**

   _____

   For example: Korean, Italian, Spanish, Vietnamese

c. **How well does this person speak English?**
   ☐ Very well
   ☐ Well
   ☐ Not well
   ☐ Not at all

18 What is your main language?
   ☐ English → Go to **20**
   ☐ Other, write in (including British Sign Language)
   _____

19 How well can you speak English?
   Very well   Well   Not well   Not at all
   ☐   ☐   ☐   ☐

FIGURE 4.4 Questions on languages in the censuses of the United Kingdom (bottom) (2011) and the United States (top) (2014).

Questions about knowledge of other languages do not usually produce comparable data. Surveys from the United Kingdom and the United States are clearly focused on the knowledge and use of English; the British one asks about "main language," whereas the American questionnaire asks for the "language spoken at home."

This diversity of treatment in the content referring to the languages of a population can also be found within a country. This is the case for questionnaires that supposedly seek the same kind of information but do so through different questions in each region, inevitably leading to the gathering of heterogeneous responses which are very often impossible to compare. In Spain, the Galician Institute of Statistics periodically carries out a "Structural Survey of Households," which includes a module about the knowledge and use of the Galician language in which it asks for the language of "habitual use" and the "initial" language. In the "Sociolinguistic Survey" carried out by the Autonomous Community of the Basque Country, also in Spain, questions are asked about the "first language" or mother tongue and the language "normally spoken," whereas the IDESCAT (Statistical Institute) of Catalunya asks specifically about "initial," "identification," and "commonly used" languages. For its part, the *Llibre blanc de l'us del valencià* (2005), compiled from surveys organized by the Valencian Academy of Language, asked respondents for the language(s) they "know how to speak" and the language(s) spoken or used in specific domains or with certain speakers.

Therefore, diversity in the methods of referring to the acquisition, knowledge, and use of languages in Spain prevents us from obtaining homogeneous information about those all too relevant linguistic absences. This conceptual deficiency is partially compensated for thanks to the detailed information that the Spanish sources provide on the domains of social and familial use of languages. In this respect, it is worth noting that, in 2001, the Government of Catalunya promoted the creation of a "System of Linguistic Indicators" (Sistema de Indicadores Lingüísticos: SIL) with the aim of compiling information about linguistic knowledge, offer in education, and use. Linguistic uses fundamentally manifested in two large areas: in relationships between people (interpersonal linguistic uses) and in relationships with organizations, both public and private (public administrations, institutions, companies…) (Solé i Camardons, 2003). The SIL, with its variants, provides the basis for the surveys in Spain that are concerned with languages.

Likewise, the conceptual diversity used in the bilingual areas of Spain is partially compensated for by the collection of data from a central entity, such as the Center for Sociological Investigations (Centro de Investigaciones Sociológicas: CIS), an autonomous body attached to the Presidency of the Government. In 1994, the CIS published the report *Conocimiento y usos de las lenguas de España* (Knowledge and Use of the Languages of Spain), which offered the results of a survey for which the same methodology and the same conceptual basis were used for all the bilingual areas of Spain (Siguán, 1994). The survey sought to study the knowledge

LLIBRE BLANC DE L'ÚS DEL VALENCIÀ:
ENQUESTA SOBRE LA SITUACIÓ SOCIAL DEL VALENCIA

Valencià 1 ☐ Castellà 2 ☐ Castellanoparlant 3 ☐

Qüestionari ☐☐☐☐ FITXA 1

Bon dia/Bona vesprada. Actualment estem realitzant una enquesta sobre la situació social del valencià a la Comunitat Valenciana (el seu ús, coneixement...).Vosté ha sigut seleccionat aleatòriament, tindria vosté inconvenient a respondre unes preguntes? Només seran uns quinze minuts. Li agraïm la seua col·laboració.

P.1. **a. Entén vosté el valencià?**
b. Sap parlar valencià?
c. Sap llegir en valencià?
d. Sap escriure en valencià?

Sexe 1. H ☐ 2. M ☐ **Edat** ☐ **Municipi** ☐☐ **Comarca** ☐☐ **Població** ☐

	L'entén	Sap parlar	Sap llegir	Sap escriure	
Gens	1	1	1	1	→ PASSE A P.3.
Un poc	2	2	2	2	
Prou bé	3	3	3	3	→ PASSE A P.2.
Perfectament	4	4	4	4	

P.2. Quin és o ha sigut el mitjà principal pel qual vosté ha après o està aprenent a...?

	Parlar en valencià	Llegir en valencià	Escriure en valencià
Amb la seua família	1	1	1
Amb els seus amics	2	2	2
En el veïnat	3	3	3
En l'escola	4	4	4
En cursets	5	5	5
Pel seu compte	6	6	6
En el treball	7	7	7
Altres ______	☐☐	☐☐	☐☐

P.3. En l'actualitat, en quina llengua parla vosté en sa casa (on viu)?

- Sempre en valencià 1
- Generalment en valencià 2
- Més en valencià que en castellà 3
- Indistintament 4
- Més en castellà que en valencià 5
- Generalment en castellà 6
- Sempre en castellà 7
- Cap de les anteriors 8

P.5. En quina llengua parla/parlava vosté amb sa mare?

- Sempre en valencià 1
- Generalment en valencià 2
- Més en valencià que en castellà 3
- Indistintament 4
- Més en castellà que en valencià 5
- Generalment en castellà 6
- Sempre en castellà 7
- Cap de les anteriors 8

FIGURE 4.5 Fragment of the survey on the social situation of Valencian.
Source: Acadèmia Valenciana de la Llengua (2005).

and different modalities of use of the languages, as well as the opinions and attitudes about these uses. The report speaks of "knowing how to speak / write" (distinguishing skills) and of language spoken or of "habitual use" in certain domains and with specific speakers but does not give clarifying definitions about the interpretation of "knowing how to speak" or about where to draw the line for "commonly used."

Considering these methodological issues, it becomes clear that the best way of avoiding conscious or unconscious divergent interpretations, as well as making information from different stories comparable, is to have, if not a unified terminology, then precise definitions about what is understood in each case for each of the terms and concepts involved (Busch, 2016; Leeman, 2020). At the same time, the objective of the questionnaire must be clearly specified, the subjects of the survey established, and the kind of linguistic and communicative information to be collected described. For example, to study the possible displacement of the languages of Turkish and Italian immigrants to the Netherlands and Belgium, Koen Jaspaert and Sjaak Kroon (1993) carried out a survey of 800 respondents about the choice of language in different situations (domains), across different kinds of communications (intragroup and extragroup), considering social, cultural, and educational background, and adding a comprehension test of their languages of origin.

During the preparation of questionnaires or after data collection, when there are doubts about the adequacy or interpretation of the questions by the respondents, about the viability of the questionnaire itself, or the validity of the data collected, demolinguistic research can fall back on "discussion groups" or "focus groups." These are small groups of people convened to express their opinions or offer information about a subject with which they have experience. Meeting with such groups is useful when working with people who don't speak a majority language (Siegel, 2018). Likewise, they can be an exceptional source for qualitative character studies.

Beyond the need to adhere to clear methodological guidelines, the truth is that surveys and censuses tend to forgo information about languages, as they do other significant aspects of identity, such as ethnicity or cultural background. In 2020, in Europe, only the censuses of Ireland and the United Kingdom specifically asked respondents about their ethnicity. In the cases of Ireland, linguistic information can be deduced from ethnic information; this is also the case in the United Kingdom, but there are cases in which this is not expressly collected, as happens with Hispanics, who are not mentioned or who don't find an unequivocal space in the questions about ethnic groups on the British census. When surveys or censuses do not offer linguistic or ethnic information, one can turn to the register of nationalities of residents or to the country's migratory register to deduce that population's knowledge of languages.

To conclude this section dedicated to surveys, it is necessary to again allude to their link with censuses and to the changes that are taking place in the methodology of data collection and analysis procedures. Currently, the sampling technique is also applied for the formalization of censuses, such that some specific questions are only asked of people included in the sample. It is often the case that shared information about a family or household is not necessarily noted for each individual, as happens with geographic origin, the characteristics of the dwelling, employment, or the languages spoken in the home. When individuals belong to groups who live at the margins of the economic structures of a country, it is necessary to attend to all people individually.

Lastly, even if current censuses can be carried out based on dynamic and continuous information from administrative and vital records, surveys remain a fundamental methodological complement. When these surveys are conducted between two traditional censuses, they are called "intercensal surveys." When they are not necessarily carried out between two traditional censuses, they can be given various names. One of these is "microcensus." In Germany, the Federal Statistical Office has carried out microcensuses since 1957. These are data collections using surveys that can be carried out on a large number of people (1% of the population), belonging to a significant number of households (several hundred thousand). These German microcensuses include questions about life events, such as migrations, which led in 2006, for example, to confirmation that one in five inhabitants of Germany has a migratory origin. Similarly, since 2017, the German microcensus (Statistisches Bundesamt, 2020) has included information about the language of primary communication in households as one of the variables to measure the level of integration of the respondents. In addition, other surveys are also carried out in Germany which ask participants for their "mother tongue," and there are other sources, such as the immigration register, that help to profile the country's language panorama.

Subjective Vitality Questionnaires

In the analysis of minority languages, subjective vitality questionnaires (SVQs) have a special political relevance and are also of great methodological interest (Bourhis, Giles, & Rosenthal, 1981). As Maria Àngels Viladot (1995) has explained, the challenge regarding the concept of ethnolinguistic vitality has been to get a "subjective" valuation of how the members of an ethnic collective judge the social conditions that affect their group or other relevant groups. Objective indexes of vitality are closely linked with subjective ones for whose study a questionnaire has been created.

The best-known and most widely tested questionnaire consists of 20 double questions and two simple questions related to a (minority) group and a (majority or dominant) extragroup. The respondents must evaluate their perception of the aspects covered by the questions using a scale to indicate greater or lesser approval. The questions refer to the following factors: status, demography, and institutional support. The complementary questions or items refer to their perception of the strength and vitality, now and in the future, of the languages of the group and the extragroup.

Studies on subjective vitality reveal contexts in which the perception of the members of the group who speak a minority language is rather realistic, as well as other contexts in which perceptions, both their own and that of the (dominant) extragroup are distorted or biased in one of the following ways:

a. Perception distorted in favor of the vitality of the group itself. The dominant group accentuates the differences in its vitality with respect to the other group, while the subordinate group attenuates them.

TABLE 4.2 Subjective vitality questionnaire.

Demographic factor
- Make a calculation of the proportion of the population comprising the following groups in this community.
- Evaluate the birth rate of each group.
- Where the following groups are concentrated, to what extent are they a majority or a minority?
- How many people from each group do you think settle (immigrate) each year?
- To what extent do you think the individuals in each group only intermarry?
- Of each group, how many people emigrate (leave) to live elsewhere?

Status factor
- What consideration do you think the following languages have in this community?
- What consideration do you think the following languages have internationally?
- To what extent do you think the following groups are well considered in this community?
- To what extent do you think the following groups are proud of their cultural history and what they have achieved in this community?
- To what extent do you think the following groups are rich in this community?

Institutional support and control factor
- How often do you think the following languages are used in official services (e.g., hospitals, social services, municipal services)?
- What influence do you think the following groups have over the economic and business affairs of this community?
- To what extent do you think the following languages are well represented in the modes of communication in this community (e.g., TV, radio, newspapers)?
- To what extent do you think the following languages are well represented in the overall educational system of this community (primary, secondary, university)?
- What political power do you think these groups have in this community?
- To what extent do you think that these languages are well represented in business-related entities?
- How often do you think the following languages are used in churches and places of worship in this community?
- To what extent are the following groups well represented in the cultural life of this community (e.g., festivals, concerts, art exhibitions)?

Source: Re-elaboration from Viladot & Esteban-Guitart (2011).

b. Perception distorted in favor of the vitality of the other group. The dominant group mitigates the differences in its vitality with respect to the subordinate group, while the subordinate group accentuates the differences.
c. Lack of agreement between perceptions of vitality.

The materials collected through questionnaires, as they are presented in the form of scales, can be treated statistically.

In general, the complexity of questionnaires about vitality can vary greatly between one study and another, depending on the goals set. SVQs are usually

TABLE 4.3 Questionnaire for the project "The Vitality of Indigenous Languages in Mexico: A Study in Three Contexts".

Lengua	*Sí*	*Poco*	*Solo entiende*	*No*
Lengua indígena				
Español				
Cuando está en casa, ¿cómo habla con? (solo en caso de hablar las dos lenguas)				

Grupo de edad	*Lengua indígena*	*Ambas*	*Español*	
Los niños (hasta 12 años)				
Los adolescentes (de 13 a 18 años)				
Los adultos (de 19 a 60 años)				
Los ancianos (desde 61 años)				
¿Cómo habla con…? (solo en caso de hablar las dos lenguas)				

Dominio	*Lengua indígena*	*Ambas*	*Español*	
Los amigos (amigas)				
En la tienda				

Source: Terborg & García Landa, 2011.

complete and complex, but there are other, simpler ones. For example, for a comparison between different contexts, it is advisable to use simplified questionnaires, such as the one used by Roland Terborg and Laura García Landa (2011) in various indigenous Mexican communities.

The questionnaire also includes a section covering personal data (name and address) and another about schooling and education.

International and Digital Sources

Along with national or regional sources, the demography of languages also finds a fundamental tool in international sources. In general, these sources belong or are closely linked to international organizations interested in supranational regions. Among the international sources most notable for demographic purposes, the following are worth highlighting.

The *United Nations* offers demographic information services from various entities within its system. For demographic purposes, the information on *Population Dynamics* offered by its Department of Social and Economic Affairs (population, fertility, mortality, migration) is relevant. Likewise, the UN annually publishes its *Statistical Yearbook* (United Nations, 2020a) and its *World Statistics*

Pocketbook (United Nations, 2020b). The first includes up-to-date information on education and migration that might be of interest for the study of the international dynamics of languages. The latter presents up to 50 indicators from more than 20 international statistical sources for 30 geographic regions and more than 200 countries or areas of the world.

For linguistic matters, information provided by UNESCO regarding endangered languages is of special interest, especially the *UNESCO Interactive Atlas of the World's Languages in Danger* (Moseley, 2010). This atlas, like other related works, is compiled by experts commissioned by the organization. UNESCO also maintains the *Index Translationum* which is a large database of book translations with information since 1979, even though records had been made by the League of Nations since 1932.

The *World Bank* provides a wealth of information on development indicators that can be viewed through the Google Public Data component. These indicators refer to income, internet access, savings, official aid, infrastructures, trade, consumption, credit, debt, education, companies, exports, and tourism, among many other aspects. The relationship of some of these with the knowledge and use of language is clear and direct, as in the case of education, for which global data is offered on the starting age of each course, its duration, the number of students, and the number of teachers.

The *International Organization for Migration* (IOM) is part of the United Nations system as the main intergovernmental organization whose purpose is to understand and manage human migrations. It is made up of member states and has a presence in over 100 countries. Among other publications, the IOM provides a *World Migration Report* (IOM, 2022) every year, which presents key data on migration with thematic chapters devoted to migration issues of interest.

Eurostat is the statistical office of the European Commission and generates data on the European Union with the aim of harmonizing the statistical methods of the states that compose it. The primary sources of data are the states themselves. Among its functions, the collection and analyses of regional data to orient structural policies of the European Union is worthy of special mention. Eurostat offers information on the languages of Europe in relation to their origin, use, and study at different levels and in different fields (Eurostat, 2021). The European Commission is also responsible for the Eurobarometers, which are periodic surveys begun in 1973 whose goal is to find out the opinions of Europeans on topics of interest through the member states. In relation to the languages of Europe, the special Eurobarometers 54.1 (2001), 243 (2006), and 386 (2012), titled "Europeans and their Languages" deserve special mention.

The *United States Census Bureau* is probably the most important national census service in the world and consequently offers very detailed information in relation to the most varied aspects of the United States population, including questions about the knowledge and use of languages. However, the information it offers on international programs is also very valuable, especially in relation to global migratory processes. It provides access to the *International Data Base* (IDB) which includes a broad set of indicators such as the total population, the population by age and sex, and demographic characteristics such as fertility, mortality, and migration.

World Population Data Sheet, under the responsibility of the non-profit organization *Population Reference Bureau*, monitors population indicators in over 200 countries and territories around the world.

The *International Union for the Scientific Study of Population*, an organization created in 1928 and supported by the French government, offers statistics and annual reports on international demographic aspects.

The above-mentioned organizations and reports are accessible almost entirely through electronic channels. In some cases, these are sources that offer their data through online interaction (charts, cross-reference tables, maps); in others, reports are offered in electronic format but are also accessible on paper. They are generally free and open access sources, although some of them require a subscription.

Along with all these, mention must also be made of the relevance that electronic resources have in themselves. In fact, contemporary demographic studies cannot be understood without electronic resources and the developments that condition methodology in the collection, transfer, and analysis of data. Among these electronic resources, those which the UN's Population Division and its Statistics Division make available to the public are worthy of mention. However, there are a great variety of sources and resources on international, national, regional, and associative levels, as well as those linked to universities and research centers, and to other official bodies.

Bearing in mind that, in relation to languages, the demographic data that are of greatest interest are those related to basic vital events, migrations, literacy, or education, here are several electronic resources of interest:

STATISTA is a private statistical information portal, focused on the world of the marketplace and opinion, which offers, according to the company, more than one million statistics on some 80,000 topics from some 22,500 sources, in 170 different sectors. Languages of the world are one of the topics covered, with information distributed across different categories: countries, studies, speakers, etc. STATISTA offers graphs and charts of all kinds, even if not all the reports and resources are free.

Demographic and Health Services (DHS) is an electronic service that offers a series of maps, modeled and produced online, which reflect survey data. The information refers to 15 indicators, although not all of them are available with the same level of updating for all countries. For demolinguistic purposes, the most relevant information refers to literacy.

Integrated Public Use Microdata Series–International is a project to inventory, preserve, harmonize, and disseminate census microdata from around the world. The project has created the largest global archive of open and longitudinal census samples which allows for comparative research. The data are offered freely over the internet as an electronic research resource. The information comes from over

80 countries, based on around 280 censuses and more than 600 million records of people and includes data on countries' languages and ethnicities.

The World Factbook (CIA, 2022) is a service of the Central Intelligence Agency of the United States that offers open information on all the countries of the world, including information on ethnic groups and languages spoken. The site provides a list of the languages of each country and specifies those which are official languages on the national or regional level. Where data is available, the languages of each country are broken down according to the percentage of the overall population that speaks each language as their first language. For countries where data is not available languages are listed in order of relevance.

Due to its growing importance, information about internet penetration and the use of social media networks in general could be added to the above resources. The portal *Internet World States* offers one of the best-documented resources in this regard.

As has already been mentioned, national sources of demographic information are usually the national, central, or federal statistics offices, departments, or institutes, often involved in the development or analysis of censuses. However, "regional sources" are also highly appreciated, especially when one is interested in data of a linguistic nature for bilingual or multilingual territories. In Spain, for example, the data offered by the Statistics Institutes of Catalonia, the Balearic Islands, Valencia, Galicia, Navarra, and the Basque Country are essential, and the institutes of other areas also offer valuable information about languages studied and learned in their territories. On a more specific level, the relevant authorities usually offer data for each country or region on specific aspects such as students by educational level, migrant registration, naturalizations, social integration, associations, and household composition.

Encyclopedias, Catalogs, and Other Sources

Encyclopedias

Worth mention among international sources are the major encyclopedias, including *Wikipedia*. Until 2012, the *Encyclopedia Britannica* published a *Britannica Book of the Year* that offered detailed information on the languages spoken in each country of the world, along with their numbers of speakers. Since 2012, the encyclopedia is only published online and offers similar annual data to the previous print editions, but not the detailed annual reports on languages. Another encyclopedia that offers data on the languages of the world and their speakers is the *Nationalencyklopedin*, promoted and financed by the Swedish government. Both works require registration and subscription in order to consult them, although some data from the Swedish encyclopedia are accessible through *Wikipedia*, which can pose additional problems.

As far as *Wikipedia* is concerned, one must recognize the effort the organization is making to compile data and harmonize sources in relation to the demography of the languages of the world, for each language and each territory. The reality, however, is that this source, indirect and secondary (or even tertiary), offers variable and scattered information. The main problem is the multiplicity of hands (experts and amateurs) involved in it (Martínez, 2012) and the diversity of the sources consulted, both over time and in the origin of the figures, which translates into insecure data that require many precautions to be taken, as the deficiencies or inconsistencies are not always foreseeable. In any event, demographic reports presented by *Wikipedia* are useful in the absence of other kinds of compilations.

However, the data offered by these encyclopedias, whether physical or virtual, usually present the same difficulties already mentioned with regard to the use of terms like *mother tongue, main language*, or *bilingualism*. In fact, those who collect and handle these data find themselves with the same problems as those who try to aggregate and analyze it: for example, the data on bilinguals (let alone trilinguals) is not offered in the same way for all countries; similarly, speakers of a language residing in countries where it is not a majority language may have been ignored or treated differently, among other factors. This reality can lead to decision-making that occasionally entails treating certain data that are known to be false as facts: at the very least, there are a number of speakers of each language who must mark it as their "mother tongue" if this is the only option, which ignores the possibilities of the existence of bilingualism and allowing an individual to be counted as speaking both languages. This circumstance can be corrected if adequate information is available, but this may undermine a comparability that, it must be acknowledged, the data collectors do not fully guarantee either.

Language Catalogs

While they cannot be considered primary demolinguistic sources, international catalogs of languages have become an obligatory reference for numerous purposes, practical as well as theoretical. Two of these catalogs stand out especially: *Ethnologue* (Eberhard, Simons, & Fennig, 2022) and *Glottolog* (Hammarström, Forkel, & Haspelmath, 2018). There is a third initiative called *Proyecto Joshua*, but its religious, proselytizing nature, together with the irregularity of its data, the lack of rigor in the use of linguistic categories, and the crossover of language data with information on religious practices make it an unreliable resource.

Ethnologue is a subscription catalog that offers information of demolinguistic value from two kinds of sources: direct sources (mainly the network of people distributed in indigenous areas) and indirect ones (data from other researchers). The origin of *Ethnologue*, as well as its primary *raison d'être*, was (and is) the mission of translating the Bible into all the languages of the world, a mission adopted by the *Summer Institute of Linguistics*, founded in the 1930s in the United States and with around 6,000 members today. To fulfill this mission, it proved necessary to send missionaries throughout the world and to give them the necessary resources to learn each language in order to translate the Bible into all of them.

These missionaries are the ones who collected the information which was later incorporated into the catalog of languages. The basic problem has been that the application of its criteria to all the peoples and ethnicities of the world has not been very restrictive when it comes to cataloging languages. This has led to many varieties being considered languages even though they don't show sufficient homogeneity or stability, don't have enough empirical support, or don't enjoy social recognition. The initiative and its results have had numerous detractors, but the truth is that the information offered by *Ethnologue* has been updated and refined over time, and the catalog has managed to become, in practice, the most accessible and consulted source of information on linguistic diversity in the world.

As for *Glottolog*, it is a project carried out by the Max Planck Institute for Evolutionary Anthropology in Leipzig, Germany, and it is not interested in demography so much as typology: the classification and counting of languages. The project is built upon a large bibliographic database that gives access to a range of information of a demolinguistic and ethnographic nature, even if the data offered do not refer to it as such.

Linguistic and Other Sources

Demolinguistic studies, especially those interested in the analysis of the vitality of languages and their processes of maintenance, minoritization, or substitution, must take into account data on aspects that make up the System of Linguistic Indicators and which have to do with the conditions of language use, rather than the number of speakers. Here, information on linguistic attitudes, languages incorporated into educational systems, communicative dynamics within communities, or the presence of languages on the internet acquire clear prominence. However, this kind of information is not only relevant for minority languages, but affects any kind of language or linguistic variety, both in its possible status as a minority language, as well as in situations of majority presence.

The factors that can affect the vitality or social life of a language or variety can be very different at any moment and may not be the same in all populations. Hence, it is difficult to establish a closed catalog of sources for these kinds of data. In fact, any information that would serve to discover or deduce the interest aroused by a language, the identification its speakers have with it, the level and depth with which it is studied, or the treatment it receives in public, among other factors, would be valid and interesting for demographic purposes, in order to learn more about the dynamics of maintenance, displacement, or substitution within a given population. However, the lack of a closed catalog of sources in this regard does not prevent some general guidelines from being followed.

These guidelines include paying attention to studies focused specifically on the linguistic and social attitudes of the population. These studies can be developed based on "psychosociological" questionnaires whose results are uniformly quantified. The questionnaires can ask directly for opinions about a language or variety or its use and meaning, or they can ask indirectly. For example, the latter is achieved by a technique called *matched-guise* or false pairings. This technique consists of using audio recordings of the same voices that speak the same content in different languages, so that the reactions to the stimuli can reflect different attitudes toward the languages. These reactions are also noted on questionnaires that can take the form of scales. In addition to questionnaires, attitudes can be gauged through "ethnographic" techniques (interviews, conversations, focus groups), which are more suitable for qualitative analysis (Baker, 1992; Preston, 2010).

These kinds of works abound and require a bibliographic investigation for each community. Let us take two simple examples. To analyze the bilingual, border-crossing community of South Texas in the United States, Esteban Hernández (2022) worked with 29 Spanish speakers, all of them born in Matamoros, Mexico, who immigrated to the United States at age 13 or older and have lived there now for at least five years. The participants were asked to fill out a questionnaire to self-identify as *American, Hispanic, Latino, Mexican American,* or *Mexican*. In contrast, to find out the linguistic experiences of Hispanic children and youth in the United States, María Carreira and Tom Beeman (2014) compiled a series of conversations that revealed this group's points of view as students in public schools and in relation to the future of the United States. The students' stories revealed the satisfactions and challenges of living between two cultures and two languages at school, in the home, and in their communities, in the context of the United States' Hispanic reality, its demographics, Spanish-English bilingualism, and their beliefs, traditions, and cultural practices.

Another line worth exploring in order to investigate linguistic vitality in specific contexts relates to associations or centers of social reference for the population: cultural centers, neighborhood associations, religious groups, and professional groups. Often, municipalities have records of these kinds of groups. Such information offers a qualitative dimension that lets one know aspects of social life that prove decisive for the maintenance or loss of a form of expression. Thus, for example, Martín Guardado (2019), in his attempt to discover the situation of Spanish as a heritage language in Canada across different generations, carried out work to collect information on different aspects of the socialization of the languages in family life, in cooperative housing, in cultural centers, Casa de la Amistad, Boy Scout troops, and Black community churches, which allowed for a microanalysis that was decisive for the knowledge of linguistic attitudes.

Likewise, for linguistic demography, all information related to or coming from educational systems is crucial. Thus, it is essential to know the number of people enrolled at each educational level, in which languages they are schooled, in which language each subject is taught, the origin and linguistic training of the teaching staff, and the sociolinguistic environment of the schools. It is also important to distinguish between compulsory and elective, fundamental and complementary, and public and private education, as well as the formative itineraries the system offers and the procedures for evaluating knowledge of the languages used in each case. Similarly, it is important to identify and characterize programs of bilingual education. This is, as can be seen here, extensive and complex information which often requires recourse to various sources.

For everything related to primary and secondary education, the main source is the respective ministry of education of each country and the corresponding administration of the state or, as is the case in the European Union, those bodies that collect the information from the member states (Eurostat, Eurobarometer, etc.). On a global level, UNESCO, together with other UN organizations, usually collects information on education. The university level, however, has serious problems in offering comprehensive data on the languages of origin of its students, languages studied, language courses offered, initial knowledge of and subsequent level attained in those languages, and the teaching staff responsible for such teaching. In this case, it is common to resort to collecting data expressly through questionnaires. Information on private or non-regulated teaching of languages also includes data of great interest, which are relatively accessible when it comes to public entities (Instituto Cervantes, British Council, etc.), but not very accessible in the cases of private centers, such as franchise language teaching schools.

Likewise, demolinguistic analysis is significantly enriched and complemented by data from areas outside language, but which have a clear projection onto it. Let us consider the information on the number of countries where a language is spoken, on internet penetration, on the level of development, or on the volume of exports and imports of the countries where a specific language is spoken. These data are found in specialist international sources devoted to each subject (World Bank, OECD, etc.) or in generalist statistical sources like those already mentioned (*STATISTA, The World Factbook*, etc.). To the previously mentioned sources, one can add those professional sources related to activities that involve a necessary use of language(s), such as communication media, translation, editorial production (including textbooks), and other cultural industries (music, gastronomy), as well as the regulations of international organizations.

Finally, for the study of minority languages, especially in indigenous contexts, it is also worth highlighting the importance of the group of works that offer detailed information on the linguistic characterization and geographic distribution (often together with demographic information) of each of the native or indigenous languages of a territory. Paradigmatic examples of this line of research and dissemination are *Atlas sociolingüístico de pueblos indígenas en América Latina* (Sichra, 2009), *Atlas lingüístico del Perú* (Chirinos, 2001), the monumental work *Las lenguas indígenas de Colombia* (González de Pérez & Rodríguez de Montes, 2000), or the most informative atlases of Asia, Africa, Europe, and the Americas created by Jean Sellier (2004a, 2004b, 2011, 2013, 2014).

As a final note in this section devoted to sources, it should be clarified that, although a differentiated treatment to each kind of source has been given, demolinguistic research usually works based on triangulation, crossing, or combination of data of different origins, as well as diverse techniques of information storage and retrieval. Only in this way is it possible to build a sufficiently solid base for the construction of well-founded demolinguistic analyses.

Summary

This chapter has presented two fundamental components of demolinguistic methodology: data and their sources. Demolinguistic data are, by their very nature, demographic and linguistic, and relationships of different natures and levels can be established between them. In general, these data refer to the number of speakers and learners of a language, the number of births and deaths among the members of different linguistic groups, the composition of households and families in their linguistic dimensions, the number and profile of members of all kinds of groups and associations, and the number of immigrants and emigrants of each linguistic group with respect to their communities of origin and destination. Most of the data collected for demolinguistic purposes do not originate from a process designed, executed, or controlled by experts in language demography; instead, demographic linguists are the ones who must search for and order this data according to the interests of their specialty. Generally, properly demolinguistic data is scarce and irregular in time and form, while purely demographic data tends to offer greater scope and continuity.

The general sources upon which demolinguistics is nourished are demographic or specifically demolinguistic in nature and can offer both dynamic and static information. The three most relevant and useful of these sources for demolinguistics are: administrative records, censuses, and surveys. Registries and censuses, created by administrative authorities, offer fundamental information for the study of the demography of languages, given that they pay attention to the composition, distribution, and dynamics of populations. There are also strictly demolinguistic censuses, but they are rare and not always transparent. Surveys, for their part, are mechanisms of data collection that are more specific and agile, due to their lower complexity and cost. Among these, within our field, it is worth highlighting those aimed at knowing the use of languages by domains and those on the subjective vitality of minority languages.

Registries, censuses, and surveys take advantage of computer and online resources that technology offers to facilitate the process of collection, storage, retrieval, and presentation of data. In addition, there are numerous sources with information related to the geographic, economic, political, and cultural dimensions of languages that prove essential to adequately analyzing the demolinguistic reality of a population, a language, or a territory.

TABLE 4.4 Demolinguistic sources.

Types	subtypes	Data	Linguistic information
Administrative records	– Civil registries – Municipal registers – Migratory records	Statistics and sociodemographic data: residence, births, adoptions, marriages, divorces, deaths, naturalizations, population movements, etc.	Inferential Nationality → language proficiency • migration and naturalization → linguistic integration (to varying degrees) • migration offspring → existence of heritage languages • composition of the families (endogamous, exogamous) → maintenance of the heritage language (more or less exposure to the language of origin)
Census and surveys	– Census – Sample census – Population-based surveys	Information on **people** (gender, age, marital status, employment status, nationality, immigration status, ethnicity, religion, languages); **households** (size, composition, characteristics); **buildings and dwellings** (condition, size, surface area, rooms, tenure, ownership)	Types of linguistic information: a) data on the mother tongue (the language that one recognizes as one's own and most enjoys speaking, the language in which one has been most fluent since childhood and in which one thinks and prays (Kertzer & Arel, 2001: 98–105); the first language that one learned and still understands (De Vries, 1986: 357)) b) data on the language of the household (languages used in the household, main language of communication, etc.) c) data on the frequency of use of one or more languages in different social spaces (leisure–reading, watching television, listening to the radio, surfing and interacting on the internet–work, family, friends) d) data on linguistic knowledge (self-assessment of linguistic competences in one or more languages according to skills–speaking, writing–or according to level) e) subjective vitality surveys (speakers' perceptions of the social and demographic reality of a language)

(*Continued*)

TABLE 4.4 (Continued)

Types	subtypes	Data	Linguistic information
International and digital sources	– International databases (UN, World Bank, Index Translationum) – Regional databases (Eurostat, ECLAC) – National databases (United States Census Bureau, INE) – Barometers (Eurobarometer, Latinobarometer) – Demographic health services	Types of data **demographic** (birth rate, mortality, migration); (education, schooling, literacy); (income, employment, poverty, inequality); **cultural** (translations, audiovisual production, languages)	In addition to being able to include linguistic data, these sources provide the necessary information to contextualize the demolinguistic processes and allow for a better understanding of the linguistic process: a) identify demographic and social dynamics; b) identify factors that influence the vitality and status of languages; c) describe the geographic and social spaces occupied by the speakers
Encyclopedias, catalogs, and other sources	– *The World Factbook* – Encyclopedias (*Encyclopedia Britannica, Nationalencyklopedin, Wikipedia*) – Language catalogs (*Ethnologue, Glottolog*) – Linguistic sources – Linguistic atlases	Population counts and estimates; statistics derived from contrasting primary data; lists of languages and spatial data on language groups; indexes derived from statistics	Types of linguistic information a) derived data and estimates, e.g., number of speakers; languages of a territory; status of languages or number of learners; b) processed data and indexes: vitality indexes; c) qualitative data: qualitative information on linguistic socialization dynamics; d) linguistic atlases: distribution of linguistic groups, estimation of the number of speakers

TABLE 4.5 List of sources mentioned.

	Data	Access
Population and migration statistics		
Eurostat	Data on European Union countries	https://ec.europa.eu/eurostat/data/database
Migration Data Portal	Global migration statistics and other resources; includes an interactive portal	www.migrationdataportal.org/
United Nations Population Division	World population statistics, demographic and migration variables	www.un.org/development/desa/pd/data-landing-page www.un.org/en/desa/
United Nations Statistical Division	Global statistics on trade, national economy, energy, industry, and demographics	https://unstats.un.org/home/
International Organization for Migration (IOM)	Periodic migration reports with statistics and analysis of migration dynamics	https://worldmigrationreport.iom.int/
World Population Data Sheet (Population Reference Bureau)	Tracking of population indicators for more than 200 countries and territories worldwide	www.prb.org/collections/data-sheets/
United States Census Bureau	Information on the US population, including questions of language knowledge and use; includes the International Data Base (IDB), a set of demographic and migration indicators	www.census.gov/
International Union for the Scientific Study of Population	Portal that offers statistics and annual reports on international demographic aspects	https://iussp.org/
Integrated Public Use Microdata Series–International	Project to inventory, preserve, harmonize, and disseminate census microdata from around the world	https://international.ipums.org
Demographic and Health Services (DHS)	Electronic service that provides a series of online modeled and elaborated maps reflecting survey data	dhsprogram.com

(*Continued*)

TABLE 4.5 (Continued)

	Data	Access
Indices of the international weight of languages		
Baromètre Calvet des langues du monde	Interactive and multidimensional index of relative importance of languages (with 2020 data)	www.culture.gouv.fr/Thematiques/Langue-francaise-et-langues-de-France/Agir-pour-les-langues/Innover-dans-le-domaine-des-langues-et-du-numerique/Soutenir-et-encourager-la-diversite-linguistique-dans-le-domaine-numerique/Barometre-des-langues-dans-le-monde-2022
Kail Chan's power index of languages	Language influence index based on five complex dimensions (geography, economy, communication, knowledge and media, and diplomacy; calculations for 2016)	http://www.kailchan.ca/wp-content/uploads/2016/12/Kai-Chan_Power-Language-Index-full-report_2016_v2.pdf
Socioeconomic and cultural indicators		
Linguistic training in the world	Information on the official status of the world's languages	www.axl.cefan.ulaval.ca/
Human Development Index	Multidimensional human development indicators of countries	https://hdr.undp.org/en/content/human-development-index-hdi
Internet World Stats	Internet user data and languages	www.internetworldstats.com/stats7.htm
UNESCO *Index Translationum*	Bibliographic database of translations (1979–2008/10)	www.unesco.org/xtrans/bsform.aspx
World Factbook	Basic intelligence on the history, people, government, economy, energy, geography, environment, communications, transportation, military, terrorism, and transnational issues for 266 world entities	www.cia.gov/the-world-factbook/

Demolinguistic Data and Sources 125

World Bank Open Data	Global development data and statistics (economic, educational, energy, environmental, etc.)	https://data.worldbank.org/
Organisation for Economic Co-operation and Development (OECD)	Global development data and statistics (economic, educational, energy, environmental, etc.)	https://stats.oecd.org/
Internet World Stats	Worldwide internet user and usage data, population statistics, Facebook statistics, and internet market research for more than 250 countries	www.internetworldstats.com/
Google Public Data	Public data and forecasts from a variety of international organizations and academic institutions	www.google.com/publicdata/directory?hl=es
Language catalogs and atlases		
Ethnologue	Catalog of the world's languages with demolinguistic information from combined sources	www.ethnologue.com/
Glottolog	Catalog of languages, language families, and dialects; includes a vitality measure	https://glottolog.org/
GlottoScope	Interactive portal combining Agglomerated Endangerment Scale (AES) and Most Extensive Description data	https://glottolog.org/langdoc/status
GlottoVis	Interactive portal with information on the vitality of the world's languages and their documentation	http://glammap.win.tue.nl/glottovis/
UNESCO *Atlas of the World's Languages in Danger*	Interactive atlas of endangered languages according to their vitality (latest version, 2010)	www.unesco.org/languages-atlas/index.php?hl=fr&page=atlasmap
Catalogue of Endangered Languages (ELCat)	Online catalog of endangered languages	www.endangeredlanguages.com
List of ISO codes for languages	List of ISO codes for languages	https://en.wikipedia.org/wiki/List_of_ISO_639-1_codes

(*Continued*)

TABLE 4.5 (Continued)

	Data	Access
Atlases of indigenous languages		
Atlas sociolingüístico de los pueblos indígenas de América Latina y el Caribe	Description of the indigenous peoples of Latin America and the Caribbean and the status of their languages	www.unicef.org/lac/informes/atlas-sociolinguistico-de-pueblos-indigenas-en-ALC
Atlas lingüístico del Perú (Chirinos, 2001)	Description of the indigenous languages of Peru	www.academia.edu/43299299/ Atlas_Linguistico_del_Peru_2001_
Las lenguas indígenas de Colombia (González de Pérez & Rodríguez de Montes, 2000)	Description of the indigenous languages of Colombia	Not available on the internet
Atlases of the peoples of Asia, Africa, Europe, and the Americas (Sellier 2004a, 2004b, 2011, 2013, 2014)	Description of the linguistic panoramas of different continents	Not available on the internet

References

Acadèmia Valenciana de la Llengua (2005): *Llibre blanc de l'us del valencià*. València: AVL.
Baker, Colin (1992): *Attitudes and Language*. Clevedon: Multilingual Matters.
Bartmiński, Jerzy (2012): *Aspects of Cognitive Ethnolinguistics*. Sheffield: Equinox.
Bourhis, Richard, Howard Giles and Doreen Rosenthal (1981): "Notes on the construction of a 'subjective vitality questionnaire' for ethnolinguistic groups". *Journal of Multilingual and Multicultural Development*, 2:145–155.
Busch, Brigitta (2016): "Categorizing languages and speakers: why linguists should mistrust census data and statistics". *Working Papers in Urban Language & Literacies*, 189.
Carreira, María M. and Tom Beeman (2014): *Voces: Latino Students on Life in the United States*. Santa Barbara: Praeger.
CEPAL (2021): *Censos de Población y Vivienda: Décadas 2000 y 2010*. www.cepal.org/es/temas/censos-de-poblacion-y-vivienda/censos-poblacion-vivienda-decadas-2000-2010 Online resource.
Chirinos, Andrés (2001): *Atlas lingüístico del Perú*. Cusco-Lima: Ministerio de Educación–Centro Bartolomé de las Casas.
CIA (2022): *The World Factbook*. www.cia.gov/the-world-factbook/ Online resource.
Cochran, William (1991): *Técnicas de muestreo*. México: Compañía Editora Continental.
De Vries, John (1986): *Towards a Sociology of Languages in Canada*. Québec: Centre International de Recherche sur Bilinguisme.
Duchêne, Alexandre, Philippe Humbert, and Renata Coray (2018): "How to ask questions on language? Ideological struggles in the making of a state survey". *International Journal of the Sociology of Language*, 2018: 45–72.
Eberhard David, Gary Simons, and Charles D. Fennig (eds.) (2022): *Ethnologue: Languages of the World*, 245th ed. Dallas: SIL International. Online version: http://www.ethnologue.com.
Esteban Hernández, José (2023): "Ideologías, actitudes y continuidad dialectal en una variedad transfronteriza de contacto". *Spanish in Context*, forthcoming.
Eurobarometer (2001): *Europeans and their Languages*. Special 54.1. European Commission. https://search.gesis.org/research_data/ZA3387 [Retrieved: 06.04.2021] Online resource.
Eurobarometer (2006): *Los europeos y sus lenguas*. Special 243. European Commission. https://europa.eu/eurobarometer/surveys/detail/518 [Retrieved: 06.04.2021] Online resource.
Eurobarometer (2012): *Los europeos y sus lenguas*. Special 386. European Commission. https://europa.eu/eurobarometer/surveys/detail/1049 [Retrieved 04-06-2021] Online resource.
FSO (2016): *Language, Religion and Culture Survey (ESRK)*. Lucerne / Lausanne / Zurich / Lugano: Federal Statistical Office.
González de Pérez, María Stella and María Luisa Rodríguez de Montes (2000): *Las lenguas indígenas de Colombia*. Bogotá: Instituto Caro y Cuervo.
Guardado, Martin (2019): *Discourse, Ideology and Heritage Language Socialization: Micro and Macro Perspectives*. Berlin: De Gruyter-Mouton.
Hammarström, Harald, Robert Forkel, and Martin Haspelmath (2018): *Glottolog 3.3*. Jena: Max Planck Institute for the Science of Human History.
INEC (2006): *Encuesta de condiciones de vida 2005–2006 v.1.4. V Ronda*. Quito: INEC.
INEGI (2020): *Censo de Población y Vivienda 2020*. https://censo2020.mx/ Online resource.
INEI (2018): *III censo de comunidades nativas 2017*. Lima: INEI.

IOM (2022): *World Migration Report*. New York: UN-IOM.
Jaspaert, Koen and Sjaak Kroon (1993): "Methodological Issues in Language Shift Research". In G. Extra and L. Verhoeven (eds.), *Immigrant Languages in Europe*. Clevedon: Multilingual Matters, pp. 297–308.
Kehl, Anika (2011): *Language Vitality in South Africa*. Nordestedt: GRIN.
Kertzer, David and Dominique Arel (eds.) (2001): *Census and Identity: the Politics of Race, Ethnicity, and Language in National Censuses*. Cambridge: Cambridge University Press.
Lagos, Cristián (2006): "Mapudungun en Santiago de Chile: vitalidad, lealtad y actitudes lingüísticas". *Lenguas Modernas*, 31: 97–126.
Leeman, Jennifer (2020): "Los datos censales en el estudio del multilingüismo y la migración: cuestiones ideológicas y consecuencias epistémicas". *Iberoromania*, 2020: 77–92.
Martínez, Cristina (2012): *Wikipedia: inteligencia colectiva en la red*. Barcelona: Profit.
Moreno-Fernández, Francisco (2014): "Fundamentos de demografía lingüística a propósito de la lengua española". *Revista Internacional de Lingüística Iberoamericana*, 12: 19–38.
Morning, Ann (2008): "Ethnic classification in global perspective: a cross-national survey of the 2000 census round". *Population Research and Policy Review*, 27: 239–272.
Moseley, Christopher (ed.) (2010): *Atlas of the World's Languages in Danger*. 3rd ed. Paris: UNESCO Publishing. Online version: www.unesco.org/culture/en/endangeredlanguages/atlas
Newell, Colin (1988): *Methods and Models in Demography*. New York: Guilford Press.
Preston, Dennis (2010): "Perceptual Dialectology in the 21st Century". In C.A. Anders, M. Hundt, and A. Lasch (eds.), *Perceptual Dialectology: Neue Wege der Dialektologie*. Berlin: Mouton–de Gruyter, pp. 1–30.
Sellier, Jean (2004a): *Atlas des peuples d'Orient: Moyen-Orient, Caucase, Asie centrale*. Paris: La Découverte.
Sellier, Jean (2004b): *Atlas des peuples d'Asie méridionale et orientale*. Barcelona: Paidós.
Sellier, Jean (2011): *Atlas des peuples d'Afrique*. Paris: La Découverte.
Sellier, Jean (2013): *Atlas des peuples d'Amerique*. Paris: La Découverte.
Sellier, Jean and André Sellier (2014): *Atlas des peuples d'Europe centrale*. Paris: La Découverte.
Sichra, Inge (2009): *Atlas sociolingüístico de pueblos indígenas en América Latina*. Cochabamba: UNICEF-FUNPROEIB.
Siegel, Jacob S. (2018): *Demographic and Socioeconomic Basis of Ethnolinguistics*. Cham: Springer.
Siguán Soler, Miguel (ed.) (1994): *Conocimiento y usos de las lenguas de España*. Madrid: Centro de Investigaciones Sociológicas.
Solé i Camardons, Joan (2003): "El Sistema d'Indicadors Lingüístics (SIL): finalitat i característiques generals". *Noves SL: Revista de Sociolingüística*, 2003.
Statistisches Bundesamt (2020): *Bevölkerung und Erwerbstätigkeit: Bevölkerung mit Migrationshintergrund–Ergebnisse des Mikrozensus 2019*. Wiesbaden: Statistisches Bundesamt.
Terborg, Roland and Laura García Landa (eds.) (2011): *Muerte y vitalidad de lenguas indígenas y las presiones sobre sus hablantes*. México: UNAM.
Tehan, Thomas and Linda Markowski (2017): "An evaluation of So language vitality in Thailand". *Journal of the Southeast Asian Linguistics Society*, 10: 45–66.
Treviño Maruri, Rocío and Andreu Domingo (2020): "Adiós al censo en España? Elementos para el debate". *Revista Española de Investigaciones Sociológicas*, 171: 107–124.
United Nations (2020a): *United Nations Statistical Yearbook 2020*. New York: Department of Economic and Social Affairs Statistics Division.

United Nations (2020b): *World Statistics Pocketbook 2020.* New York: Department of Economic and Social Affairs Statistics Division.

Viladot, Maria Àngels (1995): "Les dades demogràfiques en el concepte de vitalitat lingüística". In *Actes del Simposi de Demolingüística. III Trobada de Sociolingüistes Catalans.* Barcelona: Generalitat de Catalunya, pp. 20–33.

Viladot, Maria Àngels and Moisés Esteban-Guitart (2011): "Un estudio transversal sobre la percepción de la vitalidad etnolingüística en jóvenes y adultos de Cataluña". *Revista Internacional De Sociología,* 69: 229–252.

5
DEMOLINGUISTIC FACTORS

Speakers and Their Communities

The particularity that characterizes demolinguistics among other demographic disciplines is its attention to populations in terms of speakers (knowledge of and users) of one or more languages or varieties. This implies on the one hand giving adequate treatment to the linguistic situations that are analyzed, starting from the principles and concepts offered by linguistics and sociolinguistics; and on the other hand, adapting the demographic analysis to the peculiarities of languages and their speakers, in all their dimensions: social, psychological, and strictly linguistic.

Demolinguistics usually handles some variables that could be called "dependent" (that is, they must be explained) and other independent or explanatory variables which contribute to understanding the behavior of the former. From this perspective, speakers and their communities, within their linguistic and sociolinguistic dimensions, would be the dependent factor, and everything surrounding them in their environment could have explanatory capacities. The interest lies in discovering or confirming how and to what degree these explanatory variables act upon populations of speakers, their acquisition and learning processes, their linguistic uses and exchanges (whatever they may be in each case), as well as the possibilities of maintenance, shift, or substitutions of spoken languages. For this task, it is common to speak of languages (and their varieties) as if they were individual entities, but one must not lose sight of the possible effects the languages have in relation to their speakers, their communities, their forms, and their dynamics.

Preestablished Definitions of Speakers

Speakers and their communities can be registered directly or indirectly in all possible data sources. Generally, administrative registries allow access to information related to the language of individuals only in an indirect fashion, from traits such as nationality or geographic origin. There are not, therefore, individualized registers of speakers. Censuses, for their part, might collect specific information about language and, when they do so, allude specifically to the language with certain indicators: mother tongue, habitual language, language proficiency, and language spoken in the home. Surveys can also specifically target the collection of data about languages and their speakers, often in terms similar to those used in censuses but with more flexibility to include other indicators or aspects. Both censuses and surveys can collect information on ethnicity or race that, with due justification and demonstration, could be extrapolated to languages known.

As can be inferred from this, the conceptualization of languages and their communities can be predetermined by the way in which the data were collected. Hence the importance of knowing with exactly what values the concepts of "mother tongue" or "habitual language" are used in each case. And it is not easy to know the way in which such attributes have been purposefully attributed to each speaker, group, or community, nor to verify how their identification took place in each case. This difficulty multiplies when one wants to compare populations in which the linguistic information has been labeled in different ways. These pitfalls arise from basic questions previously explained in the concepts of linguistics for demographers: determining what is a "language" and who is a "speaker."

To address these essential questions, demolinguistics applies a principle of pragmatism that avoids endless conceptual disquisitions. That principle involves extracting theory from practice and applying it in the form of intelligent practice (Peirce, 1878). A practical way to dispel doubts about whether a language is a native language or not lies simply in giving validity to what the speaker proposes about their own language; for example, through their answers to a questionnaire. It is true that many speakers don't know, literally, what their mother tongue is because of their own linguistic biography, but it is likewise true that those speakers are not usually the majority. And something similar could be said about "habitual language" or "language spoken in the home": it is the individuals / speakers themselves who decide how the term should be applied.

In 2008, Extra and Gorter compared the treatment that non-national languages received in the censuses of 17 European Union countries, and the conclusions were very illustrative. They found that the questions on the census focused mainly on regional minority languages (RM languages) and not on immigrant minority languages (IM languages). It was also found that the three most common questions about language use referred to "mother tongue" (11 countries), "other language(s) spoken (frequently)" (six countries), and "the language(s) (most frequently) spoken in the home" (five countries). From this comparison, it was concluded that

Hungary is the country most interested in knowing about language use. It is also possible to observe other particularities, such as the fact that in some countries the collection of data on the language spoken at home was in conflict with linguistic legislation, like in Belgium, where census data on language use has not been collected since 1947 and where the traditional linguistic borders between Dutch, French, and German are established by law.

Previously, in 2004, Extra and Yağmur compared census questions referring to cultural aspects in several English-speaking countries: Australia, Canada, South Africa, and the United States. The comparison made it possible to visualize the differences in the treatment of questions regarding origin, ethnicity, religion, and language. With regard to the latter, it was observed that only Canada referred in its census to "mother tongue" and "language used at work," whereas the other countries asked for the "language used at home." In fact, this final factor, along with nationality and country of birth, are the only questions shared by the four

TABLE 5.1 Treatment of questions about languages in 17 European Union countries.

EU country	Mother tongue	(Other) language(s) spoken (frequently)	Language(s) (most frequently) spoken at home	Language(s) spoken with family or friends	Speak well/ average/a little	Understand/ speak/read/ write
Austria	-	-	+	-	-	-
Bulgaria	+	-	-	-	-	-
Cyprus	-	+	-	-	-	-
Czech Republic	(1)	-	-	-	-	-
Estonia	+	+	-	-	-	-
Finland	+	-	-	-	-	-
Hungary	+	+	-	+	-	-
Ireland	-	(2)	-	-	-	-
Latvia	+	+	-	-	-	-
Lithuania	+	+	-	-	-	-
Malta	-	-	+	-	+	-
Poland	-	-	+	-	-	-
Romania	+	-	-	-	-	-
Slovakia	+	-	-	-	-	-
Slovenia	+	-	+	-	-	-
Spain	(3)	-	(3)	-	-	(4)
United Kingdom	-	-	-	-	-	(5)

(1) Indicate the language spoken by your mother or guardian when you were a kid
(2) Only Irish; if yes, daily within / outside the educational system / weekly / less often / never
(3) Both language questions in the Basque Country; Navarre and Galicia, for Basque/Galician
(4) In Catalonia, Valencia, and Balearic Islands for Catalan
(5) Only in Wales and Scotland, for Welsh and Gaelic respectively

Source: Extra & Gorter (2008: 20).

TABLE 5.2 Overview of (set of) census questions in four multicultural countries.

Questions in the census	Australia 2001	Canada 2001	SA 2001	USA 2000	Coverage
Nationality of respondent	+	+	+	+	4
Birth country of respondent	+	+	+	+	4
Birth country of parents	+	+	-	-	2
Ethnicity	-	+	-	+	2
Ancestry	+	+	-	+	3
Race	-	+	+	+	3
Mother tongue	-	+	-	-	1
Language used at home	+	+	+	+	4
Language used at work	-	+	-	-	1
Proficiency in English	+	+	-	+	3
Religious denomination	+	+	+	-	3
Total dimensions	7	11	5	7	30

Source: Extra & Yağmur (2004).

censuses. Likewise, it is notable that Canada was the country most interested in the details of language, ethnicity, religion, and origin. On the one hand, this was probably influenced by the high sensitivity that the Canadian province of Québec has shown since the 1970s and, on the other, by the greater attention that has since then been paid to demolinguistic analysis.

Regarding the specification of "language," censuses and questionnaires also resolve the identification of "language" (including how it's designated) in a practical and direct way, although that sometimes requires offering popularly recognizable or acceptable terminological alternatives. Therefore, in addition to allowing various answers when asking about languages usually spoken at home or with family, linguistic surveys in Switzerland also offer some alternatives with double formulation, although these terms establish varying relationships among themselves:

> *Ticino or Grisons Italian dialect* (alternative designation)
> *Serbian / Croatian* (two languages or language with a double designation and double alphabet)
> *French or Swiss French patois* (two possible dialectal varieties)

Other demographic instruments also categorize and label languages with the apparent sole criterion of offering labels acceptable to the respondents and their self-ascription. The United States census, when presenting the languages spoken at home, includes alternative designations in many cases:

a. Different languages included under one general heading: "*Chinese (incl. Mandarin, Cantonese).*"
b. Different terminology for the same language: "*Tagalog (incl. Filipino).*"

1. What is your main language, i.e. the language you think in and know best?
If you think in and have very good knowledge of more than one language, please specify below.

1 German (or Swiss German)
2 French (or Swiss French patois)
3 Italian (or Ticino or Grisons Italian dialect)
4 Rhaeto-Romansch
5 Serbian/Croatian
6 Albanian
7 Portuguese
8 Spanish
9 English
10 other(s), please specify:

2. What language(s) do you habitually speak at home/with your family? (More than one answer is possible)

1 Swiss German dialect
2 High German
3 French (or Swiss French patois)
4 Ticino or Grisons Italian dialect
5 Italian
6 Rhaeto-Romansch
7 Serbian/Croatian
8 Albanian
9 Portuguese
10 Spanish
11 English
12 other language(s)

3. What language(s) do you habitually speak at work/at your educational establishment? (More than one answer is possible)
At work: include the languages you speak during work breaks.
School pupils and students should not list the individual languages they are studying, but the language(s) they use during regular teaching sessions and during breaks.

1 Swiss German dialect
2 High German
3 French (or Swiss French patois)
4 Ticino or Grisons Italian dialect
5 Italian
6 Rhaeto-Romansch
7 Serbian/Croatian
8 Albanian
9 Portuguese
10 Spanish
11 English
12 other language(s)

FIGURE 5.1 Linguistic questions in Switzerland.
Source: Switzerland's structural survey.

c. Varieties linked to the same language "*French, Haitian, or Cajun.*"
d. An entire language family: "*Russian, Polish or other languages.*"

In cases like these, the parallelism between the treatment of ethnicity and religion is clear. When asking about the origin of foreign census takers in the same United States census, alternative designations may also appear:

Hispanic, Latino or Spanish origin
Mexican, Mexican Am., Chicano

Likewise, in terms of race, some options are offered as equivalent: *Guamanian or Chamorro.*

Joint consideration of the criteria that allows for the identification of multicultural societies' population groups allowed Guus Extra and Durk Gorter (2001) to present an interesting analysis of the kind of information gathered by censuses in terms of its usefulness and drawbacks. The information analyzed referred to "nationality," "country of origin," "ethnic self-identification," and "language of the home." The advantages were immediately visible: nationality and country of origin are objective criteria and easy to establish; self-identification reveals the individual's own self-conception, along with its emotional implications; and the language of the home gives useful information for governments in matters of education and public communication.

TABLE 5.3 Disadvantages of criteria for defining and identifying population groups in a multicultural society.

Nationality
  Intergenerational weakening of identity due to naturalizations and dual nationalities
  Lack of correspondence between nationality and ethnicity / identity
  Nationality of former colonies

Country of origin
  Intergenerational weakening due to births in the country of immigration
  Lack of correspondence between origin and ethnicity / identity
  Possibility of modification of borders

Self-identification
  Subjective criteria, affected by external factors
  Possibility of multiple self-identifications
  Conditioned by historic episodes (e.g., wars)

Languages of the home
  Complex criteria: who speaks, what, and with whom
  Lack of agreement between language and ethnicity / identity
  Inefficiency in single-member households

Source: Based on Extra & Gorter (2001).

The Sizes of Speech Communities

Despite the many conceptual and terminological obstacles that arise along the way, one of the goals of collecting information on "mother tongue," "language of habitual use," or "language spoken in the home" in censuses and through surveys is to determine the sizes of speech communities. In fact, demolinguistics was born in modern times out of the desire to know the quantitative dimension of the speaking population of a language (let's say French) in a given territory (for example, Canada). From there, political, social, and educational actions of all kinds would need to be derived. At the same time, the inclusion of questions about languages in censuses was born largely as a way of constructing or reinforcing nations and nationalities based on the population that speaks these respective national languages (Kertzer & Arel, 2001).

Naturally, the tallying of speakers requires prior identification of their languages, but the effort of identifying or cataloging the languages of a given territory presents certain difficulties. The Spanish Constitution of 1978, for example, speaks of co-official languages but doesn't establish a catalog of these, leaving a wide undefined area of linguistic manifestations such as the "Asturian language" (in the Community of the Principality of Asturias) or the "Aragonese language" (in the Community of Aragón) which don't have formal co-official status. As is logical, the difficulties multiply exponentially when it comes to establishing the catalog of world languages, a task impossible to complete in a precise fashion.

Despite all this, there are various initiatives focused on determining the catalog of world languages along with their numbers of speakers. This is the task of quantifying the size of linguistic communities which is generally approached from the concept of "mother tongue," "first language," or "L1," which is specified by counting "native speakers" of the languages of a territory, a continent, or the world. As has already been explained, the concept of "native speaker" or "primary speaker" becomes extremely complex when applied to real individuals. Usually, studies of indigenous, native, minority, or minoritized languages are approached from the concept of the "mother tongue," more intimately tied to notions of identity and tradition (Skutnabb-Kangas, 1981, 2000), although these also materialize in the tallying of native speakers.

Frequently, the source used to discover the native or "primary" speakers of a language is the catalog *Ethnologue: Languages of the World* (Eberhard, Simons, & Fennig, 2022). Its data are, for example, what allowed Roland Breton to create graphs of speakers of languages in his *Atlas des langues du monde* (2003). Such a decision implies accepting the criteria used by the catalog's creators, beginning with the fact of giving priority to L1 speakers, without paying attention to other aspects, such as the vehicularity of the languages; Alain and Louis-Jean Calvet (2022) give the example of Swahili, for which there are around 700,000 native speakers, without considering the several tens of millions who have this language as an L2. The criticisms of *Ethnologue* highlight that there are cases in which the number of speakers of a language in a country exceeds the number of inhabitants, or that many data don't go beyond rough approximations, an understandable reality if one considers, for instance, that the majority of births and deaths in the world are not officially registered. In addition, there is the problem of the names of the languages (glottonymy), which are not always unique or univocal, a problem that is multiplied when the names are offered in translation and presented in a single alphabet. To some extent, these difficulties are resolved by heeding the ISO code that each language receives, although the acceptance that the code is properly attributed is also an exercise in good faith. These comments underline why it is possible for the tallying of speakers in some sources to offer very different results from others.

On the other hand, if the identification and quantification of communities of speakers of mother tongues (habitual / primary...) refer to concepts that are complex, almost inscrutable, and difficult to apply, even through self-identification, the quantification of speech communities of second languages or secondary languages with the character of "vehicular languages" presents an even more arduous task. The identification and quantification of second languages of any country or territory are normally deduced from the information offered by censuses, which is often based on speakers' self-ascription. Knowing the number of speakers of an L2 (secondary or non-native speakers) becomes an unapproachable task when the speakers themselves don't know their origin, or when they hide it, as can happen due to influences and pressures from nationalist groups or, in

TABLE 5.4 Number of native speakers of nine languages according to different sources (1964–2015).

	Muller (1964)	Salvat (1974)	Breton (1976)	Grimes (1984)	Encyclopedia Britannica (1995)	Nationalencyklopedin (2015)
Chinese	515,000,000	481,000,000	500,000,000	700,000,000	790,135,000	955,000,000
English	265,000,000	288,000,000	320,000,000	391,000,000	489,966,300	360,000,000
Hindi	185,000,000	158,000,000	350,000,000	194,000,000	354,270,000	310,000,000
Spanish	145,000,000	152,000,000	210,000,000	211,000,000	323,180,000	470,000,000
Russian	135,000,000	164,000,000	150,000,000	154,000,000	151,494,000	155,000,000
Japanese	95,000,000	97,000,000	110,000,000	117,000,000	123,830,000	125,000,000
French	65,000,000	71,000,000	80,000,000	63,000,000	98,802,000	74,000,000
German	100,000,000	121,000,000	105,000,000	119,000,000	89,401,000	89,000,000
Italian	55,000,000	–	–	–	54,414,500	60,000,000

general, from residence or host communities that don't easily accept the use of other languages.

From a different perspective, it is necessary to also remember that the size and evolution of a speech community are not only specified by the data that censuses and surveys can offer directly but can be known or deduced from the dynamism of the speech community's vital events. At this point, the term "demography of languages" takes on its full meaning. Thus, for example, the fertility rate of a population can offer valuable information about the present and future of a linguistic community. When it comes to communities of reduced size, it is possible to turn to national demographic sources to discover the most interesting vital facts in this regard. When trying to find out the population dynamic of large communities or to compare the dynamics of different countries, one usually turns to international or transnational sources such as the United Nations, which, even though it takes data from censuses, offers it in a relatively comparable and more homogeneous form.

Regarding the fertility rate, it is accepted that the higher it is, the stronger the maintenance of a speaking population. The apparent objectivity of such a rate doesn't remove all difficulties for the analysis. One of these is that the fertility index is not the same in all the regions of a country, which means it may not apply to subpopulations or minority population groups with a particular linguistic or ethnic interest. At the same time, the linguistic groups of interest might be distributed among various countries; as such, the first problem is multiplied by the number of countries involved. If it is a case of majority ethnic or linguistic groups, the fertility rates of each country where they exist can be used, adding them together to reach a global or common rate. If it is a case of ethnic or linguistic groups whose proportion within a country is known, the rate of each country can be multiplied by the proportion of the group in question (e.g., 0.45 if the group represents 45% of the population) before summing up the relative rates of each country.

Therefore, the problems of quantifying speakers in monolingual, bilingual, or multilingual communities are more than evident when it comes to identifying diverse kinds of languages in different speakers and, in general, when proceeding to a demolinguistic analysis. For this reason, it is not surprising that demolinguistics has not been limited to working directly with the concepts used by demographic sources, but instead has developed specific resources to understand the dynamics of speech communities.

Factors of Vitality and Sustainability

In the field of minority languages, especially indigenous or native languages, studies have attempted to find explanatory factors able to describe real situations, as well as to foresee future evolutions of the communities and their languages. These studies are framed in the field of the ecology of languages or ecolinguistics and are usually guided by different, although often complementary, criteria.

M. Àngels Viladot (1995) highlights three structural variables as the most influential upon the vitality of ethnolinguistic groups: demography, institutional support and control, and status. In a similar vein, other experts have specified the factors that weaken the vitality of a language. Anna María Escobar (2014) clearly summarizes:

Sociodemographic Factors

Presence of fewer than 100,000 speakers.
Small monolingual population without growth.
Dialectal diversification and lack of standardized variety.
Extended bilingualism.

Economic and Political Factors

Lack of language policy.
Reduction of domains.
Negative attitudes.
Migration to urban and culturally diverse areas.
Migration to other linguistic regions.

For their part, M. Paul Lewis and Gary F. Simons (2010) established four levels for determining the sustainability of languages: history (including the evolution of the size of the community), identity, orality, and literacy. To attain sustainability, five conditions must be met, and they are referred to by the acronym FAMED, based in turn on the criteria established by Ralph Fasold (1984) for diglossia. Those conditions are:

Functions: The functions of the language at each level of sustainability must exist and be recognized by the community. The language in question must be useful.
Acquisition: There must be a way to acquire the necessary competence to use the language with these functions.
Motivation: The members of the community must be motivated to use the language with these functions.
Environment: The external environment (political, social, attitudes) must not be hostile to the use of the language for these functions.
Niche Differentiation: The functions assigned socially to the language must be different from the functions of an L2.

All FAMED conditions must be met for the use of a language to be sustainable and to determine what components of the sustainable use are essential in each context and what the prospects for maintenance and potential development are. Factors detailed by different experts need not be present in unison nor in balanced and direct proportions for the linguistic vitality to be greater or less; instead, they combine to different degrees, contributing to a variable index of vitality (Ros, Huici, & Cano, 1994). This index will be more precise when the factors that comprise it are more easily quantifiable.

Despite the differences in the details provided, all vitality studies come to agree on the importance given to generational transmission in which the "age" factor is essential. In fact, vitality is defined to a large degree by the existence of children who learn the language in the home and who, moreover, are monolingual; such that, if there are no or few monolingual children, the language is considered "endangered" (Crystal, 2000; Whalen & Simons, 2012; Lewis, Simons, & Fennig, 2014). For this reason, a large part of the efforts made for the revitalization of languages (that is, for what Fishman called "reversal") have to do with processes of acquisition at an early age, in the home or through school. Otherwise, languages can come to have only a single speaker remaining, as has been documented in dozens of cases, after which they become extinct. The simple death of its speakers is one of the ways in which, as Zimmermann (1999) explains, a language can become extinct. The other basic form of extinction is the abandonment of the language in the process of intergenerational transmission.

The ideas that have just been presented start, in general, from the assumption that bilingualism or multilingualism is the "natural" prelude to the abandonment of minority or weak languages, treating as good and universal Joshua Fishman's (1991) outline for the displacement of languages:

monolingualism language A > bilingualism language A + language B > monolingualism language B

However, this assumption is only true if conditions are very unfavorable for multilingualism.

Demolinguistic Factors and Concepts Elaborated

While there are criteria and concepts established from censuses and surveys which are resolved differently in each initiative, along with criteria established by the ecology of the languages, there are also criteria developed from demolinguistic analysis itself. The sources and primary data are basically the same as those used in direct quantifications, but there is also the possibility of combining and crossing the data, of subjecting it to statistical treatment or reordering the data for the configuration of other categories.

When Alain Calvet and Louis-Jean Calvet became interested in quantifying the importance of the languages of the world, they used a set of factors, in addition to the number of speakers, of which there are two of interest at this moment. One of these is the "vehicularity" of the languages, which we've alluded to in various sections; the other is the "entropy" of languages. These qualities are attributed to languages which are deduced from the profiles of their speakers.

Bilingual communities, multilingual workplaces, and the possibility of gaining knowledge of second languages through school or other means makes the vehicularity of languages vary enormously. One calls the ability of a language to serve as a means of communication its "vehicularity." According to this concept, a language capable of being used as an L1 and an L2 would have a greater vehicularity than a language used exclusively as an L1. With the goal of quantifying that capacity, Alain and Jean-Louis Calvet proposed a "vehicularity rate," defined as the relationship between the number of speakers that use a language as an L2: S(L2) and its total number of speakers: S(L1) and S(L2) according to the following formula:

$$\text{Vehicularity rate} = \frac{S(L2)}{S(L1)+S(L2)}$$

The resulting rate can vary between 0, for a language that only has L1 speakers, and 1, for a language whose speakers, all of them, know it as an L2. Once the calculation has been made, the most adequate data for the application of the formula remain to be found. In fact, the decision on the number of L1 and L2 speakers for their later quantification doesn't depend solely on the goals of each study, but also on the limits of the censuses and the reliability and comparability of the available statistics on the knowledge of additional languages (Moreno-Fernández & Otero Roth 1998; Moreno-Fernández, 2014). To a large extent, the decision depends on the sources of each study which tend to *de facto* solve the problems derived from the dialectal diversity of each territory and the treatment of the languages in multilingual contexts.

The concept of "entropy," which comes from thermodynamics and information theory, was introduced into demolinguistics in 2012 by Alain Calvet and Louis-Jean Calvet (2022). Entropy serves to differentiate the languages spoken in a single country or territory from those spoken in several countries or territories. This means that entropy is not derived from a language's total number of speakers but from the way those speakers are distributed within the area or areas where the language is spoken. Thus, to calculate entropy, we may start from the proportion of speakers of a given language who live in each of the territories (countries) where it is spoken (p_i). The formula would be the following:

$$\text{Entropy} = -\Sigma \, (p_i \times \log(p_i))$$

where p_i is the probability that a language is spoken in a given territory and log (p_i) the natural logarithm of this probability, whereas Σ indicates the sum of all the possible territories (p_i). The minimum value for this function is 0 when the language in question is spoken only in one country and no maximum value is set. The Calvets gave the example of a language spoken primarily (98%) in only one country, with only a few speakers (2%) living in a second country. In this case, the entropy would be:

$(0.98 \times \log(0.98) + 0.02 \times \log(0.02)) = 0.098$

Similarly, if the speakers of a language are distributed uniformly (33%) across three countries the entropy would be as follows:

$(0.33 \times \log(0.33) + 0.33 \times \log(0.33) + 0.34 \times \log(0.34)) = 1.099$

Examples using real languages allow values of entropy to be shown to better understand the differences between languages. Data for Russian, Japanese, English, Spanish, Standard Arabic, and Mandarin Chinese are provided, with their entropy scores.

These data show that entropy is not a direct function of the number of speakers, which is why the entropy of Mandarin Chinese is lower than that of Russian, despite the difference in the number of speakers, and that of Japanese less than that of Russian, despite them having similar numbers of speakers. The entropy of Arabic is high because of the number of countries in which it is spoken (regardless of its internal dialectalization), whereas the language with a better ratio of speakers to entropy is Russian. The examples used are national or official languages in their territories, but the calculation would be of similar application with languages of minority implantation.

From another perspective, the number of countries in which a language is spoken provides information on its territorial and geopolitical dominance. The recognition of the official status or vehicularity of a language is the criterion that lets one decide which countries are integrated into that domain or not. However, the mere number of countries is not sufficiently explanatory because it would ignore the different conditions of official status which languages can hold (national, official, co-official throughout the territory, co-official in part of a territory, protected) or the linguistic diversity within each country, as well as the difference in size or economic weight of the countries themselves (Ammon,

TABLE 5.5 Entropy and number of speakers of various languages.

Language	Russian	Japanese	English	Spanish	Standard Arabic	Mandarin Chinese
Entropy	0.667	0.116	1.159	2.543	2.7?	0.160
Speakers	136M	124M	362M	443M	?	921M

M = millions.
Source: Calvet & Calvet (2022).

2010). In addition, the number of countries as an analytic factor encounters other basic complications, such as their international recognition or their status as dependents, associates, or disputed, not to mention stateless nations.

Speaker Profiles

Speech communities can also be characterized by the kinds of speakers who form them. We have already seen how L1 and L2 speakers can be identified and quantified from census and survey data, but there are ways of breaking down speech communities with the goal of reaching a more refined estimate of the overall makeup of a linguistic community. However, this doesn't mean that the result must be exact for the same conceptual and methodological reasons. The point of departure would be, once more, to determine what is meant by a language(s), specifically, and what is meant by a speaker(s) of that / those language(s).

With regard to the specific language(s) whose speaker population is to be analyzed, the task of identifying and profiling its varieties is basic, especially when the profiles are blurred in relation to prototypical modalities. Among the varieties of blurred profiles would be those who are in the process of language acquisition. Therefore, the obstacle of establishing the relationships between one or more linguistic centers (prototypical modalities) and their respective peripheries (varieties with blurred limits) must be faced. As an example, let us consider the situation of the Spanish language. The geographic domain of Spanish extends mainly within the borders of the countries in which Spanish is an official, national, or vehicular language. However, there is the possibility of identifying those who have acquired one of its varieties in other geographies as speakers of Spanish, whether through a process of learning or inheritance. Within and outside the current Spanish-speaking domain itself, there are also spaces of contact with other languages whose speakers have established a relationship of greater or lesser distance with Spanish. In these cases, the questions that must be resolved are: should the Ladino or Judeo-Spanish of Sephardic Jews, the Chavacano of the Philippines, or the Caribbean Papiamento be considered varieties of Spanish? As for contact between languages, should one include within the sphere of Spanish languages bilingual mixtures like the Media Lengua of certain groups originating from Ecuador or what is called Spanglish in the United States? Likewise, are these varieties sufficiently homogeneous as to be considered varieties and not a conglomeration of varieties? Does their self-association with the Spanish-speaking space have more weight in making them or their local idiosyncrasies worthy of consideration?

As far as speakers are concerned, limits should be established in relation to their command of their own language (in any of its varieties) and their command of other languages or varieties. In principle, there is no psycholinguistic reason at all that determines that fluency in one language by someone bilingual is incompatible with the command to a similar level of a second or third language. This means that, although demolinguistics has granted priority to mother tongues beyond their coexistence with other languages in the same person, there is no reason to exclude as speakers of an L1 / language of habitual use / primary language those who speak it as a second language. In bilingual groups, one also finds cases of "heritage speakers" whose command of the language in question can be quite varied. In the case of language learners, the moment at which they can be categorized as speakers of an L2 proves unclear. The Common European Framework of Reference for Languages (Council of Europe, 2001) establishes that a person with an A2 level "knows how to communicate when carrying out simple and everyday tasks" and "knows how to describe in simple terms aspects of their past and their environment." The questions that arise, then, would be: what treatment should be given to bilingual speakers? At what point does a "heritage speaker" cease to be a speaker of the inherited language? Can they be considered a speaker of a language when their command of it is only at an A2 level?

These borderline, blurred, or, if preferred, peripheral situations require decisions to be made by demolinguistic analysts. Decisions can be made on an operational basis, but a reasoned justification is always necessary. Given that these decisions are made in a particular way in each analysis, as an example, commentary will be given on a demolinguistic proposal from which decisions have been made with distinct levels of operativity and subjectivity. The proposal is one of the works leading to the *Atlas de la lengua española en el mundo* by Moreno-Fernández and Otero (2009), and other later demographic works by these authors.

From this demolinguistic proposal, the goal of analyzing the speakers of the Spanish language requires, as is obvious, specification of what is understood when referring to the Spanish language and what is meant by speaker. The limits of these concepts are described in the work as follows:

1. The Spanish language is considered to be any linguistic manifestation that the speakers themselves, social consensus, or political recognition understand as such, including all its varieties in any territory. In this case, the notion of the Spanish language includes, in addition to its dialectal and sociolectal manifestations (e.g., Ladino or Judeo-Spanish), its manifestations in the form of creoles in which Spanish is an acrolect (e.g., Chavacano), and its bilingual mixtures (e.g., Spanglish). The inclusion of these varieties under the general label of Spanish is due not only to historical and linguistic reasons, which are not insignificant, but also the closeness in terms of identity that these speakers show toward the language. In the case of Ladino / Judeo-Spanish, in 2020 the Akademia Nasionala del Ladino (National Academy of Ladino) was integrated as a member of the Associations of Academies of the Spanish Language; in the case of Chavacano, it is a variety clearly perceived as part of the Hispanic heritage, despite the linguistic distance that exists with regard to other varieties; in the case of Spanglish, there is a set of linguistic practices that are mostly linked to Spanish, especially Mexican Spanish, even though some

groups claim them as signs of a free-standing identity. Whatever the case, the ascription of these varieties to a generic "Spanish" would be the result of an operational decision.
2. Any person is considered a "speaker of Spanish" who knows or uses the Spanish language, in any of its varieties and in any territory, regardless of their nationality or their national or linguistic origin, independently of the number of languages they know and the order in which these were acquired.

As can be deduced from these points, this demolinguistic proposal is not made from the concept of "mother tongue" but from the concept of "language command or proficiency," which, in turn, allows the kinds of speakers that make up the linguistic community to be classified and ordered. "Command" or "proficiency" is understood as the "skill" to use a language in a way that is appropriate to its form and adequate to the communicative domains or contexts, manifesting itself at different levels conditioned by the manner and level of acquisition of the language (Moreno-Fernández & Otero Roth, 2006). The speaker with "native skills" has a linguistic or communicative capacity that corresponds with (or is close or equivalent to) those who acquire it from childhood, in interaction with their family, with members of a community, or through school. The concept refers to the ability to interact as a native speaker of a language or with native speakers of that language, as well as the possibility of being considered members of the idiomatic community of the language in question by which speakers with native fluency of a language may not necessarily have it as their mother tongue (Moreno-Fernández, 2014).

The highest degree of proficiency in a language is considered to be that of "native" speakers. This kind of command, although it can be equated to that of the mother tongue, can also be acquired through different means and in distinct contexts. Therefore, speakers could be considered "natives" if they are native speakers themselves or if they use or command the language with an equivalent proficiency. This interpretation, then, doesn't associate "native" exclusively with the speakers that Braj Kachru includes within a first circle or inner circle of a language (for example, for English, those who come from the United States, the United Kingdom, Canada, Australia, and New Zealand) (Kachru, 2017), but that "natives" can also be found in other spaces and even include speakers not born within these countries. That is why a "reanimated" concept of "native" is proposed here within the syntagm "native skills."

When quantifying the number of native speakers of a language, however, it is also possible to include those people who are not properly native, given that the demography of languages need not be limited to native, maternal, or first languages. In fact, speakers who have acquired second or additional languages contribute to increasing their communicative value and, to a large extent, their attractiveness for other speakers (De Swaan, 2001).

146 Demolinguistic Factors

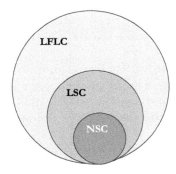

GRAPH 5.1 Levels for the categorization of speakers. NSC = native skills cluster; LSC = limited skills cluster; LFLC = learners of foreign language cluster.
Source: Moreno-Fernández & Otero Roth (2006).

The demolinguistics practiced by Moreno-Fernández and Otero Roth (1998), Moreno-Fernández (2014) or Loureda Lamas, Moreno-Fernández, Álvarez Mella, and Scheffler (2020) organizes the categorizing of speakers into three levels which are represented as three concentric circles. The relative position of each circle represents the relative cardinal or fundamental nature of the language within the communicative repertoire of a speaker or a group of speakers.

The first circle corresponds to the speakers that comprise the native skills cluster (NSC) of a language or variety. As has been explained, the concept of "native skills" refers to the ability to interact as a native speaker of a language or with native speakers of that language, as well as being considered a member of the idiomatic community of the language in question. The components of the NSC of a language may not have it as their mother tongue, and they may also be fluent in other languages.

The second circle corresponds to the limited skills cluster (LSC) in the same language or variety. It is made up of the set of individuals whose abilities to use a language is limited from a linguistic perspective (poor command of linguistic and communicative resources) or from a sociolinguistic or stylistic perspective (use restricted to certain topics, speakers, domains, or communicative situations).

Finally, the learners of foreign language cluster (LFLC) is made up of the set of individuals who are acquiring a specific language through a process of classroom learning. The proficiency in the language of the members of an LFLC can vary greatly from beginners to experts.

The linguistic community of potential users (LCPU) would be made up essentially of the members of the NSC, as the core nucleus of the idiomatic community, to which the members of the LSC and the LFLC would be added, as shown in this easy formula:

LCPU = NSC + (LSC + LFLC)

In this way, a first distinction is established between speakers with native and non-native skills; within these latter groups, a distinction is made between those with limited competence and learners, hence the fact that these two groups are included in parentheses. This methodological proposal serves to illustrate the already discussed distinction between "macrodemolinguistics" and "microdemolinguistics" (*cf.* Moreno-Fernández, 2020; Loureda Lamas, Moreno-Fernández, Álvarez Mella, & Scheffler, 2020): microdemolinguistics would allow for the identification of different kinds of speakers with native fluency, different kinds of speakers with limited competence (heritage speakers, people who may have seen their knowledge and use of Spanish limited to varying degrees and for different reasons), and different kinds of language learners.

Likewise, this typification can be adapted to the sociolinguistic situation of a language in various environments and territories, although most of the recognizable types respond to repeating patterns. Thus, in the demolinguistic study of Spanish in Germany carried out by Loureda Lamas, Moreno-Fernández, Álvarez Mella, and Scheffler (2020), the Spanish-speaking community is subdivided into the following categories:

Native Skills Cluster German Speakers (NSC)

- NSC1. Spanish-speaking immigrants not naturalized as German.
- NSC2. Second-generation heritage speakers who have socialized in environments favorable to the transmission and maintenance of Spanish.
- NSC3. Naturalized Spanish speakers with a migratory trajectory.
- NSC4. Spanish learners who have acquired native fluency.

Limited Skills Cluster German Speakers (LSC):

- LSC1. Second- or third-generation heritage speakers who have not socialized in environments favorable to the transmission and maintenance of Spanish.
- LSC2. Non-Hispanic Germans with residence in a Spanish-speaking country.
- LSC3. Ibero-American immigrants and immigrants from the Iberian Peninsula of non-Spanish-speaking origin.
- LSC4. Graduates of secondary and higher education without native fluency (including exchange students visiting Spanish-speaking countries).
- LSC5. Students who graduate from non-formal education.

Learners of Foreign Language Cluster German Speakers Learning Spanish (LFLC):

- LFLC1. Learners studying in primary education.
- LFLC2. Learners studying in secondary education.

148 Demolinguistic Factors

- LFLC3. Learners studying in higher education.
- LFLC4. Learners studying in non-formal education.

As is often the case in these kinds of intellectual exercises, this categorical division is not free from grey areas. In this way, it is not easy to determine in practice which individuals should be classified as NSC2 and LSC1, given that the knowledge and use by heritage speakers moves on a continuum. Einar Haugen explained in 1938 the intensity of the struggle between the old and new languages of those immigrants who've become heritage speakers:

> From the first day in the new land a tug of war between his old and his new self was going on in the immigrant, and nowhere was the struggle more vividly reflected than in his successive linguistic adaptations. [...] The immigrant straddles two cultures, and if he is homeless in both, it us due in no small measure to his linguistic difficulties.
>
> *Haugen, 1938*

Michal Krzyżanowski and Ruth Wodak (2008) refer to this same ambivalence when speaking of non-spatial identities, always subject to inherent and constant change. For its part, the LSC2 category presents the difficulty of determining the level of knowledge derived from living in a Spanish-speaking environment, beyond the conjecture based on experience. Other pitfalls could be added to these, such as isolating graduate students with limited competence from learners, to avoid their being counted twice.

Therefore, these established categories are not absolutes. Proposed groups cannot be understood as static for several reasons. One of these is that the property that determines them (linguistic fluency and competence) is variable. This means that the ability to communicate in a language can be acquired, developed, or lost according to different types of dynamics:

a. *Intragroup relocation dynamics.* Speakers, depending on their social profiles, can come to hold stronger or weaker positions with respect to the skills attributed to them within a given group.
b. *Inter-group transition dynamics.* Speakers can move from one group to another depending on the proficiency that is reassigned to them after a process of gaining or losing skills.

In addition, the identification of the members of speaker groups can be conditioned by two other kinds of dynamics:

c. *Extrinsic dynamics.* Changes not attributable to speakers as such; for example, the ways of registering or administratively counting the speakers of each group.

d. *Intrinsic dynamics.* Changes originating from the modification of some characteristic or condition of the speakers, either due to vital factors (for example, births or deaths) or through a modification of their linguistic competence.

This set of criteria allows the linguistic community to be analyzed in detail, even if the result will be conditioned by the reliability of the sources and always by the quality and quantity of available data. Despite all this, this analysis is oriented overall to reducing conjectures as much as possible, showing that demolinguistics wants to go beyond counting speakers with a rough estimate (Salvador, 1992).

Explanatory Factors

If a main objective of demolinguistics is to analyze the speaker populations of the languages of the world in their composition, distribution, and changes, one should consider many other external factors surrounding the languages which, because these factors affect their knowledge and use, condition their evolution and sociopolitical presence. Certainly, the size and dynamic of the speaker populations are conditioned by demography, but there are many other factors involved. Let us consider, for example, languages like Basque or Catalan: as has already been explained, a "System of Linguistic Indicators" has been created for their analysis that allows not only for their study but also for projecting linguistic knowledge and uses in different areas of society. This system includes the following factors: education, the socioeconomic dimension, media, digital, and online culture, and external projection.

The factors capable of influencing demography and the social and political life of a language, on the other hand, are not the same for all languages; for example, as just mentioned, the case of Basque and Catalan as minority languages embedded in larger state territories (Spain, France, and Italy). Along with situations of regional minority languages, a distinction should be made between ethnic, indigenous, and native languages; the minority languages of social groups (e.g., sign languages); and immigrant minority languages, as well as that of state majority languages and the majority international and transnational languages. Starting from this multiplicity of possibilities, a typology of at least seven categories could be conceived under the label of "languages," even with full awareness of its likely misinterpretation.

To present explanatory or contributing factors in demolinguistic analysis, it is possible to proceed in a way similar to constructing indicator systems. Specifically, the focus will be on factors related to the officiality and internationality of languages, the world of education, the world of economics, the fields of culture and science, and the world of digital communication. Other aspects can also be kept in mind, such as the geographic extent of each linguistic territory, the

TABLE 5.6 Typology of languages of demolinguistic interest.

Ethnic minority language (EtML)
Local minority language (LoML)
Social minority language (SoML)
Regional minority language (ReML)
Immigrant minority language (ImML)
National majority language (NaMaL)
Transnational majority language (TrMaL)

movement of tourists, the quality of the content disseminated on the internet, the volume and quality of artistic productions, and the classifications of universities in international rankings, but those won't be described at this time.

As is to be expected, working with explanatory factors of different kinds creates numerous obstacles and restrictions. One of these is recurring: access to complete and up-to-date data is not always possible. Another serious limitation would be, once more, that sources usually offer information related to countries and not their regions, areas, or provinces, nor to their cross-border areas, by which there is a territorial equalization of nations that can erase very valuable information about the effect of these factors on specific subpopulations or regions. At the same time, when working with linguistic territories which might include various countries, one must proceed with the aggregation of data that are not always comparable due to the idiosyncrasies of each country. Likewise, each specific language could require attention to be paid to some factors and not others in each of its territories. This includes the possibility that the factors presented here may not be at all relevant to certain populations.

There are numerous factors with greater or lesser demolinguistic repercussions, which are more or less direct, and their incidence must be calibrated in each case. In any event, those that are discussed here have revealed their ability to determine and explain the sociolinguistic reality for demolinguistic analysis.

Official Languages and International Languages

The languages of the world can enjoy different degrees of recognition by the political authorities of the countries where they are spoken. A language can be recognized by a state as official *de facto* or *de jure,* and it can be so for the entire territory or for a part of it. At the same time, a state can recognize one or more languages as official, giving rise to officially bilingual or multilingual countries. In this way, questions of language are also introduced into the field of law. Here it becomes relevant to consider a conceptual distinction between "official language" and "national language:"

> *National language.* A language that is considered and used as the main language of a nation state.

Official language. A language that by law must or can be used in the official and institutional affairs of a state.

Precisely because they are not recognized as "states" (with governments, parliaments, administrations, and public services) or as parts of the state, indigenous and native communities don't usually have the capacity to declare languages official. Often, these communities are geographically confined or have their territory circumscribed to domains called "reserves," "reservations," or similar terms, depending on their languages, regions, and customs.

The authorities with the power to influence official status can be local, regional, national, or international in nature. This reality makes situations regarding the officiality of languages very diverse. Ukraine, for example, has declared Ukrainian to be an official language, but grants the status of regional or minority language, with some state functions, to about 20 languages that are the mother tongue for some 10% of the population of the corresponding regions (for example Russian in the province of Dnipropetrovsk, Hungarian in Berehove) (Law 2-r/2018). A different case is that of Finland, where two official languages (Finnish or Suomi and Swedish) exist at the same legal level, but with very unequal geosocial implementation, because Swedish is only spoken by 5% of the population.

For its part, the United States is a country that doesn't have an official language *de jure*, although it does have one *de facto*. However, at the same time, there are states and territories that have declared the officiality of English within their jurisdictions, whereas others have declared the officiality of other languages in addition to English (Hawaiian in Hawaii, Sioux in South Dakota, Samoan in Samoa, Chamorro in Guam, Chamorro and Carolino in the Northern Mariana Islands); the case of Spanish in Puerto Rico, as a free associated state, is somewhat different. Therefore, casuistry is very broad.

There are also cases in which the recognition of official status is granted by local powers. The city of Fort Smith in Canada declared the officiality of its multilingual services in English, French, Chipewyan, Cree, and North Slavey, and the city of São Gabriel da Cachoeira, in the state of Amazonas (Brazil), in addition to declaring in its local regulations the officiality of Portuguese for the entire Federal Republic of Brazil, declares the adoption of three co-official languages: Nheengatu, Tukano, and Baniwa. In these cases, official status means the same as for states or regions: the obligation to offer basic services to citizens in the co-official languages, both orally and in writing; to generate public documentation in them; and to encourage their use in education and communication media.

This kind of information can be found on the website of *L'aménagement linguistique dans le monde*, by Jacques Leclerc (2020), with regard to numerous territories around the world. This portal provides information that makes evident the complexity involved in dealing with the issue of the official nature of languages

152 Demolinguistic Factors

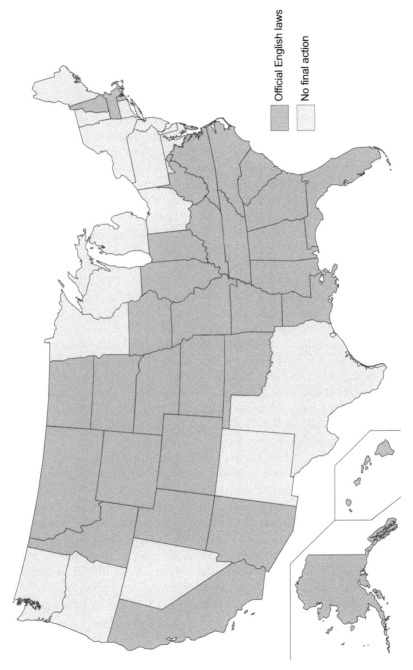

MAP 5.1 US states where English is official, with an indication of the kind of recognition, in 2021.

Source: useenglish.org.

in those states which are non-sovereign, excluded, or with limited recognition. These states, even having in many cases the sociopolitical instruments of sovereign states (government, parliament, justice system), are generally subordinate to other sovereign states whose legislation can limit or condition that of their territories when it comes to the declaration of official or co-official languages and their implementation, especially for the languages that are shared with the rest of the sovereign state. Alain and Louis-Jean Calvet (2012) use Leclerc's website when considering the "official nature of languages" factor, classifying them into three large groups: official languages of sovereign states, official languages of non-sovereign states, and languages recognized in other kinds of territories.

When a language enjoys official status within a territory, it has the privilege and the recognition of being transmitted and used in all domains and areas of public life: official bodies, education, media, and the justice system. In these cases, citizens have the right to know and use it. Therefore, official status becomes a source of social cohesion and a community instrument. This doesn't prevent, on occasion, a large gap between the spirit of the linguistic laws and the resources for their being put into practice. This happens when, in responding to internal identity demands, states declare dozens of languages to be official with equal conditions, which makes it impossible to fulfill those commitments, rights, and duties in practice in terms of knowledge and public use of such a quantity of official languages. Examples include Venezuela which, in its 2008 constitution declared 40 official languages, or Bolivia which, in 2009, made 27 languages official, some of them very close linguistically.

On the other hand, if official status contributes to the consolidation of a language within a territory, it is also a factor that implies prestige from an external perspective, so that foreign countries grant those official languages treatment they don't give to others; for example, affecting which languages are offered within their educational systems. Along with this, the importance of official recognition for a language being recognized by international organizations must be considered, as recognition must first have been granted within a country. Thus, the official status of languages in the system of the United Nations is a factor of official prestige that contributes to the reinforcement of these languages within and outside their own linguistic communities. The UN currently recognizes six languages as official: English, French, Spanish, Mandarin Chinese, Russian, and Arabic. Other international, political, and diplomatic forums recognize other official languages. In these contexts, a distinction is usually made between "official languages" and "working languages." The latter are defined as the vehicle for daily communication within an organization, for correspondence as well as for conversation.

International, diplomatic, governmental, and non-governmental organizations that have a global presence usually have English, French, and / or Spanish as their working languages, combined in different ways depending on their geopolitical environment. These languages are considered "international" largely because of their official status in numerous organizations and their status as working languages in many of them. In any case, it is worth distinguishing between the concepts of "international language" and "lingua franca:"

International language. Linguistic variety used in various countries whose inhabitants have it as their mother tongue. Linguistic variety accepted and used internationally as a communication vehicle between people who do not have it as their mother tongue.

Lingua franca. Linguistic variety used for communication between people whose mother tongues are different.

Obviously, these concepts are closely related, but that of "lingua franca" is more generic and flexible, because it can be applied to any communicative situation, public or private, official or popular; at work or with family; local, regional, or international; without need for support from an important international community of native speakers: it's enough for two speakers of different mother tongues to understand each other. From a Latin American perspective, Spanish would be an international language, because it is common in various countries, but it is not a lingua franca, except for communication between indigenous peoples of different linguistic families. That is not contrary to its growing use as an international language among non-natives or as an international lingua franca (Marqués de Tamarón, 1992), a condition enjoyed by other languages such as French and especially English. Likewise, the Amerindian vehicular languages that serve for communication between indigenous tribes would be lingua francas. These languages (Guaraní, Quechua, Nahuatl…) have long been called "general languages" (Maldavsky, Bouysse-Cassagne, Taylor, & Ramos, 2013).

Education

Education, through the official educational systems of each country, has a fundamental impact on the development of the knowledge and use of language. The greater the presence of a language in an educational system, the more students will learn and use it, and the more subjects will be taught in it; thus it will have greater stability and strength within a society, and it's more likely to have continuity. In this regard, the languages with the greatest disadvantages are without a doubt indigenous minority languages (EtMLs) and local minority languages (LoMLs).

How educational systems are organized regarding the languages of the community depends on various factors:

> Legal status of the languages used in teaching.
> Monolingual, bilingual, or multilingual nature of the community.
> Linguistic origin of the school population.

Sociolinguistic teaching objectives for each educational level.
Human and material resources available to address language teaching.

Education objectives will depend on the sociopolitical environment of each country: the United States, in general, organizes education with the goal of achieving the assimilation of minorities into the English-speaking majority of the population; Spain organizes education in its bilingual communities with the idea that individuals will complete their schooling with full competence in both of the official languages; the European Union, as a whole, promotes programs leading to the training of citizens capable of speaking two languages, in addition to their first. These factors lead to decisions regarding the organization of curricula and programs that determine which languages are included in each course and cycle, with what treatment, and for which subjects.

To facilitate comparisons, the European Union has created some diagrams made with a system of patterns and colors that characterize the training cycles, which are arranged along a time axis.

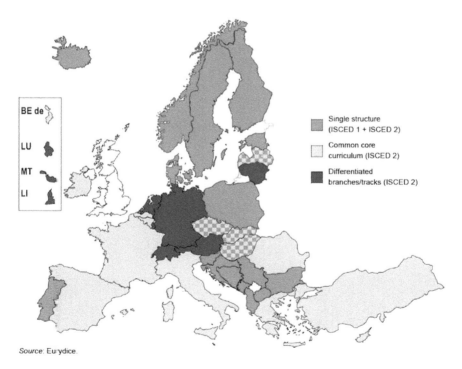

MAP 5.2 Main models of primary education (ISCED 1) and the first stage of secondary education (ISCED 2) in Europe, 2020 / 21. ISCED = International Standard Classification of Education.

Source: Eurydice, European Commission (2022).

156 Demolinguistic Factors

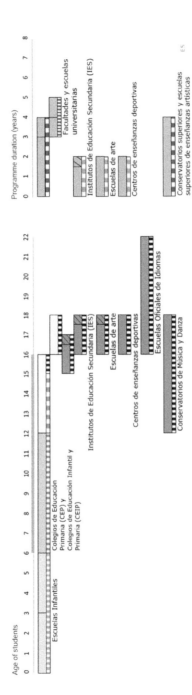

GRAPH 5.2 Educational diagram of Spain.
Source: European Commission (2022).

Indeed, this multiplicity of situations makes comparison enormously difficult for demolinguistic purposes and forces the adoption of one of two possible solutions: either a detailed level-by-level comparison, which is feasible between two countries, but very difficult among more; or to dispense with the detail of the levels and use the students' ages or years of non-university schooling (normally 12 years) as a base reference. The International Standard Classification of Education (ISCED) (UNESCO, 2011) distinguishes eight educational levels, including doctorate or equivalent.

In addition, the disparities between official educational systems, with their multiple linguistic implications, increase when professional and non-regulated education are added to the equation. For demolinguistics, the collection of all these kinds of data is very laborious. It is true that Western countries tend to have abundant and reliable statistics on compulsory education but, despite the efforts of UNESCO, this is not always the case in developing countries. Universities, which in many countries enjoy a certain degree of autonomy, often don't have data on how language teaching is practiced within their walls. And, as for non-regulated and private education, the search for data is usually oriented toward ad hoc sources whose profile doesn't always prove satisfactory in terms of the quantity and quality of the data.

The treatment that the minority languages of immigrant groups receive in educational systems deserves special mention. This is because the school fulfills an essential function for many purposes: the self-esteem of the migrants, recognition of their language and culture, support for the language to maintain its use in the family, or even the possible social maintenance of the language. This kind of teaching is given different names depending on the country: home language instruction, instruction in the native language and culture, teaching in immigrant languages, teaching in minority ethnic languages, or integration courses, among others. In turn, the persons who receive this kind of instruction are usually called "foreigners" or "immigrants".

In a comparative analysis carried out by Broeder and Extra (1998) on the European Union, it was found that immigrant minority language instruction

TABLE 5.7 Coding of ISCED levels.

ISCED 0 Early childhood education
ISCED 1 Primary education
ISCED 2 Lower secondary education
ISCED 3 Upper secondary education
ISCED 4 Post-secondary non-tertiary education
ISCED 5 Short-cycle tertiary education
ISCED 6 Bachelor's degree or equivalent level
ISCED 7 Master's degree, specialization, or equivalent
ISCED 8 Doctorate or equivalent

Source: UNESCO (2011).

(IMLI) was introduced in primary education, initially (in the 1960s) addressing the possibility of a process of return, an intention that was abandoned somewhat later and substituted by the desire to compensate for the deficit of those migrants who, by remaining in the host communities, were immersed in processes of minoritization. In this sense, the programs addressing minor languages (Lmin) were conceived to cover the distance between home and school and to compensate for the deficiencies of the migrants. However, the proposals usually underestimated the ethnocultural dimension, and this caused some countries to begin to emphasize the intrinsic importance of knowledge of the minority languages of immigration from a cultural, legal, and economic perspective. The European countries that most clearly adopted this cultural policy in the 1990s were the Netherlands, Germany, and Belgium, while France and the United Kingdom barely left any public space for the languages of migrants.

According to Broeder and Extra, the policy of recognizing the importance of immigration languages through IMLI programs has the following benefits:

a. On the cultural level, IMLI contributes to maintaining and promoting plural societies.
b. On the legal level, IMLI contributes to the recognition of the rights and the development and the maintenance of the languages themselves, as valued pieces of identity.
c. On the economic level, IMLI contributes to creating a reservoir of knowledge in a society increasingly oriented toward internationalization.

However, these approaches have not served to drag most European countries toward a greater recognition of the languages of migrants in their educational systems, but rather, in general, they usually focus on compensating for lack of knowledge about the host population. From demolinguistics, however, it's important to trace the place IMLI holds in each country to analyze with better criteria the possibilities for maintenance or displacement of the minority languages.

The extreme opposite to educational policies that are inclusive of migrant languages is linguistic genocide. This phenomenon can occur through complete disregard for and abandonment of the minority language in schools and society in general, as well as through the systematic labeling of minority languages and their manifestations as dialects, slang, patois... which ultimately leads to their becoming discredited and invisible (Skutnabb-Kangas, 2012).

The Economy

A nation's economy is, without a doubt, one of the factors that contributes most to its political, social, and cultural stability, hence its influence on languages, their prestige, and, ultimately, their vitality. Language maintains an interesting relationship with the economy. On the one hand, the socioeconomic factor is handled as an explanatory variable of many of the linguistic variations and changes that take place in all the languages of the world (Labov, 2001). On the other hand, language itself is an economic object, a good that can be produced, distributed, and managed; in short, it is a commodity, to use the language of economists and sociologists.

Languages can also move an economy or part of it. In fact, there are ethnographic and anthropological studies that show that this specific relationship between language and economy is not abstract or epistemological but can refer to discourses or linguistic uses related expressly to economic transactions (Heller, 2003; Duchêne, 2009). The economic value of language can be seen in all kinds of cultures, and it affects all kinds of languages without transactions necessarily taking place in monetary terms, as shown by the existence of barter and exchange of services. The value of language as a commodity is strongly observed in the sectors of the new globalized economy, focused on international communication. Despite lamentations about the McDonaldization of the language panorama (Ritzer, 2000; Heller, 2003), quite varied aspects of languages and identities are revealed as significant.

With regard to the Spanish language, José Luis García Delgado (García Delgado, Alonso, & Jiménez, 2012) has explained its importance within the economy through what he calls in Spanish "the three Ps:" the "peso" ("weight") that the industries related to language have in the gross domestic product (GDP) of Spain (publishers, education, technologies…), that weight is 16%; the "palanca" ("leverage") the language has, given that commercial exchanges increase fourfold when countries share the same language, while investments are multiplied by seven; and the final one is "premio" ("prize") and reflects that, as a whole, the speakers of Spanish who also have fluency in other languages can obtain a salary premium of up to 30%, although in the United States that premium does not exceed 10%.

This kind of argument is common in a discipline called the economics of language which was born in the 1970s with publications by Jacob Marschak (1965), Barry Chiswick and Paul Miller (2005), François Grin (1996), and Ariel Rubinstein (2000) (Jiménez, 2006). The economics of language is defined by François Grin as a field of research focused primarily on the analysis, theoretical and empirical, of the ways in which linguistic and economic variables influence one another, usually within the framework of orthodox (or neoclassical) economics (García Delgado, Alonso, and Jiménez 2012: 66). The major issues concerning the discipline are taken from Grin's proposal (1996): language as the defining element of the economic processes of production, consumption, or distribution; language as human capital; language teaching as social investment; the economic implications of linguistic policy; the relationship between economic income and language; and works on language as an economic sector.

Economics affirms that language has an economic function within societies and that this manifests in three characteristics: first, language is a social communication skill—without a doubt, the most powerful technology of social communication; second, language is an attribute of identity and a factor in socialization; and third, language is a creative medium. All these mean that language shows two kinds of value: an exchange value, because it gives access to other resources, and a use value, given that it is an expression of a sociocultural identity (Jiménez, 2006). On the other hand, the economics of language characterizes language as an economic good, as it could not be otherwise, and that economic good has some traits that define it compared to other kinds of goods. It is:

a) A good with no production cost.
b) A good that is not used up or exhausted with use.
c) A good with a single access cost.
d) A good whose use value increases with the number of users.
e) A non-appropriable good.

In general terms, these features characterize a "club good," in this case interpreting the "club" to which it belongs as the speakers of a given language. The economic language with which these concepts are presented and explained can link such studies exclusively to the interests of the populations of developed nations, or majority and international languages, and neoliberal trends. However,

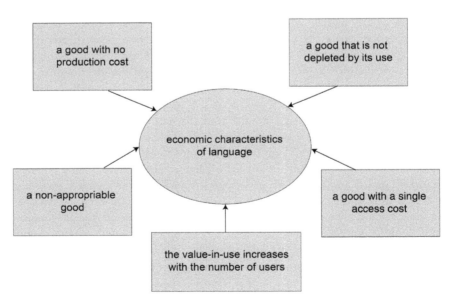

GRAPH 5.3 Characteristics of language as an economic good.
Source: Alonso (2006).

as theoretical concepts, they can be perfectly applied to minority language situations, including indigenous or native languages.

In short, a language's potential, presence, and continuity are intimately linked with the macroeconomic indices of the territories in which it is used. Among these indices, GDP, the purchasing power of the countries where a language is spoken, or their volume of exports are revealed as highly significant parameters. Thus, an analysis of world GDP (by purchasing power parity: PPP) generated by those countries where each of the six official languages of the UN has official language status reveals that English and Chinese are languages linked to the two largest economies of the world, in that order, followed by Spanish. Other calculations reveal that, in 2010, Chinese- and English-speaking communities accounted for half of the world's GDP, whereas Japanese accounted for 5.6%, Spanish for 5.2%, German for 4.9%, and French for 4.2% (Davis, 2004). However, these calculations must be taken with great reservations because of all the linguistic precautions we've been considering.

The second economic factor with a great impact on the status of languages is the purchasing power of their speakers and of the countries they inhabit, given their ability to multiply exchanges and commercial transactions. The Instituto Cervantes (2021) has calculated that the Spanish speakers of the world, not including students of Spanish as a foreign language, have a combined purchasing power of around 9% of world GDP. Within this whole, it is worth highlighting the purchasing power of the Hispanic community of the United States, whose GDP is higher than that of Spain and Mexico at current prices and twice the average for Latin America.

As far as exports and imports are concerned, these are indicators of a country's ability to influence and attract, not just from an economic point of view, but also in other areas tied to commercial activities. The annual export volume of a country enriches the previous component (the level of development) because it allows for the participation of its economy to be reflected in very different processes of internationalization. Bear in mind, for example, that 31% of the imports made from within the Spanish-speaking world come from countries in which English has official status, so the influence of anglophone countries, from this perspective, is greater than that of China (16% of imports) or the countries that speak German (7%) or French (5%). The economic weight of a language also depends, to a large degree, on the capacity of its countries and their citizens to generate activity within and beyond their borders, as well as the resources available to them. This weight is expressed through the Human Development Index (HDI).

Culture and Science

Language and culture are two sides of the same coin. For this reason, cultures can provide elements essential for the knowledge, use, prestige, and dissemination of languages. In 1952, Alfred Kroeber and Clyde Kluckhohn published a magnificent volume titled *Culture: A Critical Review of Concepts and Definitions* in which they compiled and discussed over 160 definitions of the concept of "culture" which had been published between 1871 and the middle of the last century. Among the many definitions and proposals of culture considered, those that relate culture to language(s) are of special interest. In general, the existence of some kind of link or contact between the two notions is recognized. Therefore, numerous definitions make specific mention of language, such as Tylor (1871) considering it a component of culture, Radcliffe-Brown (1949) including it as part of social heritage, or Wilson and Kolb (1949) explaining it as learned behavior. These interpretations of the relationships between language and culture apply to all the languages and cultures of the world.

For demolinguistic purposes, there are numerous cultural manifestations, understood in the broadest sense, with the ability to reflect the presence and vitality of a language, both within and outside its speech communities. The manifestations, however, are not found in all kinds of cultures, but instead are more easily recognized in societies with a market economy. These include all the so-called language industries, with special attention to the publication of printed or online works, to linguistic services, and to language technologies, which involve the development of tools and computer resources related to language and the teaching of language and the activities associated with it, such as teaching programs for foreigners or teaching materials. In this way, language itself is also presented as part of a market, as a cultural commodity, capable of being analyzed through specific parameters and indices.

Moreover, the development of culture is closely related to translation. The number of translations made from a language can be quantified as a parameter that represents the interest aroused by both the culture and the intellectual production (including the scientific-technical production) of the countries where it is spoken. According to Heilbron and Sapiro (2016), the measurement of the ebbs and flows of translation between languages reflects their level of centrality in the network of cultural exchanges and makes it possible to describe international hierarchies. Translations made from one language, in this sense, are very meaningful, as are the translations made outward into a given language. For his part, Abram de Swaan (2001) relates translation (and culture in general) to demolinguistics from a centripetal perspective: the languages with greater cultural production and dissemination attract more speakers who wish to learn them in order to consume cultural goods and even produce them.

When measuring the relative impact of translations, it is of greatest interest to consider series of years rather than isolated annual data, given that the possible cultural effect of translation is cumulative, compared to what happens with other parameters whose indexes merit annual consideration. UNESCO's *Index Translationum*, the most comprehensive source on this subject, classifies translations in nine thematic categories, specifying the source and target languages in each case: general and bibliography; philosophy and psychology; religion and theology; law, social sciences, and education; natural sciences; applied sciences; arts, games, and sports; literature; and history, geography, and biography. The problem that this database presents, aside from how up to date it is, has to do with the identification of languages and their varieties, as well as how they are named, a constant obstacle in the field of demolinguistics.

Another cultural parameter, highly regarded within francophone demolinguistics, is that of international literary awards. This factor represents the cultural recognition a language receives through the international literary prizes won by the authors who publish in that language. Thus, the awarding of the Nobel Prize for Literature means not only recognition of the winner, but also implies a renewed validation of their culture and the language they write in. The inclusion of international literary prizes among the factors of demolinguistic interest is not without objections, normally attributable to the institutions that grant them. For this reason, if this factor is considered, a sufficient number of awards (diverse in their origins and with a clear international vocation) must be used. The Calvet Barometer considers the following: the Neustadt Prize, the Man Booker Prize, the Balint Balassi Prize, the Franz Kafka Prize, the Ovid Prize, the Jerusalem Prize, the American Award in Literature, the "Golden Wreath" prize, and the Prince/Princess of Asturias Prize. The index used in this regard is the number of prizes received by authors who have written in each language, regardless of whether they write in more than one.

Published scientific production can also be considered a representative factor of the international weight of languages and their populations. To quantify this parameter, various indexes are used, such as the number of scientific journals published in a language, their international category by impact index, the number of books and articles published in each language, and the number of citations that appear in other publications.

In global terms, world scientific production is clearly located in the English language and, by country, in the United States, China, the United Kingdom, and Germany. In any case, it should be remembered that the mother tongue or native language of scientists isn't always that of the country in which they publish their work or the journal in which it is published. For demolinguistics, the quantitative management of the indexes that inform the scientific production parameter is relatively easy, given that this entire area has up-to-date and precise international metrics.

With regard to the three areas just mentioned (translations, literary prizes, and scientific production), their inadequacies as explanatory factors in the analysis of EtMLs and LoMLs should be pointed out. The reasons for this are obvious: they are languages without writing systems that, therefore, don't have formal translations or written literature, much less published scientific production. This reflection is important because only 56% of the languages of the world have a writing system

164 Demolinguistic Factors

(*Ethnologue*), while indigenous peoples make up a global community of some 359 million people distributed in more than 5,000 groups across 90 countries around the world, according to UNESCO.

Digital Communication

The so-called "digital divide" may explain why this factor is of interest for the demolinguistic analysis of some languages but not others. Languages without writing systems and peoples without any access to a large network are simply left out of the analysis of this factor. This is not to deny, however, another remarkable reality: many peoples from cultures with very precarious written manifestations or even without writing have combined some form of alphabet and internet access in order to give their ethnic minority languages a visibility that they had never previously known in their history. At the same time, other languages that have had a writing system for a long time have found a second wind on the internet, as is the case with languages like Guaraní, K'iche', Nahuatl, Quechua, Mixtec, Achi', Aymara, or Itza'. Something similar could be said of LoMLs, which have even used the internet as a stimulus for the creation of vocabularies.

Demolinguistic analysis, however, tends to draw on the international metrics related to internet penetration: the number of webpages in each language and country, or the presence of digital networks and platforms in different societies. The methodological problems that this entails are notable given that, once more, the metrics usually refer to countries, not to regions, and in the case of the internet, they can refer to internet domains whose limits are equally imprecise. The consideration of each language implies combining the data of all the countries which have their own computer domain, and this requires an exercise

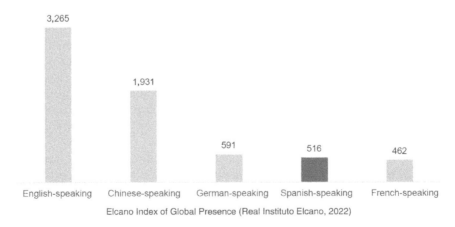

Elcano Index of Global Presence (Real Instituto Elcano, 2022)

GRAPH 5.4 Global presence of science across different linguistic fields.
Source: Instituto Cervantes (2021).

of consideration in the case of multilingual countries and paying attention to the levels of internet penetration in each country.

As far as the data is concerned, the United Nations Development Program (UNDP) reports that around 60% of the world's population has access to the internet, although most of these users live in developed countries. In less developed countries, only one in five people have access to the internet, with repercussions in the areas of education, work, and public services, given their growing dependence on access to digital technology. This confirms that lack of connectivity is an obstacle to human development. Among the most used languages online, English, Chinese and Spanish (in that order) are notable for the number of users, followed by Arabic, Portuguese, Indonesian, Malay, and French (Miniwatts, 2022). In any case, English is the most prominent language, not just because of the number of users, but also because around 60% of multilingual pages include this language, a very significant figure in terms of its global presence.

Of growing importance is also the presence of languages on digital platforms, in which the English language has a prominent presence with the prestige that this brings.

Of all the platforms considered, *YouTube*, with more than two billion active users, is the most visited website after Google. Although the most developed countries, along with their languages, are the ones that obtain the most benefits from the use of this and other platforms, the fact that some of these platforms are free has allowed access to minority groups with very diverse languages and cultures. With a view to demolinguistic analysis, presence online and on digital platforms could be a significant factor in regard to the possibilities of language development, maintenance, or shift, provided that populations with similar possibilities of internet access are used for comparison.

Something similar could be said about the activity on Wikipedia, a factor of prestige and, without question, of great cultural and informative influence. The digital encyclopedia itself provides statistics on different indexes, such as the number of articles published in each of the 325 languages (2022) included. To identify the languages, Wikipedia uses the ISO code for each of them and, in addition to the number of pages, provides interesting information on the number of edits made, and the number of administrators, users, or files.

Finally, the media currently have a close relationship with the internet, but this doesn't mean they cease to have a presence in more traditional spheres, such as radio, conventional television, or the printed press. In fact, one of the engines that is activated most strongly for the promotion and maintenance of EtMLs and LoMLs is traditional media which, in addition to conferring prestige, fulfills an essential function: keeping members of communities in contact with one another and with the corresponding authorities. In this sense, local radio stations are absolutely fundamental. However, the importance of media presence in digital formats is undeniable for all kinds of languages and peoples.

166 Demolinguistic Factors

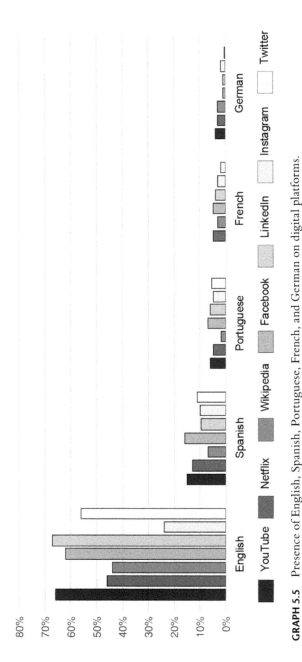

GRAPH 5.5 Presence of English, Spanish, Portuguese, French, and German on digital platforms.

Source: Instituto Cervantes (2021), based on Twinword Inc. (s.a.), Wikipedia (2021), Facebook (2021), LinkedIn (2021), OIF (2019), and GNIP (2017).

Summary

This chapter has focused on the factors usually handled by demolinguistics when preparing different kinds of analyses. These factors are naturally quantifiable and qualitative in nature and have to do with speakers (as populations), with their languages (as attributes), and with the circumstances that surround each within the different models of society around the globe.

Indeed, speakers and their languages constitute the main point of reference, the variables that must be analyzed, explained, interpreted, and projected. This is one of the main goals of demolinguistics. For this reason, it is essential to consider all the aspects that define speakers and their languages and the difficulties such definition implies. To define and identify the speakers, it is necessary to clarify theoretical and conceptual aspects that are difficult if not impossible to resolve. For this reason, demolinguistics proposes operational solutions with the ability to contribute to the advancement of the analysis. One part of these solutions involves accepting the definitions proposed directly by censuses and surveys when collecting information. Those data, in many cases focused on the mother tongue, the habitual language of use, or the language spoken at home, contribute to a basic demolinguistics for which factors such as nationality, origin, or ethnic self-ascription must also be considered.

But the analysis of speech communities supposes not just proceeding to count their members, but also studying the composition of the parts that comprise them. On some occasions, studies are carried out directly using census and survey data; on others, an ecolinguistic perspective is adopted in order to determine which factors condition the vitality and sustainability of a minority language; and in other cases, a technical elaboration is required that allows for important dimensions of the communities and their languages, such as vehicularity or entropy, to be known. Likewise, the detailed study of linguistic communities makes it necessary to distinguish different profiles of speakers, to proceed to a more detailed quantification on a microdemolinguistic level. This exercise involves differentiating native skills in a language from limited proficiency and involves treating the knowledge of languages acquired through educational systems.

As for the factors that contribute to understanding and explaining in a more complete way the dynamics of languages and communities, demolinguistics handles a wide range of possibilities, notable among which are those relating to the official status of languages and their international use, the presence of languages in educational systems, the economics of the speaker populations of each language, the cultural and scientific dimensions of languages, and the presence of languages on the internet and in social communication media. For the correct treatment of these explanatory variables, the following must be considered: firstly, not all languages are likely to be affected by all these factors, given the sociopolitical distance that exists between minority languages (of any kind) and majority languages; and secondly, available data generally allow for access only at a country level, and not at that of regions, subpopulations, or cross-border regions.

References

Alonso, José Antonio (2006): *Naturaleza económica de la lengua*. Madrid: ICEI.
Ammon, Ulrich (2010): "World Languages: Trends and Future". In N. Coupland (ed.), *The Handbook of Language and Globalization*. Oxford: Wiley, pp. 101–122.
Breton, Roland (1976): *Géographie des langues*. Paris: PUF.
Breton, Roland (2003): *Atlas des langues du monde*. Paris: Autrement.
Broeder, Peter and Guus Extra (1998): *Language, Ethnicity and Education: Case Studies on Immigrant Minority Groups and Immigrant Minority Languages*. Clevedon: Multilingual Matters.
Calvet, Alain and Louis-Jean Calvet (2022): *Baromètre Calvet des langues du monde*. Paris: Ministère de la Culture.
Chiswick, Barry and Paul Miller (2005): "Linguistic distance: a quantitative measure of the distance between English and other languages". *Journal of Multilingual and Multicultural Development*, 26: 1–11.
Council of Europe (2001): *Common European Framework of Reference for Languages: Learning, Teaching, Assessment*. Strasbourg: Council of Europe.
Crystal, David (2000): *Language Death*. Cambridge: Cambridge University Press.
Davies, Alan (2013): *Native Speakers and Native Users: Loss and Gain*. Cambridge: Cambridge University Press.
Davis, Mark (2004): *Unicode Technical Note 13: GDP by Language*. www.unicode.org/notes/tn13/ Online resource.
De Swaan, Abram (2001): *Words of the World: The Global Language System*. Cambridge: Polity.
Duchêne, Alexandre (2009): "Marketing, management and performance: multilingualism as commodity in a tourism call centre". *Language Policy*, 8: 27–50.
Duchêne, Alexandre, Philippe Humbert, and Renata Coray (2018): "How to ask questions on language? Ideological struggles in the making of a state survey". *International Journal of the Sociology of Language*, 2018: 45–72.
Eberhard, David, Gary Simons, and Charles D. Fennig (eds.) (2022): *Ethnologue: Languages of the World*, 245th ed. Dallas: SIL International. Online version: http://www.ethnologue.com.
Encyclopedia Britannica (1995): *Britannica Book of the Year 1995 (BBY)*. Charles Trumbell (ed.). London: Encyclopedia Britannica.
Escobar, Anna María (2014): "Haciendo visible lo invisible: contacto de lenguas e instrumentos de vitalidad lingüística". In L. Zajícová and R. Zámec (eds.), *Lengua y política en América Latina: Perspectivas actuales*. Olomouci: Univerzita Palackého, pp. 149–175.
European Commission (2022): *Eurydice*. https://eurydice.eacea.ec.europa.eu/ Online resource.
Extra, Guus and Durk Gorter (eds.) (2001): *The Other Languages of Europe*. Clevedon: Multilingual Matters.
Extra, Guus and Durk Gorter (2008): *Multilingual Europe. Facts and Policies*. Berlin: De Gruyter.
Extra, Guus and Kutlay Yağmur (2004): *Urban Multilingualism in Europe: Immigrant Minority Languages at Home and School*. Clevedon: Multilingual Matters.
Fasold, Ralph (1984): *The Sociolinguistics of Society*. Oxford: Blackwell.
Fishman, Joshua (1991): *Reversing Language Shift*. Clevedon: Multilingual Matters.
García Delgado, José Luis, José Antonio Alonso and Juan Carlos Jiménez (2007, 2012): *Economía del español: una introducción*. Barcelona: Ariel.

Grimes, Barbara F. (ed.) (1984): *Ethnologue: Languages of the World*. Dallas: Summer Institute of Linguistics.
Grin, François (1996): "Economic approaches to language and language planning: an introduction". *International Journal of the Sociology of Language*, 1996: 1–16.
Haugen, Einar (1938): "Language and immigration". *Norwegian-American Studies and Records*, 10: 1–43. In Haugen, Einar (1972) *The Ecology of Language*. Stanford: Stanford University Press, pp. 1–36.
Heilbron, Johan and Gisèle Sapiro (2016): "Translation: Economic and Sociological Perspectives". In V. Ginsburgh and S. Weber (eds.), *The Palgrave Handbook of Economics and Language*, London: Palgrave Macmillan, pp. 373–402.
Heller, Monica (2003): "Globalization, the new economy, and the commodification of language and identity". *Journal of Sociolinguistics*, 7: 473–492.
Instituto Cervantes (2021): *El español: una lengua viva. Anuario del Instituto Cervantes*. Madrid: Instituto Cervantes / Bala Perdida.
Jiménez, Juan Carlos (2006): *La economía de la lengua: una visión de conjunto*. Madrid: Instituto Complutense de Estudios Internacionales.
Kachru, Braj (2017): *World Englishes and Culture Wars*. Cambridge: Cambridge University Press.
Kertzer, David and Dominique Arel (eds.) (2001): *Census and Identity. The Politics of Race, Ethnicity, and Language in National Censuses*. Cambridge: Cambridge University Press.
Kroeber, Alfred and Clyde Kluckhohn (1952): *Culture: A Critical Review of Concepts and Definitions*. Cambridge: The Museum.
Krzyżanowski, Michal and Ruth Wodak (2008): "Multiple Identities, Migration and Belonging: 'Voices of Migrants'". In C.R. Caldas-Coulthard and R. Iedema (eds.), *Identity Trouble*. London: Palgrave Macmillan, pp. 95–119.
Labov, William (2001): *Principles of Linguistic Change: Social Factors*. Malden: Blackwell.
Leclerc, Jacques (2020): *L'aménagement linguistique dans le monde*. https://www.axl.cefan.ulaval.ca/ Online resource.
Lewis, M. Paul and Gary F. Simons (2010): "Assessing endangerment: expanding Fishman's GIDS". *Revue Roumaine de Linguistique*, 55:103–120. http://www.lingv.ro/resources/scmimages/RRL-02-2010- Lewis.pdf.
Lewis, M. Paul, Gary F. Simons, and Charles D. Fennig (eds.) (2014): *Ethnologue: Languages*. 17th ed. Dallas: SIL.
Loureda Lamas, Óscar, Francisco Moreno-Fernández, Héctor Álvarez Mella, and David Scheffler (2020): *Demolingüística del español en Alemania*. Madrid: Instituto Cervantes.
Maldavsky, Aliocha, Thérèse Bouysse-Cassagne, Gérald Taylor, and Gabriela Ramos (2013): "Debate sobre los significados de 'lengua general'". *Nuevo Mundo Mundos Nuevos*. Online version: http://journals.openedition.org/nuevomundo/65072.
Marqués de Tamarón (1992): "El español, ¿lengua internacional o 'lingua franca'?". *Actas del congreso de la lengua española: Sevilla, 7 al 10 octubre*. Madrid: Instituto Cervantes, pp. 189–211.
Marschak, Jacob (1965) "Economics of language". *Behavioral Science*, 10: 135–140.
Miniwatts (2022): *Internet World Stats 2022*. https://www.internetworldstats.com/stats.htm Online resource.
Moreno-Fernández, Francisco (2014): "Fundamentos de demografía lingüística a propósito de la lengua española". *Revista Internacional de Lingüística Iberoamericana*, 12: 19–38.
Moreno-Fernández, F. (2020): "La internacionalización del español y su análisis". In Instituto Cervantes (ed.), *La proyeccion internacional del español y el portugués: el potencial de la proximidad lingüística*. Madrid: Instituto Cervantes / Instituto Camoes, pp. 82–101.

Moreno-Fernández, Francisco and Héctor Álvarez Mella (2022): "Reexamining the international importance of languages". *HCIAS Working Papers on Ibero-America*, 1. https://journals.ub.uni-heidelberg.de/index.php/hciaswp/article/view/84517.

Moreno-Fernández, Francisco and Jaime Otero Roth (1998): "Demografía de la lengua española". In *El español en el mundo. Anuario del Instituto Cervantes 1998*. Madrid: Instituto Cervantes-Arco / Libros, pp. 59–86.

Moreno-Fernández, Francisco and Jaime Otero Roth (2006): *Demografía de la lengua española*. Madrid: Instituto Complutense de Estudios Internacionales.

Moreno-Fernández, Francisco and Jaime Otero Roth (2009): *Atlas de la lengua española en el mundo*. 3rd ed. Barcelona: Ariel.

Muller, Siegfried H. (1964): *The World's Living Languages*. New York: Frederik Ungar.

Nationalencyklopedin. (2010): S.v. Språk, "Tabell: världens 100 största språk 2010". http://www.ne.se/språk/världens-100-största-språk-2010 Online resource.

Peirce, Charles S. (1878): "How to make our ideas clear". *Popular Science Monthly*, 12, 286–302.

Radcliffe-Brown, Alfred (1949): "White's view of a science of culture". *American Anthropologist*, 51: 503–512.

Real Instituto Elcano (2022): *Informe de presencia global 2022*. https://www.globalpresence.realinstitutoelcano.org/es/ Online resource.

Ritzer, George (2000): *The McDonaldization of Society*. Los Angeles: Sage.

Ros, María, Carmen Huici, and Ignacio Cano (1994): "Ethnolinguistic vitality and social identity: their impact on ingroup bias and social attribution". *International Journal of Sociology of Language*, 1994: 145–166.

Rubinstein, Ariel (2000): *Economics and Language*. Cambridge: Cambridge University Press.

Salvador, Gregorio (1992): *Política lingüística y sentido común*. Madrid: Istmo.

Salvat (1974): *Enciclopedia Salvat*. Barcelona: Salvat.

Skutnabb-Kangas, Tove (1981): *Tvåspråkighet*. Lund: LiberLäromedel.

Skutnabb-Kangas, Tove (2000): *Linguistic Genocide in Education--or Worldwide Diversity and Human Rights?*. London: Routledge.

Skutnabb-Kangas, Tove (2012): "Indigenousness, human rights, ethnicity, language, and power". *International Journal of the Sociology of Language*, 2012: 87–104.

Tylor, Edward B. (1871): *Researches into the Early History and Development of Mankind*. London: John Murray.

UNESCO (2011): *International Standard Classification of Education ISCED 2011*. Montréal: UNESCO.

Viladot, M. Àngels (1995): "Les dades demogràfiques en el concepte de vitalitat lingüística". In *Actes del Simposi de Demolingüística. III Trobada de Sociolingüistes Catalans*. Barcelona: Generalitat de Catalunya, pp. 20–33.

Whalen, Douglas and Gary F. Simons (2012): "Endangered language families". *Language*, 88: 155–173.

Wilson, Logan and William L. Kolb (1949): *Sociological Analysis: An Introductory Text and Case Book*. New York: Harcourt, Brace.

Zimmermann, Klaus (1999): *Política del lenguaje y planificación para los pueblos amerindios: ensayos de ecología lingüística*. Madrid: Iberoamericana.

6
DEMOLINGUISTIC ANALYSES

Objectives and Levels of Demolinguistic Analysis

Demographic analysis of languages, as deduced from the reference works of classical demography (Henry, 1976; Pressat, 1981; Vallin, 1991), must fulfill the following main objectives:

- The *description* of the language situation of the population of a given territory or human group.
- The search for the *causes* that have led to a language situation in a given territory or human group.
- The *projection* and anticipation of a linguistic situation in a given territory or human group.

Logically, not all analyses aim to cover all of the discipline's potential objectives (descriptive, causal, predictive), which results in a diversity of research possibilities. And precisely because there is a plurality of objects of study and research objectives, it is necessary to distinguish, as pointed out in chapter 1, two kinds of approaches to demolinguistics, although the borders between them may be blurred. On the one hand, one can speak of "microdemolinguistics," interested in the demolinguistic reality of small-sized or minority communities, as well as in very specific or localized social realities. This approach would include analyzing the linguistic vitality and knowledge or use of indigenous, minority, or native languages within their respective communities. On the other hand, one can speak of "macrodemolinguistics" in relation to those investigations interested in broad or majority language communities, as well as large-scale or de-localized social realities. This would include a demolinguistics of international languages or the

DOI: 10.4324/9781003327349-7

study of the linguistic consequences of intercontinental migration processes, for example (Moreno-Fernández, 2020).

In addition to this great division, other levels of approach can be identified depending on the specificity of the object of demolinguistic study or on the nature of its content. In this way, within microdemolinguistics, a "nanodemolinguistics" could be identified if the interest were centered on small-scale communities, such as a specific community among the indigenous settlements of Brazil, or within a well-defined entity, such as a public school in a large city. When the object of study has special significance, for whatever reason, it can be given visibility through the mention of categories such as "ethnodemolinguistics" if the object is of an ethnic nature, or "sociodemolinguistics" if the object is a group or social sector.

It can be seen, then, that the objects of demolinguistic study are very diverse, of different complexities and dimensions, and that the objectives of investigation are likewise of varying scope which requires the aid of different knowledge and disciplines. With the goal of illustrating in a broader way the possible interests of demolinguistics, as well as its most important methodological strategies, some pieces of research, from different places, moments, and approaches, are presented. Later, there will be space to explain in greater detail some of the most important applications with which demolinguistic research has developed.

To go from micro to macrodemolinguistics, it is worth mentioning the research carried out by Cristián Lagos during 2003 with the goal of investigating the situation of the Mapudungun language in Santiago de Chile from a sociolinguistic and ethnolinguistic perspective, considering its functions with regard to the official language of Chile: Spanish or Castilian. Lagos builds his study based on the data of the "Housing and Population Census" carried out in Chile in 2002 and combines it with quantitative and qualitative information gathered through a questionnaire applied to a sample of informants. The analysis carried out confirmed a tendency toward integration which implied a loss of language differences in favor of Spanish. The data on the vitality of Mapudungun among subjects of Mapuche origin revealed a gradual forgetting of that language as an effective communication instrument; that is, a reduction of its vitality was observed (Lagos, 2006: 123):

> The discourse and facts show that such functions can be perfectly fulfilled using the Spanish language, but not the other way around, that is to say, that Mapudungun cannot occupy the areas that the language of the dominating (or dominant) group exclusively possess (for example, administration, mass media, education, etc.).
>
> *Lagos, 2006*

Likewise, Lagos verified that the Mapudungun language was not learned systematically, but in a fragmentary way, with isolated words or conversational

Demolinguistic Analyses **173**

routines (greetings, the more common kinship terms, utensils, food, etc.), which allows for linguistic signs of identity to be kept alive but not the language for other functions. This means that, as more young people move to the capital of Chile, the vitality of the Mapudungun language decreases. The data extracted from the questionnaire used in the investigation show that the majority of those who declare that they don't know the Mapudungun language or only know it a little were born in Santiago de Chile or emigrated to the city before they were 10 years old.

These data correspond to those collected regarding the linguistic attitudes of Mapuche residents in the city which indicate that Mapudungun is valued as a mark of group identity, but that this fact is not accompanied by either sufficient knowledge of the language or its everyday use. As such, from a demolinguistic perspective, the usefulness of both of census data and questionnaires is clear.

At a microdemolinguistic level but of broader scope is the study that John De Vries published in 1994 on the official linguistic communities of Canada from which speakers of the minority indigenous languages were left out. De Vries analyzed the demolinguistic trends observed in the English- and French-speaking communities between 1971 and 1991, a time of special significance in the history of Canadian language policy. The data came from various population censuses, and the analyses focused especially on questions related to language.

De Vries observed an increase in the proportion of speakers of English as their mother tongue, which meant that the francophone population went from 27% to

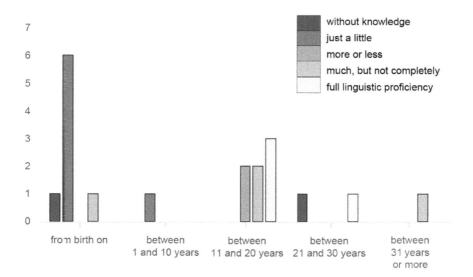

GRAPH 6 1 Relationship between age of migration to Santiago [de Chile] and fluency in Mapudungun.
Source: Lagos (2006: 107).

24% during that period. Various factors influenced the increase in the anglophone population, such as international migration and the low fertility rate in Canadian society. Between 1971 and 1991, there was also increasing territorial segregation among the official linguistic communities of Canada. Likewise, a constant increase in the proportion of the population that spoke both languages was detected: from 12% in 1951 to 16% in 1991. This increase occurred mainly in the contact areas: the Outaouais region, the metropolitan Montréal area, northeastern New Brunswick, and eastern and northeastern Ontario.

From a methodological perspective, John De Vries' study is a good example of how to manage the evolution of a linguistic situation over a period of time. Based on data from successive censuses, the analysis was interested in the processes that affected the size and composition of linguistic communities: fertility, mortality, migrations, and the displacement of languages. The analysis considered two subpopulations: English speakers and French speakers. At the same time, De Vries' analysis paid attention to the geographic variable by handling data from different Canadian provinces along with their main regions.

The macrodemolinguistic level could be exemplified by works that analyze the influence of the world's languages. These works usually concern languages of greater demographic, geographic, and sociopolitical dimensions and are interested in the situation of one or more languages in inter- or transnational contexts. They use information from censuses in order to establish the number of speakers of a language as an L1 or L2. However, this is not the only factor considered; indeed, other factors of an economic, political, social, or even technological nature are often considered and combined. This combination allows for languages to be ordered in different ways: generally, into constellations of languages in orbital arrangement or in the form of rankings. Let us look at an example.

Kai L. Chan (2016) proposed a Power Language Index from the business world's perspective. This index is built from 20 parameters grouped into five large categories: geography, which represents the ability to travel; economy, which indicates the ability to trade; communication, which indicates the ability to engage in dialogue; knowledge and means, which indicate the ability to consume them; and diplomacy, which indicates the ability to establish international relations. The parameters that are considered are the countries where the languages are spoken, their geographic size, the reception of tourists (geography), the GDP and GDP per capita, exports, foreign exchange markets, special drawing rights (economy), the number of native speakers, the number of L2 speakers, the sizes of families, outflows of tourists (communication), internet content, film production, university levels, academic magazines (knowledge), and use by the International Monetary Fund, the United Nations, the World Bank, and supernational organizations (diplomacy). The result of these calculations is presented in two ways for each language: a general ranking and a ranking in each of the five categories.

Therefore, there is great diversity among demolinguistic objectives which can respond to very different interests, as will be explained when we cover the discipline's main applications. However, it is possible to offer some basic research questions that, in one way or another, usually make up the objectives of this kind of study. Using John De Vries' (1994) proposal as a reference, the most general questions from a demolinguistic perspective could be the following:

i. How is belonging to a given linguistic group defined?
ii. How many individuals make up a linguistic group?
iii. What are the means of entrance and exit of a linguistic group?
iv. What are the relative and absolute contributions of these processes to changes in the size and composition of a linguistic group?

Here, the concept of "linguistic group" includes any set of individuals who know and use one or more languages or varieties. The size of the group can encompass the entire population of a given community or remain limited to a subpopulation (more or less extended from a collective). With their apparent simplicity, these questions hide the need to conceptually resolve some of the underlying linguistic questions already discussed: the concept of a speaker, the identification of speakers, the process of acquisition or learning of a language, and the social dynamics that favor the transmission, maintenance, or substitution of a language.

In accordance with Bruno Latour and Steve Woolgar (1979), all scientific reality is, to a certain degree, constructed, and as such the analyses themselves support their own importance if they are packaged with the acceptable covering of principles and social acceptance (Feyerabend, 1975). This should now, however, undermine the search for objectivity and the adequate application of a methodology. Even in sociolinguistics, it may happen that the research itself distorts the object of study, as shown by the "observer's paradox" (Labov, 1972), along the lines of the "uncertainty principle" (1927) of Werner Heisenberg (1989), but this should not prevent the analysis and interpretation of demolinguistic facts from reaching the clearest explanation through the most appropriate procedures.

As can be deduced from what has been said so far, demolinguistic analysis faces numerous theoretical and practical impediments. Let us take as an example the concept of "creole:" are creoles part of a common monogenetic trunk of Portuguese origin, are they part of the mosaic of their respective acrolects, or is each a branch broken off from the others (Mufwene, 2005; McWhorter, 2018)? The answers to these tricky questions may lead to the conclusion that the demolinguistic analysis of a creole can be done either independently or by relating the creole to other varieties of the same language.

On other occasions, official doctrines are what define the possibilities of carrying out a demolinguistic analysis. Thus, the General Directorate of Statistics of El Salvador ignores the existence of indigenous communities when there are sectoral reports that identify human groups in which Nahuatl is spoken (Chávez, 2008). Likewise, the official recognition of a variety as a language usually favors its demolinguistic treatment and consequently its political valuation; for this reason, the director of the National Institute of Indigenous Languages of Mexico advocated in 2013 to give the treatment of "languages" to all the linguistic modalities of the country (*El siglo de Torreón,* 2013). In Belize, the consideration of Spanish under the label of "lingua franca" (more than 65% of Belizeans know Spanish) avoids the stumbling block of categorizing a historical language of the territory as official. Finally, the identification or exclusion of ethnicities and languages can be a factor that is handled politically, depending on the interest that exists for a greater presence of these languages and their communities in public education systems.

Given those realities, demolinguistic analysis—in any of its manifestations (descriptive, causal, predictive)—has an important educational, political, social, and cultural impact, as we'll have occasion to explain when discussing its applications. For this reason, Donald Rowland (2003) highlighted the importance of safeguarding the analyses by paying attention to some cardinal qualities:

Relevance: the problems and hypotheses that are addressed; the audience of the study.
Reliability: the quality of the sources and reliability of the calculations.
Conceptual framework: the adequacy of the theoretical framework in demography and the disciplines involved.
Comparisons: the contrast with other populations or periods.

From these bases, our main interest is to know how to approach demolinguistic analysis, even with the aforementioned inconveniences. This means paying attention to the composition, structure, and dynamics of a population delimited by the knowledge and use of one language or linguistic variety (or more), as well as quantifying their components synchronously or diachronically. This will allow us to address both descriptive and projective objectives.

Qualitative and Quantitative Analysis

In demography, the analysis of languages can be organized according to different research strategies. As we have seen, there is the possibility of approaching them with a descriptive intention, but within this there is the option of addressing them longitudinally (analysis of a population over a given period of time) or transversally (analysis at a precise moment). Likewise, the demolinguistic description, based on data from a certain moment, can lead to retrospective or prospective analyses. In the case of retrospective analysis (with data of past origin), this can coincide with causal analyses: that is to say, past data is analyzed to explain the cause of the current events. In the case of prospective analyses, data from the present and the past are projected into the future to offer predictions.

TABLE 6.1 Basic typology of demolinguistic analysis.

Demolinguistic analysis	| Retrospective–Causal | Descriptive -------------------- | | Prospective–Predictive	| *Longitudinal* | *Transversal*

All these analytical possibilities are adapted to the level of approximation to be applied in each case, from the macro to the micro according to different research goals. But, in the same way, analyses can be approached from two major research perspectives: quantitative methodology and qualitative methodology.

The basic distinction between qualitative and quantitative methods operates across many other fields of research. Quantitative methodology proceeds on quantifiable data, collected expressly (number of speakers, number of emigrants, number of births or deaths...), applying statistical techniques that allow research conclusions to be obtained: analysis of regression, analysis of main components, or any other type of mathematical proof (Johnson, 2008; Macaulay, 2009). For its part, qualitative methodology brings together materials that are difficult to quantify but which are relevant for the quality and singularity of the information they provide, such as opinions about a sociolinguistic situation, life stories, or the perception of the use of languages in different communities (Johnstone, 2000).

These two methodological lines have sometimes been presented as antagonists, symbolized by the ethnographic (qualitative) and the sociodemographic (quantitative) paradigms. Monica Barni and Guus Extra (2008) explain that the ethnographic paradigm is inductive, proceeds through observations and interviews, and handles case studies or selected informants. The demographic paradigm, on the other hand, is deductive, because it handles data gathered through pre-designed questionnaires that are applied on a large scale, which assumes the existence of a previous model.

According to Barni and Extra, qualitative and quantitative methodologies or perspectives require in each case a specific type of data which is treated and interpreted in different ways. For Phil Scholfield (1994), the collection of research data can be approached in three fundamental ways: a) through "direct observation," which is a natural and non-reactive method; b) through "questionnaires," which can be closed or open; c) through "interviews." These constitute a reactive method which seeks to obtain materials and information through an interaction that tries to approximate a natural communication process. The materials obtained through interviews are gathered and organized in large collections which are often made up of transcripts of the materials obtained verbally. Naturally, such transcriptions imply the intervention of a new speaker-agent (the transcriber) who, of course, also contributes personalized attitudes, perceptions, and representations which must be evaluated in a suitable way.

TABLE 6.2 Paradigms in ethnographic and demographic research.

Research paradigm	Ethnographic research	Demo / geolinguistic research
Research methods	• Inductive / Heuristic • Participating in observation • "Qualitative"	• Deductive • Distance between researcher and informants • "Quantitative"
Usual data	• Observed data in multiple contexts • Open-ended and in-depth interviews	• Reported data in single contexts • Selective set of questions in pre-designed questionnaires
Informants	• (Multiple) case studies • Single / few informants	• Large-scale studies • Many informants

Source: Barni & Extra (2008: 5).

Logically, all the data collection techniques that have just been listed above are applicable to demolinguistics. As has been explained (*cf.* chapter 4), surveys are one of the fundamental sources, and questionnaires are the basis of a good many censuses and registries. All of these, likewise, are useful for quantitative analysis, but this doesn't prevent direct observation and interviews from providing data suitable for qualitative analysis. In fact, qualitative methodology brings important possibilities to demolinguistic study which also fully exploits the possibilities of coordinating and interweaving qualitative and quantitative analyses (Mayntz, Holm, & Hübner, 2005). It can be said that there are complementary approaches; in 1998, Isadore Newman and Carolyn Benz constructed an interactive continuum of qualitative and quantitative processes that is perfectly applicable to the research at hand. In one quantitative phase, it is possible to start from a theoretical model, duly documented in the bibliography, from which hypotheses can be constructed that must be tested and verified through analysis that leads us to conclusions which, now in a qualitative phase of analysis, once more offer the possibility of constructing hypotheses that serve as the basis for a theoretical model. A good example of the circularity and complementarity of the qualitative and quantitative approaches can be found in the studies of sociolinguistic attitudes which combine data gathered through questionnaires (closed and open) with information from personal interviews or discussion and conversation groups.

In addition to the general research strategy, demolinguistic analysis in any of its manifestations handles various fundamental concepts that must especially be considered, whether the applied methodology is qualitative or quantitative. A first basic concept is that of "correlation." A correlation is the relationship between two variables, factors, or parameters (for example, language and race, birth rate, or migration). The correlation can be established positively, when there are aligned increases of the two correlated factors, or negatively, when the increase of one

Demolinguistic Analyses 179

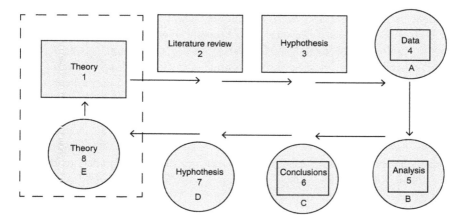

GRAPH 6.2 Interactive continuum of qualitative-quantitative philosophy. Squares: quantitative. Circles: qualitative. The 1-E overlap closes the cycle and makes qualitative and quantitative coincide.
Source: Newman & Benz (1998: 21).

Positive correlation	Negative correlation	No correlation

GRAPH 6.3 Schematic representation of positive (A), negative (B), and "no correlation" (C) correlations.

factor is aligned with the decrease or reduction of the other. Similarly, a "no correlation" or "correlation zero" is possible, when the factors are not related at all.

Correlations are a primary means of establishing causal relationships between two phenomena or processes (cause and effect), although the fact that two factors are correlated doesn't necessarily mean that one is the cause of the other, because there may be a cause external to both of them. Nonetheless, a causal relationship between two factors requires the existence of a correlation. It is important to insist that the analysis of the correlation and of the causality can be practiced both from a qualitative and a quantitative perspective. Let's give some examples. A demolinguistic study can show the correlation between the increase in the number of speakers of Basque in the Basque Country (Spain) and the number of students in that same autonomous community who follow the educational model that offers all subjects in Basque, with Spanish language as just one subject of study. Obviously, there could be a causality in this correlation, but at the same time, other social factors exist (media, volume of institutional information...) that can also be the cause of the increase in the number of Basque speakers or that could be the cause of their reduction in favor of Spanish (participation in social media, rejection of the language being imposed...). Causal analyses, therefore, must address a variety of factors of both a qualitative and quantitative nature.

On the other hand, on the quantitative level, there is a conceptual and terminological distinction that should be clearly defined. This has to do with the distinction between "index," "indicator," and "parameter"—a distinction of general use in scientific research methodology. These terms have already been used in the course of this book, but it is appropriate at this point to differentiate these concepts clearly. To move from the most general to the most specific, "parameter" is defined as the factor that is considered necessary to analyze or evaluate a fact or process. Taking as an example the analysis of linguistic vitality, UNESCO established the following as parameters (or factors) to explain its dynamic: speakers, uses, attitudes, and institutional support (Brenzinger *et al.,* 2003). These parameters must be specified, however, in "indicators" that allow for the analysis to proceed: "number of speakers" or "proportion of speakers" with respect to a total. Indicators are values calculated from primary data and can be ordered in specific scales. These scales, in turn, can be prepared with absolute figures or can be subject to a standardization. Thus, UNESCO attributes numeric values from 0 to 5 to each of the indicators it uses. From here, one can build a vitality index. These indicators are:

1. Intergenerational transmission.
2. Numerical representation.
3. Proportion of speakers in the region.
4. Public and private domains.
5. Presence of and in the media.
6. Intercultural bilingual education literacy programs and materials.
7. Government language policies.
8. Linguistic attitudes.
9. Amount of documentation on the language.

Some of these indicators refer specifically to demolinguistic questions: number of speakers, proportion of speakers in the reference community, intergenerational transmission of the languages. In this way, the greater or lesser number of speakers of a community would be expressed, not in absolute figures, but according to a five-point scale. It is true that these factors are not the only ones capable of influencing vitality, but they cannot be overlooked in any way. In fact, no factor on its own is enough to evaluate the situation of a language in its context. Lastly, the indexes can be constructed through a combination of indicators that allow a more complex concept to be quantified: for example, "human development = health + education + income" or "linguistic vitality = [indicators] 1 + 2 + 3 + 4 + 5+ 6 + 7 + 8 + 9."

Furthermore, it would be possible to bring to the field of demolinguistics a distinction that is common in sociolinguistics—that between "indicators" and "markers," under the caveat that these "indicators" are not the same ones handled in statistical analysis, although if they are quantified, they could come to be used as such. Sociolinguistics talks of "markers" to refer to features which speakers are fully aware of which let them vary their use according to contexts and interlocutors, whereas "indicators" also function in a variable way, but on an unconscious level for speakers. Regarding the use, preference, or choice of languages within a community, there can be data that function as markers (that is to say, as conscious factors) and data that function as indicators (that is to say, as unconscious factors). For example, the choice of one television channel or platform or another, for the language used in its programming, is a conscious act that favors the maintenance of a language, and as such it could be interpreted as a marker. On the other hand, attendance at religious acts of one's own community need not be a conscious act oriented toward the maintenance of a language, by which it could be interpreted as an "indicator." In this sense, the analyses of linguistic attitudes are also of great help to know when it is a case of one or the other.

The Statistical Elements of Demography

Demography builds its methodological edifice upon a solid quantitative foundation. The description of a population's components and dynamics cannot dispense with quantification, nor can its projections, or comparisons with other populations. For this reason, it is essential to present the statistics with which demography describes its fundamental concepts and obtains the quantifications. Given that our interest is demolinguistic, the criteria and concepts that usually have greater weight in this kind of analysis will be considered. At the same time, given that those interested in demolinguistics are not often expert demographers, the statistical measures and formulas will be presented in a clear and simple way.

Demography works with measures or "statistics" on the compositions, distribution, and changes of populations. The quantification of vital events and other elements can be made through absolute (n) and relative (%) values or through "demographic indicators" which indicate the average variation of a specific demographic event in a given period, generally over one year. These measures are, to a large degree, in the form of "rates," arrived at through the application of formulas to data from quantified or quantifiable sources, the results of which must be interpreted as aggregate and not individual measures.

The rates indicate the relative frequency with which certain events occur in the average of a population during the time in which such events are recorded.

Thus, the rates are obtained by dividing the number of factors or events that took place during a period of time (a flow of events) by the average population that existed during that same period; for example, the mortality rate is the quotient that results from dividing the number of deaths during a period by the average population in that same period. The concept of "rates" should not be confused with that of "probability," which results from dividing the events that occurred in a population during a period by the population at the start of that same period. Nor should rates be confused with "indicators," which are more generic and can include different calculations, including rates (Pérez Díaz, 2010).

Rates can be "crude rates" when they are calculated for the whole of a population or as the average of a total (the entire population appears in the denominator) or "specific rates" when a specific segment of a population appears in the denominator; for example, those under 18 years of age. For their part, the "net rates" or "balances" indicate the difference between two rates; for example, the difference between the total number of immigrants and the total number of emigrants in a population. Regarding the time periods considered, beyond specific years, demography recommends separating the indicators of "cohort" and "period." A period refers not to a cohort, but to several, and makes it possible to consider the births and deaths in different age groups, constructing a hypothetical or synthetic cohort (Preston, Heuveline, & Guillot, 2000).

Basic Demographic Indicators

Let us highlight three of the most used demographic indicators:

Birth rate: the frequency of births in a population; the total annual number of births in a population per 1,000 inhabitants.
Mortality rate: relative frequency of deaths in a population; the total annual deaths in a population per 1,000 inhabitants.
Migratory balance: the annual difference between the number of immigrations from abroad and the number of emigrations abroad per 1,000 inhabitants.

In addition to these indicators, demography (and with it, demolinguistics) also works with "ratios," which simply quantify the relationship between two magnitudes in the form of proportions. Among the fundamental ratios is the sex ratio. The sex or sex / gender ratio simply expresses the proportion of men and women within a population:

$$\text{Sex ratio} = \frac{\text{Men}}{\text{Women}} \times 100$$

This ratio can also be calculated specifically for subpopulations or groups of members of a population, such as the number of male births per 100 female births. In any case, the ratios or proportions are calculated to find out the relationship between any two groups within a population, including groups that speak different languages.

These indicators are common in demographic analyses with repercussions concerning the knowledge and use of languages. These demographic indicators are calculated based on data recorded in "vital records," "migratory records," and other registries linked to demography, especially those involved in linguistic and sociocultural issues. From the primary data, statistics are prepared that allow not just real situations to be described but also "population projections" to be made; that is to say, estimates about the future of the structure and evolution of the demographic factors within a population.

Along with these fundamental rates, ratios, and balances, there are other demographic indicators that directly affect linguistic communities: life expectancy, fertility rates, and demographic aging. Let's take a closer look at these.

Life expectancy at birth. This is the average number of years that a person is expected to live based on a population's mortality levels. It is a decisive indicator for calculating the Human Development Index (HDI) of a country, which is related to the sex / gender breakdown, education, economy, and health of a population and also has effects on the population's languages. Life expectancy is calculated from the mortality table of a real generation (longitudinal analysis) or from data from a given moment (transversal analysis). Thus, one begins with the number of years lived by all the members of a population starting from a given age (usually zero) and divides that figure by the number of members of the population who survive to a specific age. This calculates for each specific age how many years of life can be expected from that age onwards. It is important to forewarn that the calculation is made based on mortality tables and not on the population tables by age, given that life expectancy is independent of a population's average age.

Fertility rate. As has already been explained, fertility is the ability to reproduce. As a demographic indicator, it refers to the fruitful life of an "ideal" generation of women; that is, without assessing the possible mortality that might affect them individually. Fertility is calculated by adding together all the children that 1,000 women of each age would have (so many per thousand) and from this calculating the number of children per woman. Fertility is also related to other indicators, such as:

Birth rate: the average number of children of each woman in a generation or cohort.

Replacement level fertility: the total fertility rate at which a population exactly replaces itself from one generation to the next, without migration.

Fertility is often considered in relation to "birth rate" and willingness to have children, but the total number of births also has to do with other factors, such as the proportion of people of childbearing age at a given moment. Hence the convenience of handling the concept of fertility. For demolinguistic purposes, it is interesting to use both the birth and fertility data without confusing the concepts. In the analysis of measures such as life expectancy (for a given period) or the overall fertility rate, demography also advises using periods of time (synthetic cohorts), and not specific cohorts, as a reference.

Demographic aging. Social aging is a process by which an elderly population survives more years within a population. This concept refers to the average age of people in a population, especially those over 65 years of age; this means that a reduction in the proportion of the population who are young or children translates into an increase in the proportion of the elderly or those of advanced years. The aging of a population is usually taken to correspond with a period of social, as well as demographic, decline, for its possible repercussions for health or pension systems. Such repercussions can also reach the processes of language maintenance or shift, given that generations can be identified by different linguistic repertoires and practices. The matter, however, deserves to be treated in a way that distinguishes the cultural and ideological factors that make up each society. To a certain degree, old age is an ideological construct, relativized by the traditions and conditions of each society. Even from a linguistic perspective, the elderly population may have a social projection associated with prestige in some cases and loss of prestige in others (Moreno-Fernández, 2009). In the field of languages, it is possible to find cases in which the older generations can represent the final stages of maintenance of some linguistic repertoires within a community (the case of dying languages), or they can act in a decisive way to prevent a rapid and complete displacement of a minority variety to a majority one, as happens in the United States with Spanish, which finds "abuelitas" (little old grandmothers) to be a decisive factor for its maintenance among young second- and third-generation immigrants (Parra, 2021).

Subjective Categories

Beyond demographic statistics, the management of demolinguistic indicators and the calculation of the corresponding indexes can come up against specific methodological difficulties due to the very nature of languages and their speakers as members of linguistic communities. Among these difficulties are, as already mentioned, those that affect nationality, the residence of the speakers, and their self-ascription.

The various nationalities of the components within a population are one of the features that can be used to identify the speakers of a language when there is no direct information about it. This supposes making mother tongue or first language (L1) equivalent to nationality, along with all the problems (and falsehoods) that this entails. Obviously, having a nationality is not the same as speaking a language, although they are variables that frequently establish a correlation that must be verified. The problem is that registry data often doesn't allow for such a correlation to be established. For example, there are people who hold dual nationality, which introduces an element of doubt or complete ignorance, and there may be situations in which nationality doesn't reflect a population's linguistic condition; for example, in Italy, nationality is not automatically granted to the children of immigrants, but rather they retain that of their parents (*jus sanguinis*) although the reality is that these young people may perfectly well have Italian as their first language. This explains the need to verify in each case to what extent nationality and language correspond.

On the other hand, the fact that a population is located within a given country or region doesn't imply that all its members speak the same languages on a regular basis. In the 1970s, Susan Gal (1978) described the situation of Oberwart, an Austrian community segregated from Hungary after World War II. This situation resulted in the men and the elderly population being monolingual in Hungarian and the younger women displacing their Hungarian in favor of German. The women's linguistic choice was explained in the context of their social position, strategic life choices, and the symbolic value of each language. In this case, age and sex were conditioning factors of language preferences. In terms of languages, therefore, homogeneity of their knowledge and use is an assumption that must be subjected to verification or evidence.

Other categories that pose methodological difficulties are "race" and "ethnicity," as has already been mentioned (*cf.* chapter 3). It is common for populations that can be included in one category or another of this type to be identified by "self-ascription" and not by objective traits described in a register. Thus, in the 1990 United States census, the people registering were asked to identify themselves using the following racial categories: white, black, American Indian, Eskimo or Aleut, and Asian and Pacific Islander. This last category offered nine alternatives: Chinese, Filipino, Hawaiian, Korean, Vietnamese, Japanese, Asian Indian, Samoan, Guamanian, plus an "other" category with space to answer freely. In addition to this question, a second asked respondents to indicate possible Spanish or Hispanic origin, with the possible answers "Yes" or "No," followed by the alternatives "Mexican," "Mexican American" or "Chicano," "Puerto Rican," "Cuban," and "other Hispanic origin," with space to write in other options.

In cases like these, the calculated size of the population of a given origin can depend on the information offered by that same population. This being the case, demographic calculation depends on the way in which the very people who are registered by the census interpret their reality. In this sense, it was shown in the 1980 and 1990 United States censuses that nearly 90% of Hispanics identified as white, but no small number identified with the racial category of "Other," simply because they were uncertain as to how to answer that question. Another widely used category to refer to non-Hispanic whites is "Anglo;" however, such a category cannot be identified through the direct information of the census but requires a cross-check of population and ethnoracial data. Therefore, the qualitative analysis of populations must be adequate for the quantifications to have sufficient support.

Population Dynamics

Populations have a dynamism that translates into "population changes." In general terms, a population change is calculated through an equation that includes the number of births, deaths, and migrations at the start and end of a given interval of time. In this way, a (final) population is obtained by adding the number of births and the number of immigrations to the initial population, and then subtracting the number of deaths and emigrations. As already anticipated, when the final population is larger than the initial population, there is "demographic growth;" the difference between the number of people who are born and those who die indicates the "natural growth" of a population. Therefore, processes of change concern the fertility, mortality, and migrations of populations. This leads us to a first fundamental concept for understanding demographic change: the "growth rate:"

Growth rate: the average annual increase of a population; the annual increase in the number of individuals of a population for every 1,000 inhabitants.

There are various ways to analyze and interpret population growth, but in general, growth is the rate at which a population increases or decreases during a year, due to natural events and net migration (that is, the total immigrant population less the total emigrant population). Thus, the growth rate considers basic movements of the population: births, deaths, and migration. In its simplest terms, the growth rate is calculated by adding the rate of natural increase to net migration. This means finding a balance between the "gross" rates of birth, mortality, immigration, and emigration.

Growth rate = Rate of natural increase + Net migration rate

$$P^{t+n} = P^t + (B^{t,t+n} - D^{t,t+n} + I^{t,t+n} - E^{t,t+n})$$

(P = population; t = initial moment; t+n = final moment; B = births; D = deaths; I = immigrations; E = emigrations)

Likewise, the growth rate can be calculated in relation to the average population through a formula in which the numerator contains the annual number of events (births in a year, minus deaths in a year, plus the net migration for the year) and whose denominator is the population during the observed period.

$$R_{t,t+n} = \frac{\left(P^{t,t+n} - P^t\right)/2}{\left(P^t + P^{t+n}\right)/2}$$

From these calculations, one might be tempted to equate population growth with the growth of the number of speakers of a language. And indeed, this is the case in the simplest situations. However, the reality is that this shortcut cannot always be made, given that other factors worthy of investigation intervene in the growth or reduction in the number of speakers of a language (in its maintenance or shift), such as the sociolinguistic profile of the speakers and the social conditions of the acquisition and use of the languages.

In the case of the immigrant population in Catalonia, it could be thought that its growth should be directly detrimental to the use of Catalan, given the volume of immigration from within Spain and from other places. However, the sociologist Anna Cabré (1999) developed a theory about the "Catalan system of reproduction" according to which low fertility and high immigration are two factors which are not consecutive but are linked from the outset and may be related to the patrimonial transmission system: the ease of incorporating the migrant population, first from the Catalan countryside, then from outside Catalonia, had the effect of reducing fertility. This system, characterized by insufficient fertility for economic growth, did allow for patrimonial transmission, including, one assumes, linguistic heritage. Faced with this formulation, it could be said that, in Catalonia, as a result of migration, two large population pockets of Spanish speakers gained access to Catalan through the creation of an educational system based on immersion rather than by a system of heritage transmission. In any event, this is not the moment to debate two theories about the maintenance of Catalan, but to warn of the importance of evaluating different factors, alongside pure demography, to understand the dynamics of languages within a society.

Finally, Donald Rowland (2003) proposed a series of crucial considerations for the adequate interpretation of demographic changes. These considerations refer to essential concepts, such as:

Immediate causes: the existence of a sufficient basis of data to address the causes of population changes.
Underlying causes: the involvement of hidden or correlated factors or variables.
Consequences: analysis of the effects of the changes on the population and related aspects of interest.
Implications: the possible repercussions of the population changes for different aspects of social life: education, health, wellbeing/welfare, politics, culture…
Prospective developments: the evolution over time of the population changes and their institutional or organizational implications.

Comparing Populations

One of the most interesting analytic dimensions of demolinguistics is that it allows for comparisons to be made between populations that speak one or more languages, as well as observing their evolution within a single society. To make comparative approaches of a demolinguistic nature, it is essential to keep in mind two basic concepts: "standardization" and "weighting."

"Standardization" involves operating from the idealized data of two or more parts of a population, and not from primary data. In other words, to standardize a population, one calculates the rate that one would expect to find in each subpopulation if all the subpopulations (for example, by age group) had the same composition. It can be used, for example, to calculate the level of knowledge of a foreign language that is being learned by a group of students. Within the group, it would be expected that each student had a different level of proficiency in the language learned. In this case, to work with the mean knowledge of the language within this group of students, the grades obtained at the end of the course would be averaged. In this way, the group's level is standardized, and it can then be compared with the level of other groups of language learners.

Standardization is likewise equivalent to a statistical "normalization" with the goal of making heterogeneous data comparable. Thus, when within a linguistic corpus (collection of samples of written and/or spoken language) there are distinct kinds of texts of quite different lengths and it is necessary to analyze the frequency of a word within those texts, a "normalization" can be carried out. This normalization is made to compensate for the inequalities between samples or subsamples (in the example, kinds of texts) and consists of using as a reference not the total volume of data but instead some "normalized" values or frequencies; for example, the frequency with which a word appears for every million words (Molina Salinas & Sierra Martínez, 2015).

Demography standardizes populations, accepting that all the groups or strata (for example, of age) that compose them have the same structure. These idealized strata are arbitrary and subjective, it is true, but analysts must try to ensure that they correspond to or approximate as closely as possible the populations under analysis. In the field of demolinguistics, standardization supposes, for example, treating as equivalent or identical the knowledge and use of one or more languages in different strata of a population. In this case, standardization is resolved with a qualitative-based decision.

As for "weights", these allow for certain values to be assigned to each of the variables that make up a given indicator in order to adjust these values to their real incidence in relation to a given event. Thus, weighting allows for the correction, through a statistical resource, of the imbalances that may occur between data collected from various sources. A common kind of weighting is that applied a priori to combining indicators and calculating indexes. With three cases, each indicator receives a weight that reflects an influence or a specific assessment with respect to the others. Thus, if we want to calculate the international weight of a language, for example, we can use explanatory factors such as the number of native speakers, the number of countries where it is an official language, and its official status in international organizations. Each of these indicators can lead to a quantified value to which a weight can be applied, in order that, for example, the number of countries has a greater weight than the number of speakers in the calculation. One of the easiest ways of applying a weight is to multiply by

1 those factors that you do not wish to modify and by a decimal (0.5 or some other value) the factors whose incidence you wish to reduce. It is understood that the assignment of the coefficients of weighting (and therefore the weight of each indicator) is subjective and arbitrary and depends on each investigation.

> The assignment of weighting coefficients is arbitrary, and in fact responds to a previous hypothesis.
>
> *Otero Roth, 1995*

Weighting can also be applied to compensate for differences that may exist between strata in which a sample of informants who have been surveyed is subdivided. A clear and well-known example of this has to do with surveys collected from men and women. There may be circumstances in which the data handled in a survey come from 100 men and 25 women, for instance. In this case, in order to rectify the imbalance, the weighting helps us to reduce the overall weight of the answers from men and to increase the weight of the answers from women.

Demographic Projections

Projections are an essential component of demographic analysis, mainly because they are the gateway to an activity that is essential for societies: planning. In the field of demolinguistics, projections offer information about the possible evolution of a linguistic community, but they also allow for the planning of actions aimed at maintenance, majoritization, prestige, or language spread. Let us remember that censuses are traditionally carried out every 10 years and that such a period seems long when it comes to forecasting possible difficulties or social needs. That is why the evolution of demographic events must be analyzed and projected over time. This projection is made by distinguishing key variables, such as age, sex, or education, such that the projection can include different scenarios in the future. When the scope of the evolution is considered almost immediately, it is usually referred to as "estimations;" when the forecast period is larger, one speaks of "short-term" or "long-term" projections.

The calculation of projections has frequently been applied to the minority languages of Western countries, both to anticipate future educational or cultural needs and to glimpse the possible strength of the languages a few years in the future. In fact, in the case of Spain, discussions about the reduction or possible disappearance of languages such as Basque or Catalan are common and recurring, even through centuries of history, as well as the will of these linguistic communities themselves, support the impossibility of such a disappearance taking place.

In this regard, one of the best-known projection exercises in the field of demolinguistics was carried out by Anna Cabré on the Catalan language. Cabré (1995) made a calculation that consisted of projecting the population of 1900 with

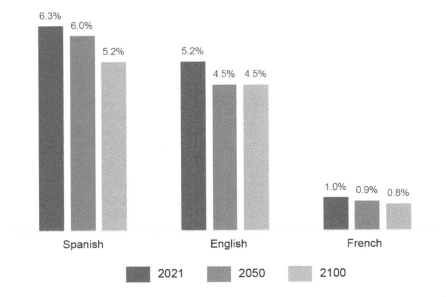

GRAPH 6.4 Projections of communities of native speakers of Spanish, French, and English in 2012, 2050, and 2100.
Source: Instituto Cervantes (2021).

the historical fertility and mortality rates of Catalonia over the course of almost a century. Counter to the mid-twentieth century theses that maintained that the population would diminish in a Catalonia governed by its own demographic dynamics, Cabré showed that not only did this decrease not occur but in fact the Catalan-speaking community had benefited. In this same fashion, projections have been made of the percentages of English, Spanish, and French speakers in the world population over the course of the next century, even if these projections are solely based on demographics; that is, they don't take into account other social or linguistic circumstances.

Another projection exercise was undertaken by David Sankoff (2008) in Papua New Guinea. Sankoff made a population projection based on village patrol reports and birth records from a small sample of hospitals. In light of this, he studied literacy rates in Tok Pisin and English in Papua New Guinea and the social conditioning of the spread of these languages. Based on this experience, Sankoff developed a demolinguistic model to project the evolution of other bilingual communities (Casesnoves & Sankoff, 2003; 2004).

The way in which projections are made is based primarily on data provided by censuses and records collected by statistical institutes or the respective census offices. For demolinguistic purposes, the inclusion of information on language knowledge is fundamental, in correlation with other factors such as age, sex, migrations, and geographic areas affected. However, this is not always the case,

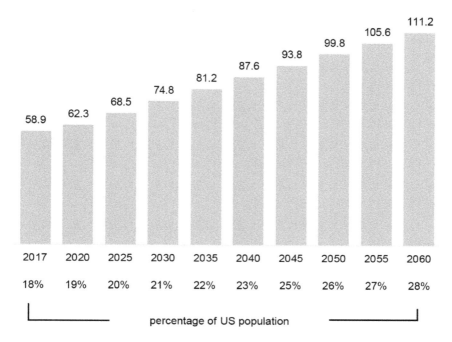

GRAPH 6.5 Projection of the Hispanic population in the United States between 2020 and 2060.
Source: US Census Office.

unfortunately. In general, the organizations mentioned offer demographic projections of different kinds, such as the projection of the Hispanic population between 2020 and 2060 made by the US Census Bureau. In this case, the correspondence between Hispanics and Spanish speakers is not exact, given that one would need to subtract the number of Hispanics who don't know the language and add the number of non-Hispanics who do know it. Nonetheless, the total number of Hispanics projected, together with other factors, makes it possible to anticipate an increase in the number of Spanish speakers.

In general, statistics institutes offer precise information about how their projections were made. When projecting demolinguistic information, various non-demographic values are considered. In 2012, Guus Extra produced a report on European indicators of language policies and practices in which he compared data regarding education, legislation, services and public spaces, media, and businesses. Any projection should take into account such indicators. This (Yağmur, Extra, & Swinkels, 2012) implies crossing data from diverse sources, such as statistics institutes, immigration offices, and international organizations.

Other clear examples of projection include vitality scales or intergenerational transmission scales, such as EGIDS (Expanded Graded Intergenerational Disruption

192 Demolinguistic Analyses

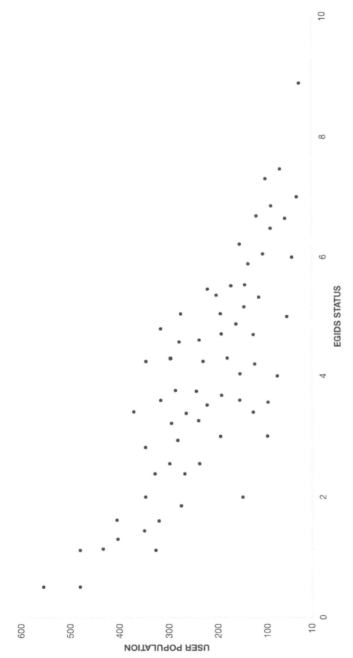

GRAPH 6.6 Simplified scatter diagram for intergenerational disruption scale. STATUS: 0: International. 1: National. 2: Provincial. 3: Wider communication. 4: Educational. 5: Developing. 6a: Vigorous. 6b: Threatened. 7: Shifting. 8a: Moribund. 8b: Nearly Extinct. 9: Dormant. 10: Extinct.

Source: Based on Lewis, Simons, & Fennig (2014).

Scale) (Lewis & Simons, 2010). The Ethnologue Project has used scatter diagrams to locate each language of the world at a point on the scale. These diagrams show the status or level of each language (on EGIDS) on the x axis and the number of speakers in millions on the y axis.

Vitality scales, when calculated periodically, can help to project the future of the languages analyzed. Nonetheless, these scales, especially those applied on a global level, have the drawback that they usually handle data from different moments in time and, moreover, among their dependent variables, they use qualitative data that are poorly defined (level of fluency) or quantitative data that are complicated to equate in absolute terms (for example, use by "many" or "few" speakers). In any case, projections can have a revelatory qualitative dimension and offer a determining impression of the social perception of the factors of language.

Errors, Biases, and Changes in Criteria

Errors

Errors are no minor issue when it comes to demography. It can be said that one must live in a constant struggle to avoid them, as well as to justify the decisions taken at each moment. Despite this struggle, it is common for people unrelated to demolinguistic research or those who approach it in a circumstantial way to use errors as an ideal excuse to destroy the theses of others or justify their own. Errors are so common, in the form of biases or simple mistakes, that demography manuals usually include them in their general indexes. Colin Newell (1988), for example, explains two kinds of fundamental errors: "coverage errors" and "errors of closure."

Error of closure: this is an indicator of the consistency of the demographic data and the quality of their collection; it occurs when there are differences in the definition of the populations, especially if they are compared to one another. The measurement of births, deaths, migrations, and population size is often imprecise and is a process with a high propensity for error.

Coverage error: this occurs when a sector of the population is not considered, giving rise to incomplete coverage or an underestimation: in many cases, the parts of the population that are homeless, nomadic, student, traveling, or which belong to closed congregations or communities are not included. Errors of overestimation or overrepresentation also occur and are no less common in demolinguistics.

Newell also expressly mentions "accidental errors," which can be due to unforeseen or unforeseeable circumstances, especially in administering questionnaires: errors in the answers, misunderstanding questions, and inappropriateness of the questions to a specific cultural environment. Another classic demographer, Roland Pressat (1961), does not hesitate to state in relation to errors:

> A catalog of the errors in judgement caused by an erroneous analysis of the numerical data would be valuable for multiple reasons.
>
> *Pressat, 1961*

Pressat expressly refers to some errors that are frequently repeated, such as ignoring the effect of the age structure of a population, not appreciating the effect of occasional migrations, comparing parameters of different dimensions, or not considering cultural factors in the interpretation of demographic factors. He adds to this a more subtle error: that of getting carried away by reasoning or a perfectly logical or convincing line of argument, leaving aside two principles as simple as the value of "common sense" and the weight of the primary data.

In developing this work, it is possible to point out some areas where errors are most frequent. Let us remember the possible confusion in Spanish between "fertility" and "fecundity," because of the influence of these terms in English, or the closeness of the concepts of birth rate and growth rate, which leads to them sometimes being confused. In demolinguistic practice, there are many more causes or sources of inaccuracies or inadequacies. One of these is the establishment of a direct correlation between ethnicity and speakers of a language. In this regard, the case of Hispanics in the United States has been pointed out, but there are many examples: the Estonian census offers data on ethnic groups of origin, and that would allow information about the possible languages of origin of those people to be deduced, but this is a deduction, not an empirical confirmation.

The same problem arises when it comes to data referring to nationality in relation to the languages known and spoken. Spanish nationality does not guarantee having Spanish as a mother tongue, for it could well be Catalan, Galician, or Basque (among others). The question is different if the case is not the mother tongue, but a native command of the language, where the deduction is more plausible. The operation of deducing linguistic information based on nationality proves even more delicate when it comes to second languages. For example, it is known that Spanish is, along with English, the best-known and most used foreign language in Brazil. In this way, if there is a minimum of half a million Spanish speakers in Brazil, who represent 0.23% of the overall population of the country, without considering those who study this language, one could deduce that among the Brazilian emigrants who arrive in other countries, there would be a parallel proportion of Spanish speakers. The error could lie in not taking into account the stratification of that population by educational level or regions of origin within Brazil where the proportion of Spanish speakers could be higher. This question has to do with one of the aforementioned errors: omitting attention to specific segments of the population, whether this be related to age, sex, educational level, or any other aspect.

Often, the problems for demolinguistics arise from the sources themselves. Thus, it is common for data migration records, data from central demographic services, or those provided by international sources like Eurostat or the UN not to coincide. In these cases, researchers are the ones who decide on what basis to build their calculations or interpretations. One option is to always handle the same kind of source at some agreed-upon level; another is to follow the most reliable sources available, generally those closest to the territory; that is, to the original facts.

Likewise, it is not surprising for the criteria handled by researchers or by a research institute to change over time, which can lead to doubts when it comes to interpreting the evolution of the events analyzed. One example of this is offered by the calculation of the Human Development Index (HDI) by country. The HDI is expressed in values from 0 to 1, calculated based on a series of parameters and indicators that relate to education, health, and income. For the first HDI, established in 1990, the life expectancy in a country used health as the indicator, the literacy rate was used as an indicator of educational level, and the GDP per capita as an indicator of income. Despite their clarity and usefulness, these criteria were modified over time, such that in 1991 the average years of schooling was considered, only to be replaced in 1995 by the enrollment rate at different educational levels, and in 2010 all these previous indicators of education were substituted by the expected years of schooling and the average years of instruction of the adult population. Likewise, the GDP per capita parameter was substituted by the gross national income per capita, adjusted for purchasing power parity (Villar, 2010; Mohanty & Dehury, 2012). The relationship between the indicators of the three general parameters was established by means of an arithmetic mean until 2009, when it was decided to opt for a geometric mean, recommended for data of geometric progression because it normalizes the values of different ranges.

As is well known, the HDI ranking is a value used for numerous applied purposes in which temporal progression is significant. Does this mean that all calculations generated from 1990 until 2009 for the HDI have been rendered useless by these changes in statistical criteria? The answer must be determined for each investigation, but the possibility of assimilating the older indexes with the current ones should not be dismissed out of hand, because the object of study may be sensitive to the changes in criteria. Although it does not seem a feasible task, it would be possible to recalculate the HDI since 2010 with the earlier criteria. In any event, the change of practical, technical, or statistical criteria is a frequent practice in demography and in many other disciplines that always seek to offer the most reliable data. Sometimes, it is the adequacy of the data that makes a change of criteria advisable; at other times, it could be the discovery of a new criterion; and at others, finally, it is the evolution of reality itself that recommends the change of criteria.

But without a doubt, it is in the field of linguistic concepts and in the delimitation of categories related to the knowledge and use of languages where confusion or inconvenient interpretations can happen with greatest ease. This matter has already been addressed in presenting the concepts of linguistics for demographers. Let us remember the blurred boundaries between categories such as mother tongue, first language, and main language; and the difficulty of specifying the exact knowledge bilingual people have of their languages, or of knowing to what degree the heritage language can be considered native or not for the second generation of immigrants. The problem is not really with using some concepts or others, or some interpretations or others, but in not knowing what concept each term used refers to or in comparing categories that reflect different concepts or dimensions. Hence the need to provide all the information available in this regard, although the formats of publication also condition the possible revelation of the information and sometimes do not allow for the necessary length of text, certain graphs, or notes, among other components.

Biases

Beyond the errors of execution or concept, there is another stream of errors that refers to the interpretation of the data, the sources, and the results of the analyses. These are known as "cognitive biases" that cause deviations, distortions, or inaccurate judgments about the available information. These biases include predispositions, as well as prejudices and beliefs of all kinds. Psychologists have identified dozens of biases, a good number of which could appear in demolinguistic studies (Baron, 2000; Gilovich, Griffin, & Kahneman, 2002). Some of the most common biases in scientific research in general, and in demolinguistic research in particular, will now be briefly presented.

Among scientific biases, collectively understood, "confirmation bias," "hindsight bias," and "motivated reasoning" deserve mention. "Confirmation bias" means favoring that information that confirms one's own hypotheses or beliefs and disfavoring that which contradicts or is inconvenient to one's own hypotheses or beliefs; "hindsight bias" presumes the ratification of a hypothesis as if it had been formulated previously, without that being the case; and "motivated reasoning" consists of an a posteriori argumentation that justifies the initial beliefs, or the actions carried out by researchers. Biases possible in the field of demography (although not exclusive to it) include "representative bias," which consists of ignoring the probability of the results and the size of the sample. Thus, sometimes the same judgments are applied to both large samples and small ones, and sometimes greater validity is given to the results obtained from a large sample without considering that the validity is subject to the sample's representativity and not its size.

On the other hand, in demolinguistics, biases that respond to beliefs or prejudices are relatively to be expected; that is, to motivate reasoning both from the analysts and their critics. According to Karl Popper (1972), scientists always try to refute the conclusions of other scientists or themselves to advance science. However, it is more common for scientists to seek above all to verify their discoveries or those of likeminded scientists, which presupposes the rejection of those analyses that contradict them, accusing these of being irrelevant or erroneous, if not biased or skewed. This last accusation is usually based on prejudices of diverse kinds: ethnic, political, ideological. In this way, in the field of languages, it is usually assumed that the studies carried out by official institutions or by people linked to them are tendentious by nature. Of course, it is irrational to deny this possibility absolutely, but the matter should be treated with great care, especially if the accusations are made in the name of anti-institutional tendencies or of a supposed critical pronouncement that is sustained merely by criticism itself and not by the practice of alternative studies.

As for other biases, there are many, coupled with various cognitive effects, with fallacies, and with heuristics or shortcuts that simplify decision-making in conditions of insecurity. Among these other biases, some related to researchers and the analysis process itself could be mentioned (Behavioral Research Group, 2020):

a. Biases relating to researchers

Framing effect. This involves building a discourse that highlights the positive and negative aspects of a situation according to the interests of the researchers or their discursive strategy.

Honesty bias. If a person is convinced of their own honesty and integrity, they tend to exhibit this self-concept, even if this implies an attack on the honor of everyone else. This can occur when the honesty of some demolinguistic analyses is criticized or questioned, emphasizing the honesty of the critic.

Habit bias. This consists of making statements or drawing conclusions that coincide with repeated or learned facts which usually appear in a particular context. Sometimes, when a statement has been repeated many times (for example, that English will become the only global language), statements to the contrary may be avoided.

b. Biases relating to the analytical process

Conjunction fallacy. This is the tendency to assume that the specific conditions are more likely than the general conditions. This fallacy can occur when minorities are analyzed. For example, if a person is of indigenous heritage, is 30 years old, and lives in a rural area, there is a tendency to think that this person self-identifies as indigenous and that they speak a native language when the probability of both these conditions occurring together is less than the probability that each condition occurs independently.

Law of small numbers. This consists of the belief that small samples should resemble the population from which they are drawn. This usually occurs when reduced environments or minority situations are analyzed without considering that, although there is a law of large numbers, no law of small numbers exists.

WYSIATI (what you see is all there is) bias. This involves drawing conclusions on the basis of limited evidence using intuitive thinking.

Criticisms and Disputes

The reasons and arguments that have just been presented explain the relative frequency with which, not just criticisms of studies, but true scientific disputes occur, when they don't turn personal. In 1977, Stanley Lieberson noted the following regarding a criticism made by John De Vries (1977) about one of his works (Lieberson, Dalto, & Johnson, 1975):

> The objections might easily be called charming except for the mounting evidence that they can cause stomach ulcers.
>
> *De Vries, 1977*

Lieberson, Dalto, and Johnson's work tried to offer a way to handle a wide variety of available data on numerous languages throughout time and across geography. De Vries criticized their handling of data taken from secondary sources, the undue mixing of measures (mother tongue, habitual language, and ability to speak a given language), and the use of data of questionable reliability. Lieberson recognized at that moment the error of having misinterpreted some data and of not having heeded the information offered in footnotes for a secondary source. Footnotes often appear in the criticisms, either because they are needed in greater abundance and detail (as they already abound in demography and demolinguistics) or because more attention is demanded for the notes provided by others. To a significant extent, the criticisms Lieberson met with had to do with the relationship established between concepts like "urbanization" and "linguistic diversity" or the interpretation of the change of language as an intergenerational or intragenerational process; Lieberson considered it to be intergenerational "for the most part," which, in itself, doesn't deny the possibility of "intragenerational" change, even less so if data from different countries and time periods are considered. As was to be expected, the interpretation and use of the concept of "mother tongue" was once more brought up in connection with the situation of various countries.

Logically, criticisms are to be expected in any scientific endeavor and are a constructive element that not only helps in correcting errors and misinterpretations, but also contributes to an improvement of methods and investigations. As happens with developing dictionaries, no demolinguistic work is immune from detailed criticism, due to the complexity and ambiguity of the concepts handled, the erratic reliability of the sources, the quantity of data from diverse origins (across both time and space), the interaction (not always evident) of the parameters and indicators handled, the need to operate by conjectures, and the inevitability of human error. However, it is not constructive for criticisms to be seasoned with qualifications or assessments capable of "provoking stomach ulcers," such as those that allude to greater or lesser liking of the data by the people criticized or their desire to "disguise" reality in answer to obscure motives. It also frequently happens that criticisms of errors are made directly and without nuance while the nuances expressed in the text under review are ignored. Gregorio Salvador published a chapter titled "Los alegres guarismos de la demolingüística" ("The Happy Figures of Demolinguistics"), which was a clear accusation of frivolity, superficiality, and lack of rigor among the entities interested in counting speakers (Salvador, 1992), with an attitude of moral superiority that earned it not few followers.

In the field of demolinguistics, the most critical texts are usually directed against works focused on comparing languages or on international languages, but not against those that deal with minority languages. It gives the impression that any criticism against the study of a minority language must be interpreted as an attack against the minority language itself, a view with little scientific basis. Equally without foundation is that the demolinguistic study of a transnational language has as a consequence the minoritization of the languages that coexist with it. "Critical sociolinguistics," in whose name many of the aforementioned criticisms are made, is only truly critical when it focuses on scientifically based arguments, because it fails to offer, due to its *de facto* epistemology, alternative studies that can be substituted, without any criticism, for the criticized works. When its arguments reveal prejudices or ideological overtones, critical sociolinguistics becomes nothing more than "hypercritical" and condescending sociolinguistics.

Graphic Representations

The graphic representations offered by demolinguistics don't substantially differ from those handled by demography and geodemography. This means that demolinguistics, on the one hand, responds to the growing importance that society attaches to data, figures, and statistics and, on the other, that it turns to the methodologies that are currently most used, including the geographic information systems (GIS) which give a visible face to the results of the interaction between statistics, cartography, and computing.

The repertoire of possible graphic representations that are useful in demolinguistics include numerous possibilities beyond numerical and statistical tables and charts: population pyramids, line graphs, bar graphs, pie charts, scatter plots, box-and-whisker plots, or area graphs; histograms, matrixes, distribution graphs, and binary and ternary or triangular diagrams, among others. In the field of cartography, the possibilities are also multiple: cartodiagrams; symbol maps; gravitational maps; choropleth maps; anamorphic maps or cartograms; point, isoline, surface or three-dimensional maps; flow maps; and focal density maps, among others (Breton, 1990; Ambrose & Williams, 1991). Specific samples of the most used graphic representations in demolinguistics will be presented later, but first, it is worth reflecting briefly on some key aspects of the application of these techniques which have been treated in a clear and straightforward way by Pedro Reques Velasco (2011).

The first aspect refers to the process of applying graphic representations and, more specifically, statistical cartography. To do this, there is a preliminary phase which involves: a) considering the reality analyzed in its social and geographic dimensions; b) identifying the data most likely to be represented; c) assessing the goals of the research; d) checking the technical resources and execution times available in each case. Once these preliminary aspects have been reviewed, a succession of phases commences which concludes with the graphical portion of the analysis. These phases are:

1. Observation and preparation of the initial information.
2. Statistical and, where appropriate, spatial treatment.
3. Graphical and / or cartographic representation.

It is important to bear in mind, however, that the arrangement of the successive phases, both in the preliminary tasks and in the execution, need not follow a strictly linear development, but rather the tasks and phases can ultimately have a round-trip or circular development in which modifications and corrections are not the exception.

Regarding linguistic cartography specifically, Joshua Fishman stated in the prologue to Roland Breton's *Atlas des langues du monde* (2003):

> Languages do not take up any space. Only their speakers and institutions can be located spatially. For this reason, the mapping of languages always depends upon demographic data, usually information provided by governments, such as the number of speakers of a living language in a given region or place.
>
> *Fishman in Breton, 2003*

This task, however, is not so simple, as can be deduced from the difficulties highlighted by Reques Velasco (2011):

1. Determine the information to be represented in terms of the subject treated and the geography represented.
2. Determine the categories to be represented, how they will be ordered, and the numerical values (discrete or continuous, positive and / or negative, central, scattered) that express them.
3. Determine the best kinds of maps or cartographies to be used in each case.

With regard to this third difficulty, it is important to know the technical resources available in each case, as well as the virtues and drawbacks of each option. Let us now look at some of the graphical and cartographic resources most used in demolinguistics. The possibilities when it comes to graphic representation are many, so only some of the most frequent are outlined here.

Line Graphs

This type of graph, as effective for representation as it is easy to construct, consists of simply drawing the relationship between the value of two variables, generally one independent or explanatory and the other dependent, by means of a line.

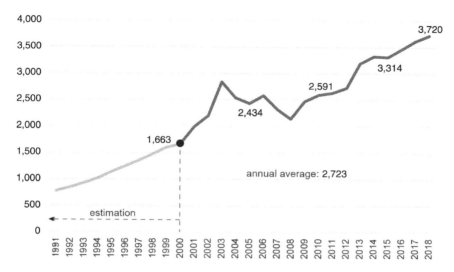

GRAPH 6 7 Naturalizations of Spanish-speaking migrants in Germany (1991–2019), based on data from the *Statistisches Bundesamt* (2020).
Source: Loureda Lamas, Moreno-Fernández, Álvarez Mella, & Scheffler (2020).

Bar Graphs and Pie Charts

Bar graphs represent the (absolute or relative) frequencies or values of discrete variables; that is, they are not mutually or necessarily required; for example, the continents of origin of an immigrant population. Normally, the total of the values represented in the bars or sections adds up to 100%.

This kind of information can also be represented through circular graphs in which the variants of the variable considered form sections or portions of a circle which is why they are often called "pie charts." In the illustration of the oral uses at home and with friends in the Valencian community, it can be seen that the position of the variants could be interchanged and that the total frequencies add up to 100%.

Histograms

Although bar charts and histograms are often confused, they use different base data. Both represent the frequency of a given value on cartesian axes by means of bars, but while bar graphs offer the frequencies or values of discrete variables, histograms present the values of variables arranged in the form of intervals or non-discrete variables, such that the variants must follow a specific order (for example, age ranges). In other words, in bar graphs it would be possible to change the order in which the bars appear, whereas in histograms the bars must be ordered in the progression that indicates the corresponding intervals, hence they are usually represented as adjacent bars.

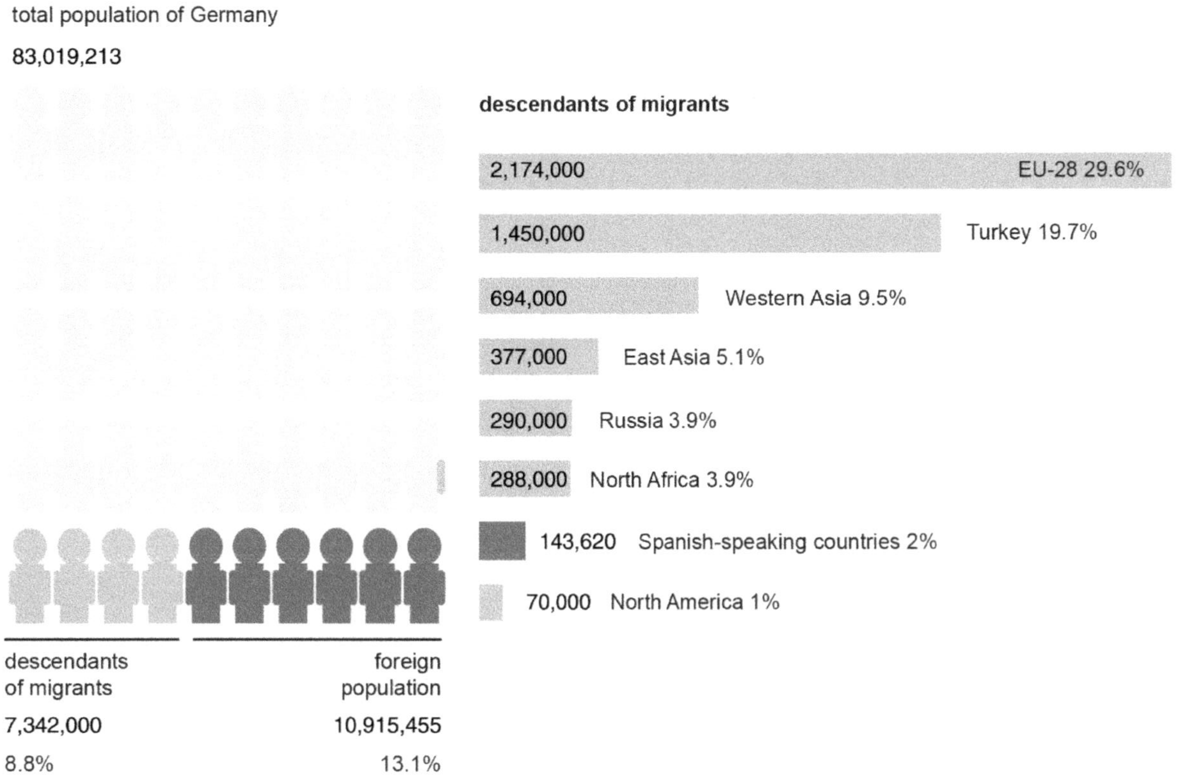

202 Demolinguistic Analyses

total population of Germany
83,019,213

descendants of migrants

- 2,174,000 — EU-28 29.6%
- 1,450,000 — Turkey 19.7%
- 694,000 — Western Asia 9.5%
- 377,000 — East Asia 5.1%
- 290,000 — Russia 3.9%
- 288,000 — North Africa 3.9%
- 143,620 — Spanish-speaking countries 2%
- 70,000 — North America 1%

	foreign population
	10,915,455
	13.1%

descendants of migrants	
7,342,000	
8.8%	

GRAPH 6.8 Descendants of migrants in Germany (1/1/2019) (typical development), based on data from the *Statistisches Bundesamt* (2020).

Source: Loureda Lamas, Moreno-Fernández, Álvarez, & Scheffler (2020).

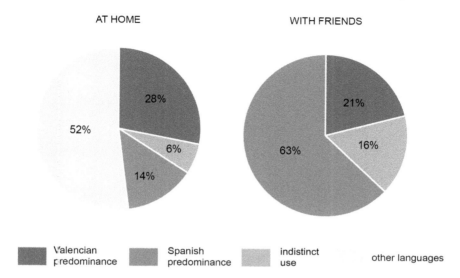

GRAPH 6.9 Oral use at home and with friends. Prevalence of Valencian / Spanish / other languages or indistinct use.
Source: Acadèmia Valenciana de la Llengua (2005: 67).

The width of the base of histogram bars is usually calculated to a specific formula, depending on the total range of the data and the number of categories that are considered. Consequently, the width of the bars in a histogram need not be the same, although they can be averaged. When such a calculation is not made, the result resembles a bar graph more closely, as occurs in this sample of the evolution of the Basque-speaking population by age group in the Basque Country.

The information in histograms can also be presented in circular graphs, such as this one that presents the level of competence of speakers of Mapudungun of Mapuche origin in the city of Santiago de Chile. In this case, the sum of the relative frequencies must be 100% and the variants are ordered in intervals, although these are presented qualitatively.

Radar or Spider Charts

On the one hand, these graphs can present the distance between some real and ideal values relative to a series of factors or variables. On the other, they can represent the degree to which each factor or variable is represented within a whole. This illustration represents the main varieties of Spanish that are supposedly used most in each of the federal states of Germany.

204 Demolinguistic Analyses

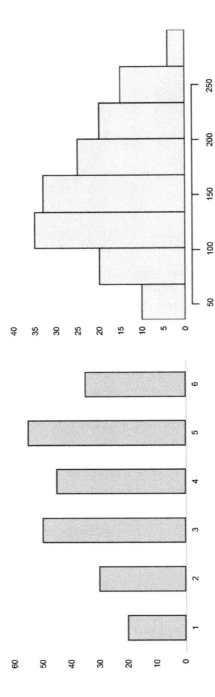

GRAPH 6.10 Bar graph (left) and histogram (right).

Demolinguistic Analyses   **205**

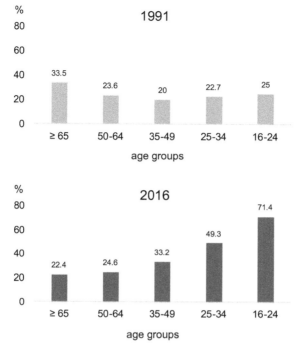

GRAPH 6.11   Evolution of the Basque-speaking population by age group. CAE (Comunidad Autónoma de Euskadi) 1991–2016 (%).

Source: Basque Country Government / Gobierno País Vasco (2016).

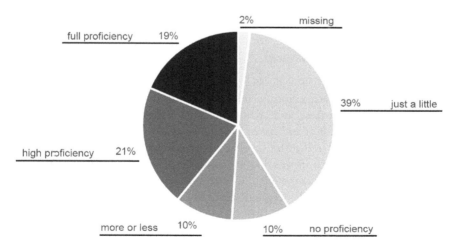

GRAPH 6.12   Competence in Mapudungun of members of Mapuche communities in Santiago de Chile.

Source: Lagos (2006).

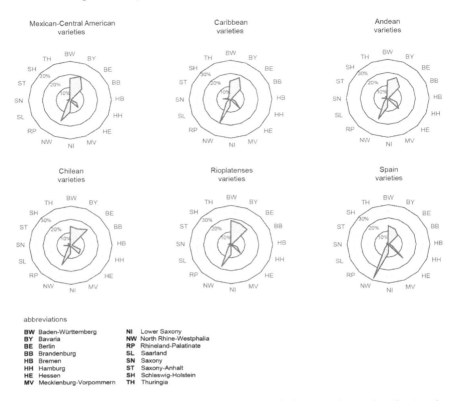

GRAPH 6.13 Varieties of Spanish in Germany and their speakers: distribution by federal state, based on data from the *Statistisches Bundesamt* (2020).

Source: Loureda Lamas, Moreno-Fernández, Álvarez Mella, & Scheffler (2020).

Pyramids of Speaker Populations

A population pyramid is a double histogram of frequencies, understanding histogram as the representation by means of rectangles whose widths represent intervals of classification and whose heights represent the corresponding frequencies. In the case of pyramids, the bars or rectangles of the histograms are arranged horizontally so that the vertical intervals represent age groups, normally in intervals of five years. In this double histogram, it is customary to arrange the information about men on the left side with information about women arranged on the right. In this way, the frequencies form a pyramid, occupying a space that is more or less broad on one side than on the other. The elaboration of a pyramid requires distributing the ages in equal intervals and ensuring their comparison forces are the same dimensions in all the compared pyramids. In this case, the pyramids can be juxtaposed or superimposed.

Demolinguistic Analyses   **207**

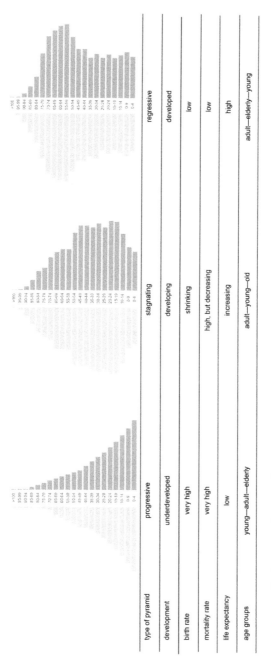

GRAPH 6.14 Basic types of pyramids.
Source: Alonso (2022).

208 Demolinguistic Analyses

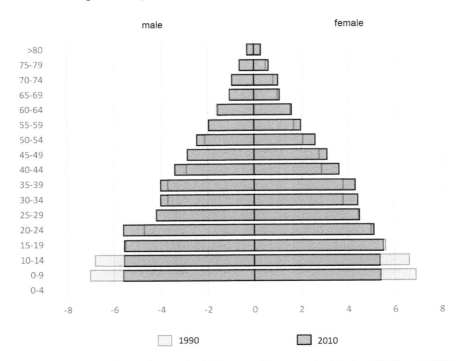

GRAPH 6.15 Population that speaks indigenous languages in Mexico, 1990 and 2010. Superimposed pyramids.

Source: Vázquez (2013).

The shape that a pyramid finally adopts helps to predict how a population will evolve over the course of generations, such that three basic types of pyramids are distinguished: progressive population (with a wide base and thin top), regressive population (base thinner than the center and / or the top), and stagnant population. This typology doesn't prevent intermediate or even unbalanced forms from occurring, if a population has experienced an event that has altered its structure, such as a war or a mass emigration process.

The progressive population pyramid represents a developing population; the regressive population pyramid represents a population with a low birth rate and higher life expectancy; and the stagnating or stationary population pyramid represents a population in transition between progression and regression. In the pyramids of speaker populations of different languages, different pyramid shapes can be seen that reflect different states of demolinguistic structure.

When communities are stable in a territory, their shape corresponds to the basic types outlined above, as can be seen in the populational representations of Mexico. When it comes to migratory communities or groups, the pyramid shape is usually that of an inverted top, where the base is small, given that migration is usually carried out by groups ranging in age from 20 to 50 years old.

Demolinguistic Analyses **209**

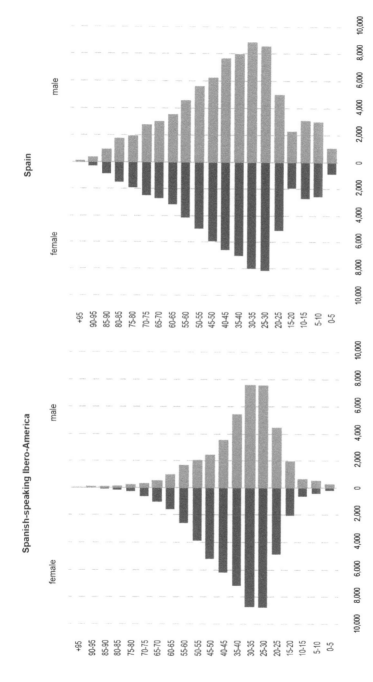

GRAPH 6.16 Population pyramids of the Spanish-speaking immigrant population in Germany according to their origin (1/1/2019), based on data from the *Statistisches Bundesamt* (2020). Juxtaposed pyramids.

Source: Loureda Lamas, Moreno-Fernández, Álvarez Mella, Scheffler (2020).

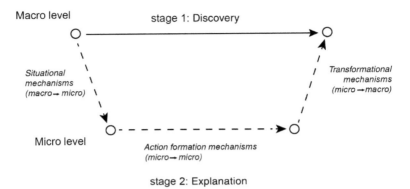

GRAPH 6.17 Coleman diagram for social mechanisms of demography.
Source: Billari (2015).

Other Diagrams

Among the many possibilities offered by current infographics to represent the data and analyses of demography and demolinguistics, the Coleman diagram, also known as Coleman's boat (1986) is worthy of mention because of its interpretive potential. This diagram serves to represent the relationship between factors that concur in a given phenomenon or process and which establish a causal relationship between themselves, especially when the potential causes and interactions distinguish between a macro and a micro level. The relationships between factors are usually indicated through arrows of diverse kinds, and the succession of the factors over time is represented through their disposition from left to right. For example, in the field of demography, Francesco Billari (2015) has proposed a model of social mechanisms that distinguishes between situational mechanisms (ways in which the macro level is considered to affect individual outcomes; for instance, how the decline in mortality in a society affects individual fertility choices) and transformation mechanisms (ways in which, through the aggregation of the individual results or the interactions between individuals, macro-level results are generated). All this is represented through a Coleman diagram.

Cartography

According to Reques Velasco, the main options available to researchers when deciding on their maps are the following: to make a point map ("point expression mapping"); to make a map of lines or flows ("linear expression mapping"); or to make a map of zones ("zonal expression mapping"). There are also other possibilities in which data of different natures are combined or where maps receive different forms.

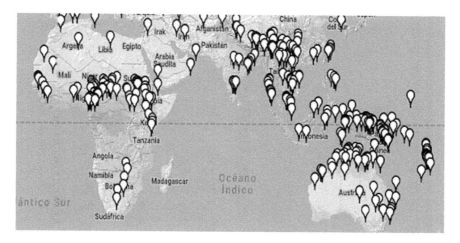

MAP 6.1 Point map of languages in a critical situation in Africa, Oceania, and South Asia.
Source: UNESCO Atlas of the World's Languages in Danger (Moseley, 2010).

Point Expression Mapping

Point maps are quite common in linguistic research because they allow specific linguistic phenomena, dialectal areas, or different languages to be located in space. An example of point mapping is that offered by the UNESCO Atlas of Endangered Languages, with the advantage that the maps can be generated interactively online, using reader preferences.

Linear Expression Mapping

Flow or line maps represent any type of movement between two points or areas. They can represent, for example, the dialectal areas of origin of a contingent of immigrants who arrive in a certain place (for example, Latin American migrants in Europe).

Zonal Expression Mapping

Maps of zones or areas represent the (simple or compound) data of interest localized in the corresponding geographic zones. The shape of the maps can be very varied. Choropleth maps, for example, divide the space into zones (conventional or non-conventional) on which qualitative or quantitative data are represented by assorted colors, patterns, or intensities.

In cartograms, the areas into which a space is divided are linked to specific statistical information represented in the form of graphs; for example, pie charts,

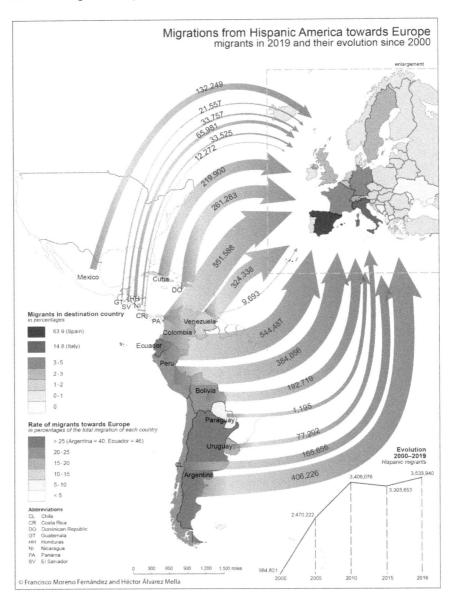

MAP 6.2 Map of origins of Hispanics in Europe.
Source: Moreno-Fernández & Álvarez Mella (2019).

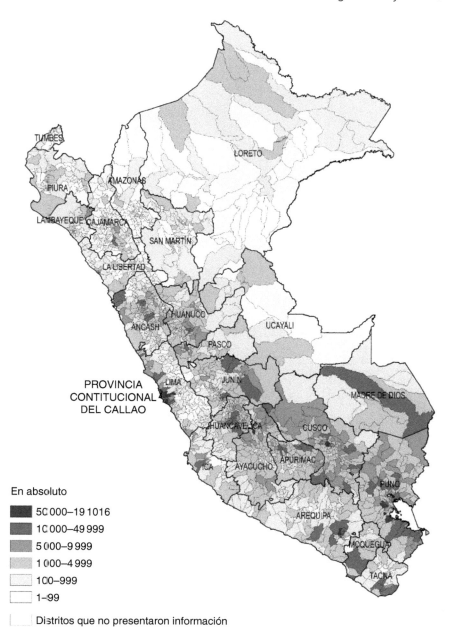

MAP 6.3 Map of areas of the population that self-identifies as indigenous or native to the Andes according to districts of Peru (2017).

Source: Instituto Nacional de Estadísticas e Informática, Perú.

214 Demolinguistic Analyses

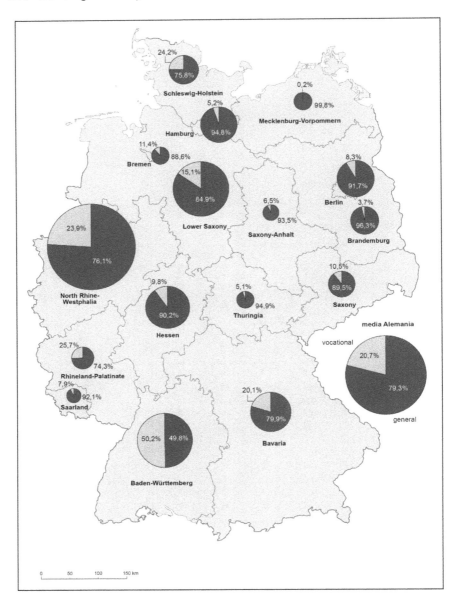

MAP 6.4 Students of Spanish by federal state (2018/19 academic year), based on data from the *Statistisches Bundesamt* (2020).

Source: Loureda Lamas, Moreno-Fernández, Álvarez Mella, & Scheffler (2020).

bar graphs, or histograms. Map 6.5 shows the map of the proportion of students of Spanish by federal state in Germany.

Summary

This chapter has explained fundamental aspects of the tasks that make up the true core of demolinguistic research: analyses. These analyses can pursue different objectives and therefore be located at a macro or micro level. In turn, the objectives established determine whether to proceed through qualitative or quantitative analyses, assessing the close and unavoidable implications that connect them.

For quantitative analysis, it is essential to know the fundamentals of the statistics or tests that control it. These statistics affect the composition, distribution, and changes of populations, considered here as populations that know or use a specific linguistic repertoire. These statistics will put researchers in a position to make comparisons between populations, as well as projections into the future based on data from the present or from specific time series. Biases and errors are possible at all stages of analysis and must be avoided or justified as far as possible.

Graphic representations are an essential component of demolinguistic research because they allow for multiple or complex factors to be visualized in an uncomplicated way. To do so, demolinguistic research relies on the entire graphic catalog that is common in statistics and in demography itself. Given the link between languages and geography, cartography—more specifically, statistical cartography—becomes a fundamental instrument for analyses.

References

Acadèmia Valenciana de la Llengua (2005): *Llibre blanc de l'us del valencià*. València: AVL.

Alonso, Jaime (2022): *Jaime Alonso's Blog for Social Sciences @ IES Lope de Vega*. https://jaimelopedevegasociales.wordpress.com/author/jaimegeografiaehistoria/ Online resource.

Ambrose, John E. and Colin H. Williams (1991): "Language Made Visible: Representation in Geolinguistics". In C.H. Williams (ed.), *Linguistic Minorities, Society and Territory*. Clevedon: Multilingual Matters, pp. 298–314.

Barni, Monica and Guus Extra (eds.) (2008): *Mapping Linguistic Diversity in Multicultural Contexts*. Berlin: Mouton–de Gruyter.

Baron, Jonathan (2000): *Thinking and Deciding*. 3rd ed. Cambridge: Cambridge University Press.

Behavioral Research Group (2020): *Bias: Encyclopaedia of Biases and Heuristics*. Not specified: Behavioral Research Group.

Billari, Francesco (2015): "Integrating macro- and micro-level approaches in the explanation of population change". *Population Studies*, 69: 11–20.

Brenzinger, Matthias, Tjeerd de Graaf, Arienne Dwyer, Colette Grinevald, Michael Krauss, Osahito Miyaoka, Nicholas Olster, Osamu Sakiyama, María Villalón, Akira Yamamoto, and Ofelia Zepeda (2003): *Language Vitality and Endangerment. UNESCO Ad Hoc Expert Group Meeting on Endangered Languages*. Paris: UNESCO.

Breton, Roland (1990): "Indices numériques et représentations graphiques de la dynamique des langues". In L. Laforge and G. McConnell, *Diffusion des langues et changement social*. Québec: Travaux du CIRB, pp. 211–230.
Breton, Roland (2003): *Atlas des langues du monde*. Paris: Autrement.
Cabré, Anna (1995): "Factors demogràfics en l'ús de la llengua: el cas de Catalunya". *Actes del Simposi de Demolingüística. III Trobada de Sociolingüistes Catalans*. Barcelona: Generalitat de Catalunya, pp. 9–13.
Cabré, Anna (1999): *El sistema català de reproducció: cent anys de singularitat demogràfica*. Barcelona: Proa.
Casesnoves Ferrer, Raquel and David Sankoff (2003): "Identity as the primary determinant of language choice in Valencia". *Journal of Sociolinguistics*, 7: 50–64.
Casesnoves Ferrer, Raquel and David Sankoff (2004): "The Valencian revival: why usage lags behind competence". *Language in Society*, 33: 1–31.
Chan, Kai L. (2016): *Power Language Index: Which Are the World's Most Influential Languages?*. Fontainebleau: Institut Européen d'Administration des Affaires. Accessible at http://www.kailchan.ca/wp-content/uploads/2016/12/Kai-Chan_Power-Language-Index-full-report_2016_v2.pdf
Chávez, Carlos (2008): "El náhuat se extingue". *Séptimo Sentido*, 13 July.
Coleman, James S. (1986): "Social theory, social research, and a theory of action". *American Journal of Sociology*, 91: 1309–1335.
De Vries, John (1977): "Comment on 'The course of mother-tongue diversity in nations'". *American Journal of Sociology*, 83: 708–714.
De Vries, John (1994): "Canada's official language communities: an overview of the current demolinguistic situation". *International Journal of the Sociology of Language*, 1994: 37–68.
Feyerabend, Paul (1975): *Against Method*. London / New York: New Left Books.
Gal, Susan (1978): "Peasant men can't get wives: language change and sex roles in a bilingual community". *Language in Society*, 7: 1–16.
Gilovich, Thomas, Dale Griffin, and Daniel Kahneman (eds.) (2002): *Heuristics and Biases: The Psychology of Intuitive Judgment*. Cambridge: Cambridge University Press.
Gobierno País Vasco (2016): *VI encuesta sociolingüística*. San Sebastiàn: Comunidad Autónoma de Euskadi.
Heisenberg, Werner (1989): *Encounters with Einstein and Other Essays on People, Places, and Particles*. Princeton: Princeton University Press.
Henry, Louis (1976): *Population: Analysis and Methods*. New York: Academic Press.
INEI (2018): *III censo de comunidades nativas 2017*. Lima: INEI.
Instituto Cervantes (2021): *El español: una lengua viva. Anuario del Instituto Cervantes*. Madrid: Instituto Cervantes / Bala Perdida.
Johnson, Keith (2008): *Quantitative Methods in Linguistics*. Oxford: Blackwell.
Johnstone, Barbara (2000): *Qualitative Methods in Sociolinguistics*. Oxford: Oxford University Press.
Labov, William (1972): *Sociolinguistic Patterns*. Philadelphia: University of Pennsylvania Press.
Lagos, Cristián (2006): "Mapudungun en Santiago de Chile: vitalidad, lealtad y actitudes lingüísticas". *Lenguas Modernas*, 31: 97–126.
Latour, Bruno and Steve Woolgar (1979): *Laboratory Life: The Construction of Scientific Facts*. Beverly Hills: Sage.
Lewis, M. Paul and Gary F. Simons (2010): "Assessing endangerment: expanding Fishman's GIDS". *Revue Roumaine de Linguistique*, 55: 103–120.
Lewis, M. Paul, Gary F. Simons, and Charles D. Fennig (eds.) (2014): *Ethnologue: Languages*. 17th ed. Dallas: SIL.

Lieberson, Stanley (1977): "Response to De Vries's comments". *American Journal of Sociology*, 83: 714–722.
Lieberson, Stanley, Guy Dalto, and Mary Ellen Johnston (1975): "The course of mother-tongue diversity in nations". *American Journal of Sociology*, 81: 34–61.
Loureda Lamas, Óscar, Francisco Moreno-Fernández, Héctor Álvarez Mella, and David Scheffler (2020): *Demolingüística del español en Alemania*. Madrid: Instituto Cervantes.
Macaulay, Ronald K. (2009): *Quantitative Methods in Sociolinguistics*. New York: Palgrave.
Mayntz, Renate, Kurt Holm, and Peter Hübner (2005): *Einführung in die Methoden der empirischen Soziologie*. Munich: Westdeutcher.
McWhorter, John H. (2018): *The Creole Debate*. Cambridge: Cambridge University Press.
Mohanty, Sanjay K. and Bidyadhar Dehury (2012): "Human development indices: old and new". *Artha Vijñāna: Journal of the Gokhale Institute of Politics and Economics*, 54: 19–38.
Molina Salinas, Claudio and Gerardo E. Sierra Martínez (2015): "Hacia una normalización de la frecuencia de los corpus CREA y CORDE". *Revista Signos*, 48: 307–331.
Moreno-Fernández, Francisco (2009): *Principios de sociolingüística y sociología del lenguaje*. 4th ed. Barcelona: Ariel.
Moreno-Fernández, Francisco (2020): *La lengua y el sueño de la identidad*. Rome: Aracne.
Moreno-Fernández, Francisco and Héctor Álvarez Mella (2019): "Muestra cartográfica de las migraciones hispánicas". *Archiletras Científica*, 2019: 353–377.
Moseley, Christopher (ed.) (2010): *Atlas of the World's Languages in Danger*. 3rd ed. Paris: UNESCO Publishing.
Mufwene, Salikoko (2005): *Créoles, écologie sociale, évolution linguistique*. Paris: L'Harmattan.
Newell, Colin (1988): *Methods and Models in Demography*. New York: Guilford Press.
Newman, Isadore and Carolyn Benz (1998): *Qualitative-Quantitative Research Methodology: Exploring the Interactive Continuum*. Carbondale: Southern Illinois University Press.
Otero Roth, Jaime (1995). "Una nueva mirada al índice de importancia internacional de las lenguas". In Marqués de Tamarón (ed.), *El peso de la lengua española en el mundo*. Valladolid: Fundación Duques de Soria / INCIPE / Universidad de Valladolid, pp. 235–282.
Parra, María Luisa (2021): *Enseñanza del español y juventud latina*. Madrid: Arco Libros.
Perez Díaz, Julio (2010–2021): Curso de demografía. https://apuntesdedemografia. com/2017/01/04/el-concepto-de-familia-en-las-fuentes-censales/ Online resource.
Popper, Karl (1972): *Objective Knowledge*. Oxford: Clarendon.
Pressat, Roland (1961): *L'analyse démographique*. Paris: Presses Universitaires de France.
Pressat, Roland (1981): *Les méthodes en démographie*. Paris: Presses Universitaires de France.
Preston, Samuel, Patrick Heuveline, and Michel Guillot (2000): *Demography: Measuring and Modeling Population Processes*. Oxford: Wiley.
Reques Velasco, Pedro (2011): *Geodemografía: fundamentos conceptuales y metodológicos*. Santander: Universidad de Cantabria.
Rowland, Donald (2003): *Demographic Methods and Concepts*. Oxford: Oxford University Press.
Salvador, Gregorio (1992): *Política lingüística y sentido común*. Madrid: Istmo.
Sankoff, David (2008): "How to Predict the Evolution of a Bilingual Community". In M. Meyerhoff and N. Nagy (eds.), *Social Lives in Languages—Sociolinguistics and Multilingual Speech Communities*. Amsterdam: John Benjamins, pp. 179–195.
Scholfield, Phil (1994): *Quantifying Language*. Clevedon: Multilingual Matters.
Statistisches Bundesamt (2020): *Bevölkerung und Erwerbstätigkeit. Bevölkerung mit Migrationshintergrund–Ergebnisse des Mikrozensus 2019*. Wiesbaden: Statistisches Bundesamt.

Vallin, Jacques (1991): *La démographie.* Paris: La Découverte.
Vázquez Sandrin, Germán (2013): *Dinámica demográfica de las poblaciones indígenas en México: 1970–2010.* México: Instituto de Investigaciones Jurídicas de la UNAM.
Villar, Antonio (2010): *El desarrollo humano: 1980–2010.* Valencia: Instituto Valenciano de Investigaciones Económicas.
Yağmur, Kutlay, Guus Extra, and Maries Swinkels (2012): "Towards European Indicators of Language Policies and Practices". In G. Extra and K. Yağmur (eds.), *Language Rich Europe: Trends in Policies and Practices for Multilingualism in Europe.* Cambridge: Cambridge University Press, pp. 28–73.

7
APPLICATIONS OF DEMOLINGUISTICS

Manuals on demography frequently conclude with a section or chapter dedicated to its possible applications. Donald Rowland (2003) comments in this regard that the interest in the practical aspects of demography has a long history, above all because the *raison d'être* of censuses and vital statistics is precisely to provide useful information for political, administrative, and planning decisions.

Another common comment within demographic discourse consists of specifying the fields or tasks in which application proves most convenient. Rowland himself mentions demography's commercial applications, especially in the field of life insurance. He also speaks of an "applied demography" based on projections and prospections of populations of potential clients for organizations, consumer markets for companies, and labor forces for companies and governments. Likewise, Reques Velasco talks about the numerous applications of geodemography (health, immigration, employment, housing…) and points out three fundamental fields: urban planning, public health, and consumption (*geomarketing*).

Throughout its previous chapters, this book has unraveled the ways in which demolinguistics is interested in the composition, distribution, and changes of a population which is characterized by the knowledge or use of one or more languages or linguistic varieties, and how those speakers are quantified, either at a specific moment or over a period of time, whether for descriptive or projective purposes (Moreno-Fernández, 2014). In this way, the goal of demolinguistic studies is to know how linguistic groups spread territorially, how intergenerational linguistic transmission occurs, and what immigrant integration processes are like (Casesnoves & Sankoff, 2006; Potowski, 2018), among other strands. This knowledge makes it possible to contemplate more specific goals, such as approaching the revitalization of a language, facilitating its adaptation to the communicative needs of a community (Mackey, 1968), planning the schooling

DOI: 10.4324/9781003327349-8

of a community, including the teaching program, establishing sociolinguistic indicators such as bilingualism or diglossia within a community, or providing basic information about the social evolution of a language and its community.

The applications of the demography of languages are connected in one way or another with the applications foreseen for general demography. Projections of immigrant populations, for example, affect the possible provision of education and health services in the language(s) of those who are to arrive, and a focus on bilingual communities can project the growth of their population to properly attend to citizenship. Likewise, land use planning can be tied to ethnolinguistic groups with particular characteristics within a state or region, and information about the knowledge of language can prove useful for hiring bilingual employees for companies or administrative services.

Indeed, the list of possible applications of demolinguistics is very long, but it is worth trying to highlight and summarize the most relevant ones. To do so, two different strategies can be contemplated. The first would consist of putting the focus on the objectives pursued; the second concerns applying it to the diversity of situations which can be the focus of demolinguistic analysis. According to the first strategy, it's possible to speak of political, organizational, educational, anthropological, properly linguistic, ideological, or basic research interests, among other possibilities. The list of interests could be very long and, moreover, if these criteria were followed, it would highlight the problem of identifying autonomous interests to the exclusion of other possibilities, which is a very difficult task: doesn't education involve politics? Doesn't linguistics affect education? Doesn't the political offer an ideological backdrop?

Therefore, the approach based on linguistic situations will be followed, without failing to mention the possible interests specific to each analysis. According to this approach, it is possible to order the applications of demolinguistics according to the languages affected in each case, although once more the treatment of different situations plunges us into a conceptual spiral that is difficult to escape: how are the languages identified? What are the limits between them? What are the limits between dialectal varieties? In any case, as is typical in demolinguistics, the spiral can be resolved through practical or operational decisions, providing a *de facto* way out of what reality itself and its theoretical trappings do not otherwise allow us to resolve.

Let us start from a list of linguistic situations that includes the varieties presented with regard to the demolinguistic factors of greatest incidence (see Table 5.6). Among those considered, the following are included for both minority and majority situations, even if such determinations refer to relative or proportional magnitudes, not absolute ones. The kinds of languages handled also reflect the principal attributes that characterize them: ethnic, local, social, regional, immigrant, national, transnational. It is therefore of interest to present some of the principal applications of demolinguistics through some basic types of situations characterized by being located in specific (although diverse) geosociolinguistic domains. At this level of approximation to reality, analyses are usually plural and include data from various sources.

Ethnic, Local, and Social Minority Languages

The study of minority language situations is one of the favorite objectives of demolinguistic analysis. Thus, one of the applications of demography of minority languages it to describe and analyze the demo- and sociolinguistic situation of indigenous, original, or native languages, to know their real situation in contexts that normally do not favor them. However, these studies don't typically place themselves within a demographic discipline, but instead within the field of linguistic ecology and within the study of "linguistic vitality." Nevertheless, this epistemological position does not impede, and in fact demands, that the analysis of minority languages incorporates a quantitative demographic component (Lagos, 2006). In this way, minority languages are clearly possible objects of microdemolinguistic or even nanodemolinguistic analysis.

The Study of Vitality

One of the most expected and demanded objectives of the demographic analysis of languages is knowledge of their vitality. Aspects related to the sources and methods of analysis of the contexts of use of indigenous minority languages (EtMLs) have already been pointed out in the previous chapters. However, it is still appealing to dwell on other experiences with the goal of illustrating the applications of this kind of research. Roland Terborg and Laura García Landa (2011) coordinated a research project titled "The Vitality of the Indigenous Languages of Mexico: A Study in Three Contexts," ("La vitalidad de las lenguas indígenas de México: un estudio en tres contextos") from the National Autonomous University of Mexico (UNAM) which was oriented to both the quantitative analysis of those contexts and studying the pressure that such languages receive within their respective ecolinguistic systems. The Mexican contexts considered in the project were: suburban (San Cristóbal Huichichitlán, near Toluca), rural with easy access (e.g., Santiago Mexquititlán), and rural with difficult access (e.g., Camotlán).

Starting from this division, the Mexican project determined the degree of isolation of the communities where an indigenous language was spoken and their exposure to the maintenance or displacement of their language. The objective was to measure the vitality of each language, the degree of knowledge of Spanish and the indigenous language, their transmission to the next generation, their use in different areas, and the attitudes (speakers' own and that of those outside their communities) toward the languages, as well as to calculate the "maximum shared facility" (MSF). This final factor is ascertained by deciding if the respective languages are "spoken well," "spoken only a little," "understood but not spoken," or "neither spoken nor understood." The fieldwork involves interaction with

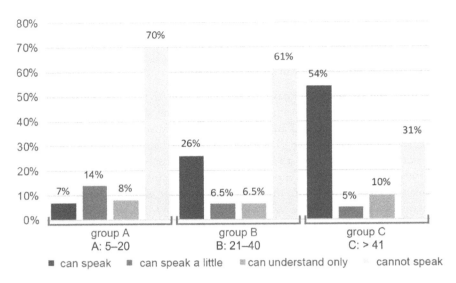

GRAPH 7.1   Knowledge of Totonac in Mecapalapa by age group (Neri, 2011).

samples of speakers of different ages, and the analysis would allow comparison of indigenous languages in different contexts.

The questionnaires used in the Terborg and García Landa project showed some affinities and overlaps with national population surveys. However, the project made it possible to investigate qualitative questions about knowledge of the languages which the census, due to its more generic nature, doesn't usually address. This was achieved through a team of researchers specifically trained in linguistic questioning. On the other hand, the sample of subjects used was smaller than that of the census. The graph shows quantitative information about the use of the Totonac language by age group in Mecapalapa, Puebla (Mexico).

There are numerous studies on indigenous minorities that offer quantitative information regarding their populations, information that on occasion can be interpreted from the perspective of knowledge of languages. Examples of this are the analyses by Vázquez and Quezada (2015) on the Mexican population self-ascribed as indigenous in the years 2000 and 2010.

These analyses and results are the most clearly connected with demography. The way in which the connection between populations and languages is resolved is particular in each case and must confront the multiple conceptual and methodological barriers posed by the task. Cristián Lagos (2006) states in this regard:

> Although there are no quantitative parameters that define when a language possesses greater or lesser vitality, its effective use as a communication tool is the indication of such a condition.
>
> Lagos, 2006

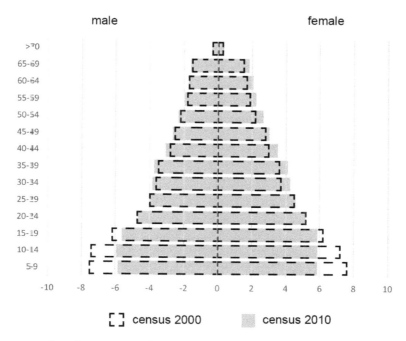

GRAPH 7.2 Population pyramids of persons self-ascribed as indigenous in Mexican censuses of 2000 and 2010.
Source: Vázquez & Quezada (2015).

Indeed, in studies on minority languages, the objective of describing the speaker populations from a demographic perspective (either based on censuses or surveys) tends to extend (or better yet, be subordinate to) the objective of approaching a qualitative description and considering any other factors that affect the vitality of the languages (Breton, 2008). In fact, works on vitality often fail to treat the degree of vitality based on complex statistics but instead qualitatively assess the weight of the variables that can explain and predict the use of minority languages in relation to other majority ones. Along these lines, Fernando Teillier (2013) makes a critical reading of the vitality data present in quantitative research and proposes a qualitative reading that would demonstrate that the vitality of a language can be greater than is indicated by the survey data.

Likewise, it is important to bear in mind that theories of linguistic vitality have the capacity, mainly, to explain situations of linguistic contact in which an "inequality" exists between the coexisting languages and to account for how these situations will evolve over time. This approach places the studies of vitality beyond indigenous or native populations, given the infinite number of situations and contexts in which languages with different degrees of vitality coexist in the world (De Vries, 1994): let us think of French and English in Canada; English and Welsh or Scots in Wales or Scotland; Gaelic and English in Ireland; Basque, Catalan, or Galician and Spanish in Spain. Naturally, this perspective must overcome theoretical and practical drawbacks, given that studies of vitality, for example, tend to treat languages holistically. Nonetheless, on paper, nothing prevents the attempt at an analysis.

The World Map of Minority Languages

Leaving aside studies on the linguistic vitality of specific languages in their respective contexts, one of the lines of work with the greatest international consequence is that of evaluating the level of vitality and the danger of disappearance of minority languages as a whole. For this, it is also necessary to systematize in a general framework all the factors that can influence vitality and the status of languages. The ultimate objective is, through detecting the needs of languages in danger, to contribute to the creation of language policies that allow adequate safeguarding measures to be implemented.

To this general end, UNESCO commissioned an international group of linguists to develop a model that would make it possible to determine the degree of vitality of languages. This group of experts on languages in danger of disappearance created a document titled *Language Vitality and Endangerment* (Brenzinger *et al.*, 2003) that allowed them to address the UNESCO *Atlas of the World's Languages in Danger* (Moseley, 2010). Following this initiative, others have emerged, such as the already mentioned catalog *Ethnologue* or the University of Hawaii's Catalog of Endangered Languages (ELCat) (Campbell, 2017; Lee & Van Way, 2018). ELCat establishes four variables to determine a language's level of danger: intergenerational transmission, absolute number of speakers, speaker number trends, and domains of use of the language. Based on these four variables, ELCat identifies six degrees to measure the state of vitality of languages.

Likewise, computational tools have been developed to understand the state of vitality of the world's languages based on the *Glottolog* language catalog, combined with available data. *GlottoScope* and *GlottoVis* are tools that make use of a mathematical model that groups and establishes correspondences between the primary models for measuring linguistic vitality. This model is called the *Agglomerated Endangerment Scale* (AES) (Hammarström, Forkel, & Haspelmath, 2018).

An interesting exercise in applying demographic information is that practiced by Bromham *et al.* (2021) to predict the future of endangered languages and of linguistic diversity. In their analysis, this team combined the actual size of the population of L1 speakers with the degree of vitality (threat) of the languages, according to the EGIDS system (Lewis & Simons, 2010) (see chapter 2), along with demographic information about the age structure of the population. This allows for a prediction of how many L1 speakers there will be between 2060 and 2100. In this interesting study, the use of demographic information is very

Applications of Demolinguistics 225

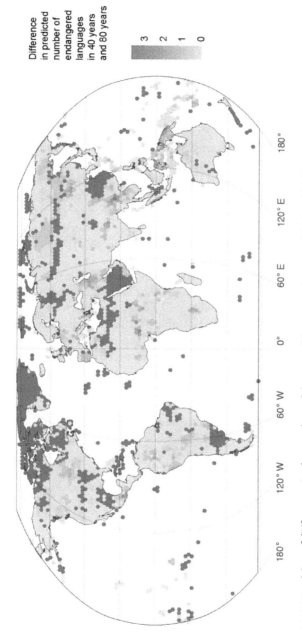

MAP 7.1 Map of differences in the number of threatened languages between 2060 and 2100.
Source: Bromham et al. (2021).

limited, as it simply predicts when all current L1 speakers would have died, in cases where there is no transmission of the language to children. The ideal would have been to work on language transmission rates, but such information is not available for most of the world's languages.

Without action to increase the transmission of languages to younger generations, it is projected that by the end of the twenty-first century, at least 1,500 languages will no longer be spoken. The "hot spots" of future language loss will be the west coast of North America, Central America, the Amazon rainforest, West Africa, the north coast of New Guinea, the north of Australia, Borneo, the southeast of China, and the areas around the Caspian Sea. The greatest proportional loss of languages is predicted to take place in the Arctic, the interior plains of North America, the temperate zones of Chile, and the Sahara. Predictors of language loss include demographics and education, but not contact with other languages. Previously, Gary Simons and Melvin Lewis (2011) calculated that more than 75% of the languages used in 1950 are now extinct or dying in Australia, Canada, and the United States, and that 19% of the world's living languages are no longer learned by children. On the one hand, speculations about the causes of a phenomenon of such dimensions point to widespread settler colonies (Mufwene, 2001) and, on the other, to rampant urbanization across the globe.

What is called the "Rosetta Project" could be interpreted as a complementary objective to the desire to catalog the world's languages in danger. This project, sponsored by the private Long Now Foundation, aims to create a database with all the languages currently in danger of disappearing. Faced with the prospect that, in a few decades, the number of the world's languages will be drastically reduced, an interdisciplinary team joined forces to help conserve the languages that are most clearly in danger of extinction. To do this, a 7.5-centimeter diameter nickel disk was created on which the same text was engraved in numerous languages of the world, including transliterations of languages without writing systems, along with a world map indicating the location and description in English of some 1,000 languages. The text chosen was the first verse of Genesis. The Rosetta Disk, a modern Rosetta Stone of which numerous copies have been made, has been placed in a spacecraft bound for a distant comet and distributed to many places around the world, protected in steel spheres, so that it can be an object of knowledge and study thousands of years in the future.

Controversies Around Vitality

Analyses of linguistic vitality and the catalogs derived from them are no strangers to criticism, either as an object or the subject of the criticized facts. One of the criticisms received by this line of work claims that they represent ideologies from above (top-down) that hide the initiatives and efforts made from the communities from below (bottom-up). This line leads to the apparent paradox of considering endangered languages that have a sizable and solid speech community, as is the case of Quechua and its varieties in the Andean region (Moseley, 2010). Anna María Escobar calls attention to factors of a sociological and anthropological nature, generally "invisible" ones, that should be incorporated as instruments to measure vitality, especially in the case of Amerindian languages. Among these invisible factors would be sociocultural spaces (clubs, restaurants, dances, religious centers...); new genres (popular music, movies, code-switching...); linguistic expressions (poetry, use of characteristic linguistic features...); semi-structural expressions (native alphabets, animation of native stories, audiovisual repertoires of traditions, training of native language teachers...) (Escobar, 2014).

In turn, other ways of treating indigenous minority languages have been severely criticized by vitality studies. One of these refers to the way in which governmental authorities treat the social space of indigenous communities and their cultural manifestations in official statistics. Governments are accused of treating minority contexts superficially and peripherally, specifying that ethnolinguistic differences are ignored, which leads, for example, to official statistics speaking of 350 linguistic varieties in Spanish-speaking America, when for some there are no fewer than 725, leaving the difference in a vague category of "others." As has already been mentioned, these kinds of controversies have two undeniable facts at their root: the difficulty of establishing limits between languages and dialects (or between varieties) and of identifying members of native communities without self-ascription or self-identification.

Studies interested in linguistic ideologies have also dealt with the treatment of indigenous minorities by governments and international bodies. From this perspective, the weight that majority, national, official, or vehicular languages have in the cultural and educational policies of countries is criticized. This being the case, it is taken for granted that the attention to majority languages has two clear effects: on the one hand, the "homogenization" of linguistically diverse territories; on the other, the "invisibilization" of minority realities (Irvine & Gal, 2000) to the point of reaching an insensitivity that facilitated what Louis-Jean Calvet called "linguicide" (Calvet, 1974, 1999) These linguistic consequences oppose the legitimation of majority languages to the exclusion of minority languages, while at the same time overvaluing native-speakerism (Holliday, 2006) which normalizes a use of the majority language without particular accents, especially those derived from the influence of minority languages.

There have been diverse ways of explaining the hegemony of majority languages. One of these is that of Terborg and García Landa (2011), when they speak of the "ecology of pressures."

This ecological system includes basic factors, such as beliefs, values, ideologies, or needs, that determine interests that lead to pressure on the minority groups, also conditioned by the limited knowledge and use of the languages themselves. A related line has followed the ecology of Salikoko Mufwene (2001), based on the concepts of pressure and adaptation. Mufwene has also insisted that languages move with people, for various reasons, including nomadism, long-distance trade,

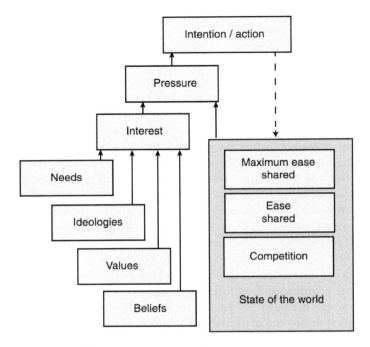

GRAPH 7.3 Ecology of pressures in minority language contexts.
Source: Terborg & García Landa (2011).

colonization, exile and seeking refuge, or deportation. These reasons, which are not mutually exclusive, allow for a better understanding of the differential evolution of languages in the country of origin and in their diasporas due to the different population structures and other ecological conditions resulting from different kinds of migrations (Mufwene, 2017).

Linguistic Revitalization

Language catalogs and specific studies of linguistic vitality make up a necessary information base to address another of the objectives of demolinguistics: the practice of language planning and linguistic policies aimed at linguistic reversion or revitalization. The revitalization of languages is a field of research that emerged in the early 1990s when sociolinguists and anthropologists studying endangered languages began to use the available data on the processes of change and disappearance of the languages with the goal of halting or reversing that disappearance (Fishman, 1991; Friedman, 2011).

Revitalizing policies need some basic information upon which to operate and make decisions, and demolinguistics contributes to providing that. Thus, demolinguistics reveals that there are territories with a large diversity of indigenous minority languages spoken by a very low percentage of the population, as is the case in Brazil, where linguistic diversity affects less than 1% of the total population, whereas in Mexico, Guatemala, or Bolivia, the reference population is much broader. Therefore, diversity and vitality are factors that must be analyzed in a particular way.

Language policies, on the other hand, must take into account the specific characteristics of each context. Therefore, the vitality of the languages and the possible actions that affect them usually use a theoretical model of ecology of the languages (Haugen, 1972; Mühlhäusler, 1996). This model is well established in works on maintenance, displacement, and loss of languages and, therefore, in works about linguistic revitalization. With this goal, linguistic revitalization guides have been proposed (Flores Farfán & Córdova, 2012, 2020), and repertoires of practical cases that illustrate how processes of reverse in diverse places across the world, such as Latin America, Europe, Asia, and Africa, have been developed (Yin, 1989; Malone & Premsrirat, 2005; Flores Farfán, 2011; Essegbey, Henderson, & McLaughlin, 2015). The work of Flores Farfán and Córdova (2020) bears a fairly transparent title in this regard: *Guía de revitalización lingüística: para una gestión formada e informada* (*Linguistic Revitalization Guide: for an Educated and Informed Management*). It covers many aspects that must be considered for adequate management, such as the kinds of speakers, and the treatment of orality, writing, and audiovisual media. Likewise, the rights of linguistic and cultural minorities, not just ethnic ones, have been included in international charters and declarations such as the *European Charter for Minority and Regional Languages* (Council of Europe, 1992), the *Universal Declaration of Linguistic Rights* (UNESCO, 1996), and the UNESCO *Universal Declaration on Cultural Diversity* (UNESCO, 2001).

Local Languages

The world's minority languages are not exclusively located in areas of indigenous populations but are also found in localities of non-indigenous territories. Starting from the division of contexts established by Terborg and García Landa (2011), regional minority languages (ReML) would largely correspond with those used either in suburban or easily accessible contexts. Due to their particular linguistic and cultural history, ReMLs are frequent in European and Asian countries, and this is reflected in the UNESCO *Atlas of the World's Languages in Danger*. This reality contrasts with the indigenous minority languages of America, Africa, and the Pacific.

In terms of their vitality, ReMLs are affected by most of the factors mentioned in relation to EtMLs. In fact, the criteria for considering them as vulnerable, endangered, seriously endangered, or critically endangered languages are identical in both cases. And in both cases, they experience processes of invisibilization and exclusion which linguistic ideology studies have criticized. Like majority languages, these regional minority languages can rely on their ISO country code, but that gives them no guarantee of political recognition beyond the will to protect a cultural heritage that is often not accompanied by any practical or effective actions with a view to maintaining them.

One of the most frequent lines of political and educational action on this type of language, with views to revitalizing them, has been to apply an alphabet and elaborate an orthography. This has been very common in relation to African languages (Essegbey, Henderson, & McLaughlin, 2015), as well as the languages of the Americas, including the North American ones (Reyhner, Cantoni, St. Clair, & Parsons, 1999); it was also an important task of Soviet linguistics with regard to the many minority languages of that territory (Švejcer, 1986). Obviously, writing offers a tangible image of the existence of a language, but this image can be pure illusion if it is not accompanied by a process of maintenance. In this sense, the creation of a writing system reflects a Western model of literacy which requires great institutional support, not always available, and which restricts the process of maintenance to the classroom when small communities often base their communication on other kinds of images and on sound.

Demolinguistic studies focused on regional minority languages are usually interested in three fundamental aspects: the number of speakers, the domains of use, and the treatment the languages receive in schools. Let's look at two examples that are not even included among the 2,464 languages represented in the UNESCO *Atlas*: Mirandese (Portugal) and Palenquero (Colombia).

Mirandese is a linguistic variety from Miranda do Douro (Portugal) and some surrounding villages, historically related to Asturleonese from the north of Spain. In fact, the UNESCO *Atlas* offers Mirandese as an alternative name for Asturleonese used in Portugal. Once more, the question of glottonymy arises and, above all, the question of borders between languages and their varieties, as well as between the varieties themselves. In 2002, Quarteu and Frías offered the figure of 12,000 speakers of Mirandese, divided between residents and migrants. However, Gómez Bautista (2013) states that it is the language of between 6,000 and 10,000 people who live in 29 localities of the municipality of Miranda de Douro and in three settlements of a neighboring municipality. This author also makes mention of the Mirandese speakers of Porto and Lisbon, but without offering any specific quantification.

The demolinguistics of Mirandese reveals that 87.6% of the population surveyed for the study (Gómez Bautista, 2013) understands Mirandese, and 64% knows how to speak it, with larger percentages in the more rural areas. Mirandese was transmitted from parents to children; however, the majority of those surveyed don't speak it with their children, as a result of which the intergenerational transmission might be interrupted, at least in semi-urban contexts. It proves interesting to contrast this last data point with the fact that more than three fourths of those surveyed are of the opinion that it is important that children learn Mirandese.

As of 1999, Mirandese began to be used in municipal assemblies, at public events, especially cultural ones, in some radio broadcasts, and in schools. All

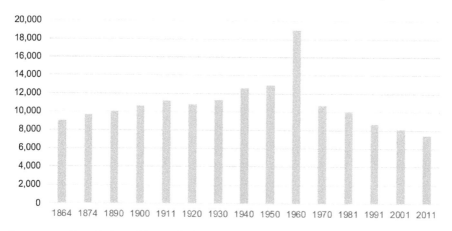

GRAPH 7.4 Population of Miranda do Douro according to the censuses of 1964–2011.
Source: Gómez Bautista (2013).

this was through political will, but especially because of private initiatives or the efforts of professional sectors, such as teachers (Martins, 2008). Despite everything, Mirandese is in danger because of the influence of the national media, the prestige of the majority language, and especially due to the loss of population. The graph shows the intensity of this process since 1960. On the one hand, the loss of population is a factor in the interruption of intergenerational transmission and, on the other, in the reinforcement of the majority language already spoken by emigrants when they return temporarily to their communities of origin.

The introduction of majority languages by populations originating from minority communities is widespread throughout the world and affects local and ethnic groups of all kinds, as occurs in Palenque de San Basilio (Colombia) with the Palenque Creole language. Palenquero is a variety created starting in the eighteenth century in a community near Cartagena de Indias founded by Black Maroons who fled the city seeking freedom. The African origin of the slaves and their coexistence in Cartagena favored the formation of the creole language that survives to this day. The condition of being a "transplanted people" (Ribeiro, 2007) that Palenque de San Basilio has leads us to consider Palenquero as a regional minority language. Demolinguistic analysis of the Palenquero population clearly shows a process mentioned before: the reduction of the population in the age groups with the most intense labor activity.

The population of Palenque, although partially dedicated to the countryside and farming, is sustained mainly by the street vending of traditional sweets, a trade practiced by women for the most part who carry out their sales outside the community. The women travel to the urban centers of Colombia and Venezuela which entails their absence from Palenque for between two and ten months each year. As the men are by and large dedicated to working in the fields, their children are cared for by their grandparents.

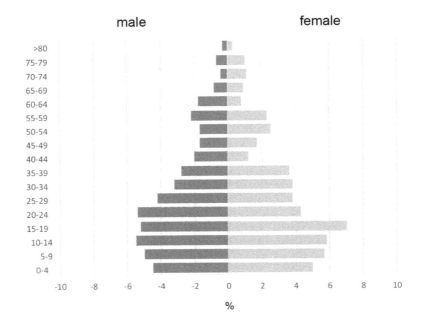

GRAPH 7.5 2009 population pyramid of Palenque de San Basilio. Sociolinguistic self-diagnosis.

Source: Ministry of Culture PPDE, Colombia.

In general, the number of people from Palenque residing in cities like Cartagena, Barranquilla, Maracaibo, and Caracas is significant and, as such, intergenerational transmission, of both language and traditional cultural elements, has been weakened. Added to this is the fact that these trips abroad bring back a lower use of the minority language and a greater presence of the majority language with an inertia that is transmitted within the community. It is true that those Palenqueans who settle in urban contexts conserve some elements of their culture, but these are not usually transmitted to their children. Demolinguistics helps to understand and calibrate these processes, but its contributions do not always imply the practice or effectiveness of political actions.

Social Group Languages

Minority languages can also gain that status for social reasons, not linked to a specific territory or locality. They are social group languages or varieties which are characteristic of or unique to a population identified by sharing a specific relevant attribute. These cases are also susceptible to demolinguistic treatment with the possibility of applying it to the exercise of a language policy. Let's look at two examples of these languages: sign language and Romani—the language of the Roma people.

When it comes to sign languages, let us begin by remembering two basic facts: first, that they have nothing to do with oral languages and are completely independent systems, and second, that it is calculated that there are some 300 sign languages in the world, often one per country, although that is not always the case, given that in Spain, for example, two sign languages exist: Spanish Sign Language (Lengua de Signos Española: LSE) and Catalan Sign Language (Lengua de Signos Catalana: LSC). While having widespread use throughout the United States, American Sign Language (ASL) is also known in other places due to the many means that exist for its dissemination, although the variety that is used in international forums (World Congress of the Deaf, Deafalympics), is International Sign Language.

The World Health Organization (WHO, 2021) reports that the number of people with hearing loss in the world is 360 million (5.3% of the population). In Europe, France is the country with the largest number of sign language users ("signers"), leading to a coding system being created there. In Spain, a country with an oralist tradition, the number of signers is higher than in the United Kingdom, despite the latter having twice the population. The census of deaf people in Spain is made up of approximately one million people, which is equivalent to 2% of the population. In the field of demographic prospections, the WHO reports the existence of 1.1 billion young people worldwide at risk of hearing loss, which points to a possible growth in the population that uses sign languages.

The application of demolinguistics in the field of sign languages is not as easy as it might seem for three reasons. Firstly, because a part of the deaf population communicates orally through lip reading, imitating mouth shapes and breathing patterns, but not through signs. Secondly, because the diversity within the population with hearing loss is very large, including semilingual deaf people who have not managed to acquire an oral language or learn a sign language natively. And thirdly, because there is a non-deaf population, normally with close ties to the deaf community, which knows and uses sign language to communicate with deaf relatives and friends.

Probably as a consequence of the fact that 80% of the world's population lives in developed countries, the demands for rights and political actions that protect them are very visible and often successful. In Spain and Brazil, for example, LSE and Brazilian Sign Language have the status of official languages. However, the list of demands is still long, to a large degree because official status doesn't translate into practical actions. Thus, it is demanded that sign languages be expressly recognized in the *European Charter for Minority and Regional Languages of Europe* (Council of Europe, 1992) but, in addition to that, the removal of all kinds of barriers is also demanded: in education, in justice, in health, in cultural services, in interpreting services, in the media, in public communication, and in emergency telephone numbers, among other areas.

As far as the Romani people are concerned, the European Union has recognized that they constitute the largest ethnic minority in Europe. Between 10 and 12 million Romani live on this continent, of which approximately six million are citizens or residents of the EU. The Roma population presents two defining characteristics when it comes to linguistics: on the one hand, their lack of affiliation to a territory with demarcated borders; on the other, their linguistic diversity. Regarding the first characteristic, one of its consequences is that protective legislation is created in a fragmentary fashion, country by country or even region by region. The ultimate goal is to guarantee the inclusion of the Romani and to implement a genuine European policy, but this task is hampered by the lack of precise data about the Roma population and its distribution, which are often assessed through estimates.

With regard to its linguistic diversity, it is necessary to consider that the Roma population participates in the majority languages of each territory in a very high proportion, and that this is not an obstacle for the maintenance and inter-group use of Romani or any of its varieties, with the added problem that not all of them are conserved intact nor are they subject to equal knowledge by the entire population. The numbers of Romani speakers are extremely varied in Europe and do not always correlate with the Roma population. Thus, it is calculated that in Romania, there must be more than one million speakers of Romani (Bakker & Kyuchov, 2000), whereas Caló, the Romani of Spain, no longer maintains the necessary elements for communication across all domains, while at the same time the majority of Gitano Romani people in Spain have a very limited command of the remaining components.

TABLE 7.1 Estimate of Romani speakers in Europe.

Country	Speakers	Country	Speakers
Albania	90,000	Latvia	18,500
Austria	20,000	Lithuania	4,000
Belarus	27,000	Macedonia	215,000
Belgium	10,000	Moldova	56,000
Bosnia-Herzegovina	40,000	Netherlands	7,000
Bulgaria	600,000	Poland	56,000
Croatia	28,000	Romania	1,030,000
Czech Republic	140,000	Russia	405,000
Denmark	1,500	Serbia & Montenegro	308,000
Estonia	1,100	Slovakia	300,000
Finland	3,000	Slovenia	8,000
France	215,000	Spain	1,000
Germany	85,000	Sweden	9,500
Greece	160,000	Turkey	280,000
Hungary	290,000	Ukraine	113,000
Italy	42,000	United Kingdom	1,000

Source: Bakker & Kyuchov (2000).

This does not deny the ethnic and linguistic reality that the Roma people face in Europe, nor does it justify the absence of a European policy, as the European Union itself acknowledges that many of the Roma people continue to be victims of prejudice and social exclusion, despite this discrimination being forbidden in all the member states. The European policy in this regard is established in the document called the *EU Roma Strategic Framework for Equality, Inclusion, and Participation* (2020).

Immigrant Minority Languages

Immigrant minority languages (ImMLs) play a leading role in many contexts, and their number may also be increasing, given the breadth and intensity of migratory movements in the twenty-first century. The applications of demolinguistics in this field can therefore affect millions of people who find themselves in foreign territories confronting problems of integration in the fields of education, work, justice, and many other aspects of community life.

Language and immigration are closely related phenomena as Einar Haugen pointed out in 1938. François Grin (2003) has distinguished four lines of research that concern the consequences of the contact between languages caused by immigration:

a) The study of discrimination due to the immigrants belonging to a specific linguistic community.
b) The study of the value derived from knowing the majority language of the destination community.
c) The study of the value derived from knowing a useful minority language in the destination community.
d) The study of the value derived from the use of the mother language of the immigrants in the destination community.

These points explain why the social integration of immigrants is affected by their language skills, although the incidence of purely linguistic integration could be more confusing and less direct than would be supposed in principle.

When speaking of sociolinguistic integration, one must systematically appeal to the linguistic and communicative dimensions of the process. The study of these dimensions requires consideration of different aspects related to the coexistence of languages (in this case, one resident language (or variety) and one immigrant language (or variety)) in the destination community and makes it necessary to explain the integration process in relation to the use of the language(s). With regard to the current situation of the languages of Europe, Auer and Hiskens (1996) understand that social and cultural changes are affecting the nature and position of traditional dialects very quickly. European languages are finding themselves immersed in processes that affect different dimensions, one of which is large-scale emigration which provokes the convergence between the dialects imported by large groups of immigrants, as well as the relationship between those new social groups and native geolects.

As has been shown in different contexts of immigration, the volume of the immigrant population, its low cultural level, or the constancy of the flow of new immigrants arriving are factors that influence the maintenance of the immigrant language within the host community. The host community may put into effect public communication mechanisms (administrative, advertising, media) in the language of the immigrant group of largest demographic weight or feel the need to rely on the work of cultural mediators. On the other hand, the social presence of the immigrant language can be increased if it proves useful in economic activities (e.g., tourism). Likewise, when the host community is bilingual or multilingual, the maintenance of linguistic diversity can find itself favored.

The sociolinguistic dynamics of these contexts develop in the individual a proclivity and some positive attitudes to multilingualism (Ambadiang & García Parejo, 2006). In these cases, Richard Fardon and Graham Furniss (1994) speak of a greater ability to adapt to changing sociolinguistic circumstances, taking advantage of the language skills of the people involved in the communicative exchange. When the host community is bilingual, the preference of immigrants for one language or another will be determined by factors such as:

- The distribution of public and private domains of the resident languages.
- Prior knowledge of the resident languages by the immigrants.
- The affinity of the language of the immigrants with each of the resident languages.
- The attitudes of the immigrants toward the resident languages.
- The attitudes of the residents toward the language of the immigrants.

The social, economic, educational, labor, and linguistic importance of all the factors mentioned shows the need to address them from a detailed demolinguistic perspective which is not always considered. In the case of Europe, a good part of the studies on immigrant populations and their languages were done by Guus Extra, who explores issues highlighting the progressive attention that multilingualism has received in Europe. This has involved focusing on the following factors (Extra & Verhoeven, 1993):

a. The sociopolitical context of (non-indigenous) immigrant languages at a macro level.
b. Attitudes toward minorities and their speakers.
c. The use of minority languages in conversation.
d. The interaction between the dominant and minority languages.

e. The process of acquiring the mother tongue in contexts of immersion or submersion.
f. The factors that determine the maintenance, displacement, or loss of the first language.
g. The emergence of new varieties due to the limited domain of the minority language with the dominant ones.

From a demolinguistic perspective, the European Union recognizes four main groups of immigrants: people from the Mediterranean countries of the Union itself; people from the Mediterranean countries outside the Union; people from former colonies; and political refugees. However, statistics do not always allow for a complete and up-to-date picture of immigrants in Europe, and even less so for their linguistic resources, although the European Union does collect, albeit irregularly, information on education and skills, including the linguistic skills of first- and second-generation immigrants through the EU Labour Force Survey (Eurostat, 2014). This survey shows, for example, that only 9% of those born in another EU country and 12% of those born in a non-EU country are considered to have only a basic knowledge of the main language of the host country. Clearly, first-generation immigrants' language skills improve over time. However, even among people who have lived in their host country for ten years or more, 4.1% of those born in another EU country and 7.9% of those born in a non-EU country will only be classed by the EU as having basic knowledge of the language(s) of their host country.

As for asylum seekers, in 2020, nearly half a million requests were presented by people from some 150 countries, among which those that don't require a visa stand out (Venezuela: 7.3%; Colombia: 7%). These statistics do not have a linguistic

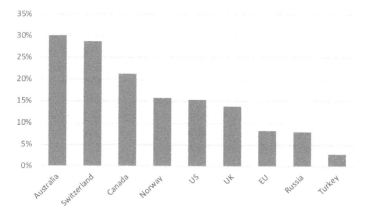

GRAPH 76   EU residents not born in the EU, by country of origin.
Source: Eurostat, OCDE, UNDESA (2020).

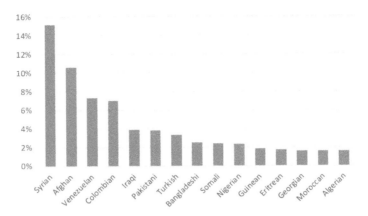

GRAPH 7.7 Main nationalities of people who applied for asylum in the EU for the first time. 2020.

Source: Eurostat.

correlation, so if information is needed about the languages of the immigrants, for educational purposes for example, these must be deduced from nationality. In recent years after the wars in Syria and Ukraine, the number of refugees in Europe has undergone a serious upheaval.

Let us add to the above that the presence of immigrant minority languages does not always originate in people who have crossed borders. In addition to the development of a language in territories where it is not official, there can also be migratory flows and educational processes, as well as internal demographic growth. Take the case of Germany as an example. The group of German users of Spanish is explained by the combination of three factors: Germany is a country relatively favorable to the study of Spanish (Loureda Lamas, Moreno-Fernández, Álvarez Mella, Scheffler, 2020); it is a priority destination for Spanish-speaking immigration to Europe (Bayona-i-Carrasco, 2018; United Nations, 2019); and it features significant migratory demographics. In this context, the group of Spanish speakers in the country shows behaviors aimed at the conservation of the Spanish language (Loureda Lamas, Moreno-Fernández, Álvarez Mella, & Scheffler, 2020). The demography of the languages of migration in their host communities is concerned not only with the state and the evolution of those languages as native languages, but also with their development in speakers with limited proficiency and in language learners of different levels.

Regional and National Languages

Regional minority languages (ReML) have many aspects in common with indigenous minority languages, so it will not be necessary to outline all of their characteristics. In both cases, their relationship with the respective majority languages proves decisive for an analysis of their situation and their possible future developments. In the case of the ReMLs, however, there is a differentiating circumstance with regard to indigenous minority languages, which is the possibility of competing for social space with the majority language, according to the legislation of each country for its territories. This competitive coexistence between the majority language and minority language makes the contribution of demolinguistics more necessary, for its results become more decisive for the possible success of language planning and policy tasks. In this case, the applications of demolinguistics refer to politics and its action in the most diverse social spheres, with special significance for the educational field.

The situation of ReMLs requires the application of demolinguistics for its relevance in the fields of language planning and policy, both in terms of the corpus (form) and the status of the languages. This research provides essential knowledge on intergenerational language transmission, as well as the integration of immigrants (Casesnoves & Sankoff, 2006). In this sense, demolinguistics proves essential for planning the schooling of a community in qualitative and quantitative terms. What's more, its importance is also decisive in the field of language revitalization or its adaptation to the communicative needs of the community. At the same time, demolinguistics contributes to the specification of sociolinguistic indicators, particularly when working with data from specialized surveys, given that these tend to better contextualize the uses and functions of all the languages or varieties that make up the repertoire of a community.

The ways of establishing comparisons between the majority and minority languages of a country can refer to very different aspects and levels. Charles Ferguson (1966), for example, proposed comparing the relationships between the languages within a nation according to their status and function. To that effect, he defines three subcategories of languages: major language (Lmaj), minor language (Lmin), and language of special status (Lspec). An Lmaj within a given country would be that spoken: (a) as a native language by more than 25% of the population; (b) by at least one million people; (c) or used as a language of education. An Lmin would be spoken by at least 5% of the population or at least 100,000 people, and an Lspec would be any language that doesn't reach any of the thresholds established for the other two categories. Ferguson uses demographic criteria to establish differences between the categories.

Throughout the previous chapters, we've shown examples from countries in which the ReMLs have been the most studied demolinguistically and where language policies have taken them most into account, as is the case in Canada, Switzerland, and Spain. It does not seem necessary to insist on this to understand the applications of demolinguistics to these kinds of situations. However, it may be worthwhile to dwell on some aspects related to the coexistence of the national majority languages (NaMaL) and ReMLs, whose analysis and interpretation can be of interest in fields such as political science or ideology.

The first aspect has to do with the connection between "languages" and "nations." This is nothing new, given that we've seen that the identification and delimitation of nations constituted one of the first arguments for including questions about languages in censuses. Even the forerunner to comparative linguistics, Lorenzo Hervás y Panduro (1880), alluded to this in his *Catalog of the Languages of the Known Nations* (*Catálogo de las lenguas de las naciones conocidas*):

> Mankind, then, in the situation and circumstances in which the human race currently finds itself, can be distinguished into nations by means of their customs, and the great diversity of accidents in their corporeal figure: but it has always been possible, men can and will be able to distinguish themselves into nations with greater clarity and exactness by means of the diverse languages they speak. Of these, the wise and ignorant at all times have used and still use this as the most efficient, safe, and certain means by which to distinguish the diverse nations of the human race.
>
> *Hervás y Panduro, 1880*

On the other hand, the matter is intimately linked to the phenomenon of nationalism, no matter whether it is regional and self-identifying or state and official. Here, the concept of "own language," as ascribed to minority language, would also enter the debate, although nothing impedes that "ownership" from also being claimed by the native speakers of a majority language in the context in which it is (Spanish in Mexico) or in those in which it is not (Spanish in the United States). And in this regard, attention to legal questions and the law is of no minor importance, for it must resolve the conflict between minority claims and the exercise of sovereignty (Kraus, 2018).

Generally speaking, for nationalism, language is considered to be an attribute of the territories that administrations and managing bodies or their leaders must protect, support, and spread to the point of exclusivity if possible. It is common for languages to be not just the object of a nationalist treatment, but also of a "nationalist" or "statist" conception (Pohl, 1972); that is, as part of the role of the state or the nation as the center of decisions in the economic, social, and cultural life of a country. On the other hand, this conception is usually accompanied by the naturalization and normalization of a supposed "monolingual" speaker in the language of the nation, a "native" in terms of the supposed "purity" of the accent that they use, which is also denounced as "native-speakerism." In fact, native speakers have become a point of reference for questions as significant as the legitimacy of documentation, the origin of immigrants or refugees, and integration in minority contexts.

Indeed, demolinguistic analyses are in high demand in the field of politics, especially language policy, whose derivations affect education, social services, administration, culture, and social communication media. And it is precisely its use for political goals that requires many precautions to be taken when it comes time to interpret and evaluate demolinguistic analysis. One must consider that often political authorities or entities and institutions controlled from the political sphere are the ones responsible for both compiling the demolinguistic data, through the organization of censuses and surveys, and analyzing these data. It could be said that, to the degree in which the political leaders are conditioned by their particular ideology and electoral interests, the demographic (and also demolinguistic) analyses may be conditioned and even distorted by those same guidelines and interests which would lead us to the conclusion that population statistics are a fallacy.

And in effect, both the data gathered and the analysis practiced could be the object of manipulation, with greater or lesser subtlety. If the "statistical lie" exists then one can also talk of the "demolinguistic lie," although sometimes a lie is confused with an error or imprecision (forced or not). In any event, this does not necessarily need to be so.

At the same time, it should be appreciated that censuses and surveys can be in themselves a mechanism for the production of identities when respondents are asked to specify their social identity and are offered closed identity options from which to choose, or when they are forced to negotiate their identity with the surveyors, with unpredictable results. Added to this is the need to resort to indirect factors, such as nationality or origin, to deduce identity or linguistic information, when censuses are not specifically interested in ethnicity, race, or the language of those surveyed. Such situations also favor the appearance of subjectivity in political decisions.

Nationalism and other political movements are likewise strongly linked to linguistic ideologies, which are guessed at and even presupposed in any demolinguistic approach. Any attention to a majority language, whether promotional or not, is usually interpreted through regional nationalism as an ideologically based decision that leads, if not to "linguicide," then to the invisibilization of the minority language, the iconization of the majority language and identity, and the application of fractal recursive hierarchies (Irvine & Gal, 2000). As the word indicates, invisibilization supposes rendering the minority reality invisible or unappreciable through exclusive or emphatic attention to the majority language. Iconization implies an identification between a language and the social images with which it's associated: languages become iconic representations as if they represented the inherent nature or essence of a social group. Fractal recursion implies the projection of the same criterion on different levels: for example, the correct model of a language can be recognized in a center (the Spanish of the Iberian Peninsula, the English of England) but not in its periphery; in the same way it could be interpreted in any center (Spanish from the Canary Islands, English from Hong Kong) with regard to their respective peripheries. These same criteria would apply, then, to different scales.

These principles of linguistic ideology are complemented by the ideological systems of "anonymity" and "authenticity" proposed by Kathryn Woolard (1998).

In the system of anonymity, languages are understood as abstract subjects, as common voices, a reflection of a "view from nowhere," a socially neutral, objective, and anonymous view. In the system of authenticity, languages are interpreted as a genuine expression of a "self" rooted in a context through which speakers are linked to specific places. Woolard applies these conceptualizations respectively to majority languages (paradigm of anonymity: languages of everyone) and minority ones (paradigm of the authentic and legitimate: autochthonous languages).

Linguistic ideologies can be detected in contexts of diglossic bilingualism, such as that which exists in the United States between English and other second languages, among which Spanish stands out precisely because of its demographics. It is its demographic weight that intimidates broad sectors of American society with an exclusively anglophone base which try to counter other languages through political movements like English Only or U.S. English to eradicate Spanish from the field of public life through various instruments, such as education or the officialization of English in all the states of the union. This ideology of the supremacy of English is deeply rooted in the country from its very constitution and has given rise to numerous episodes of linguistic repression (MacGregor-Mendoza, 2000) that multiply further when the political atmosphere is more radical and populist, as occurred during Donald Trump's term of office (Moreno-Fernández, 2018).

On the other hand, ideological considerations are very palpable in contexts where there are ReMLs that enjoy a very generalized knowledge and recognition, as occurs with Catalan in Catalonia. The question becomes more delicate when the ReMLs are not collectively accepted as such. In these cases, political action becomes more complex and polemical at all levels. Let us take as an example the case of what is called Asturian or Bable in the Asturias region of Spain. In this context, as in others, demolinguistics does its job by offering information about the knowledge and use of the variety in different domains, as well as its acceptance.

TABLE 7.2 Use of Asturian/Bable in formal and semi-formal situations by bilingual speakers.

	More Asturian	*Indistinct*	*More Castilian/ Spanish*	*Indistinct*
Shopping	22.5%	22.5%	37.8%	2.8%
Work	20.3%	20.3%	37.6%	10.2%
Church	19.4%	19.4%	39.8%	10%
Bank	17.5%	17.5%	51.6%	0.9%
Doctor	18.5%	18.5%	51.8%	-
Politics	16.2%	16.2%	42.9%	10.8%
City hall—official paperwork	13.9%	13.9 &	58.6%	1.1%

Source: Llera Ramo & San Martín Antuña (2003).

Demolinguistics shows that the use of Asturian is not majority in any of the expected domains; the indistinct use of both languages is not even the majority. However, the sum of indistinct use and use of Asturian, even if it is not majority, is not quantitatively negligible either. To these arguments one could add that of the diversity of linguistic practices in the use of Asturian. This is the situation that the political class faces when it comes to deciding if Asturian should be considered a language, for reasons of convention, and if that language should have the seal of official status, with all that this entails. Demolinguistics does its job accordingly.

Transnational Majority Languages

The applications of demolinguistics also reach transnational majority languages (TrMaLs). Here "transnational" is understood as those that are spread across various nations, although such languages can also be considered multinational (that is, belonging to many nations) or international (that is, belong to two or more nations, or to countries other than where they originated). As can be deduced from this characterization, majority languages can be native (mother tongues or first languages) or non-native (second languages). In turn, the fact that they function as transnational does not contradict the possibility that, in many contexts, they are minority languages, or social group or immigration languages. In any case, at this time what interests us is their transnational, multinational, and international nature. In fact, in the field of English studies there is an entire line of work called World Englishes that also has a demographic basis (Kachru, 1990, 2017; Kachru, Kachru, & Nelson, 2009).

Transnational majority languages can also be the subject of language policies, as well as of complaints of an ideological nature. In some cases, these languages experience processes of majorization, especially in relation to minority languages, as happened with French in Russia at the time of the Tsars and in the central African republics, or with Spanish in the Americas after 1700. In other cases, majorization is not usually tied so much to cultural interests as political ones: in the 1980s, Soviet linguistics denounced US foreign language policy whose goal was to influence the "Third World," to which end it financed specific centers such as the *Center for Applied Linguistics* or the study group at the University of Hawaii (Švejcer, 1986). From a critical point of view, these international policies have contributed to the formation of an idiomatic oligarchy that competes for the top positions in terms of capacity for influence (Moreno Cabrera, 2014) and which has contributed to the spread of neoliberalism in the world (Martín Rojo & del Percio, 2020).

Demolinguistics is a discipline that allows us to tackle a problematic task: estimating or quantifying the international weight of languages. Likewise, the analysis of the weight of languages raises two fundamental questions: why and for what purpose such analyses are carried out. Obviously, part of these studies is tied to the interest in knowing the number and volume, in terms of quantity of speakers, of the languages of the world. It could be said that this interest has always existed in one way or another, from Lorenzo Hervás y Panduro's *Catalog of the Languages of the Known Nations* to more contemporary initiatives, such as *Linguistic Composition of the Nations of the World* (1974–1984) by Heinz Kloss and Grant McConnell, the *Glottolog* project (Hammarström, Forkel, & Haspelmath, 2018), or the *Ethnologue* catalog (Eberhard, Simons, & Fennig, 2022).

The applications that have been derived from this kind of approach stem from quite varied motivations: from the satisfaction of the enlightened spirit and the development of a long-term investigation, such as those responsible for the Glottolog at the Max Planck Institute, to the desire to know all the languages of the world in order to translate the Bible into them, as happened in the initial development of *Ethnologue* (Paolillo & Das, 2006). However, the analysis of the international importance of languages has been linked to interests that have to do, fundamentally, with politics and economics.

An example of the work that is carried out for political purposes can be found in the publications of the *Organisation International de la Francophonie* (OIF) produced by the *Observatoire de la langue française*. The OIF is a clearly political institutional body dedicated to the promotion of French and the implementation of political, educational, and economic cooperation which functions through summits of heads of state and government, and supports the action of various agencies, such as the OIF itself or the International Association of Francophone Mayors. The reports titled *La langue française dans le monde*, published by the OIF with editions from 2014 and 2019 (Wolff, 2019; Wolff & Aithnard, 2014), offer data on the importance of French in relation to other languages, both in numbers of speakers and domains of use, as well as in geographic distribution.

As examples of studies with economic or commercial aims, those by David Graddol on English (1997, 2006), commissioned by the British Council, might be mentioned. This institution has among its interests the promotion of one of the most notable and idiosyncratic lines of business in the UK economy: the teaching of English. Concerns about this business have already been made clear in Brian McCallen's book (1989), and the conclusions of Graddol's work (2006) are presented as a reference for British providers of English language training and for the broader educational business sector. Likewise, studies derived from the project "El valor económico del español" (The Economic Value of Spanish) (García Delgado, Alonso, & Jiménez, 2012) have been interpreted as studies for commercial purposes, given that the project was sponsored by Fundación Telefónica and that it began at the moment of the company's expansion in Ibero-America (Moreno Cabrera, 2014; De Laurentiis, 2018). This international and interdisciplinary project originates from scientific interests that belong to the "economics of language," a discipline whose results and research questions are relevant for any study that seeks to understand the social conditions in which the languages are used (Heller & Duchêne, 2016; Mufwene & Vigouroux, 2020).

How to Measure the Importance of Languages

Throughout ancient and more recent history, the importance of languages has been established or advocated for following absolutely impressionistic guidelines. Demolinguistics, however, has contributed to approaching this task through analysis of verifiable results which have been consolidated as the phenomenon of globalization has affected culture. It is evident that languages in themselves cannot be ordered by their weight, given that none of them is ahead of the others, neither from a biological point of view nor from an ethnological understanding of language. Despite everything, society, in its public and published opinion, in its institutions, in its educational, social, and economic organizations, demands a hierarchy of languages in the same way that information is demanded about the wealth of nations, best-selling books, most-successful young people, most-beloved teachers, the world's greatest fortunes, the number of visitors to state museums, or the number of doctoral theses presented at universities. Everything is weighed and measured to determine its value, even in the case of things that are difficult to measure. Santiago de Mora-Figueroa, Marqués de Tamarón, stated in 1992:

> But perhaps some of the most-determining foundations of the international importance of a language are completely imponderable, and I use imponderable in its triple meaning: "that which cannot be weighed," "that which exceeds all consideration" and "an unforeseeable circumstance or one whose consequences cannot be estimated."
>
> Marqués de Tamarón, 1992

Those approaches aimed at estimating the international weight of languages can be grouped according to the criteria on which their elaboration is based: the perception of importance, the estimation of scores, and the calculation of complex indices.

a. Perceived importance

Perceived importance is a parameter that is estimated and observed in very different fields of the individual and social life, and so, naturally, it is not foreign to languages, neither because of their linguistic characteristics, nor for the cultures to which they belong, nor for their use in social life. This perception can be calibrated or measured in different ways. One way to assess the perceived importance of languages is simply to ask the subjects about their perception. Thus, the Eurobarometer reports of the European Union titled "Europeans and their Languages" (2006, 2012) include information obtained through questions such as these:

> Thinking about languages other than your mother tongue, which two languages do you think are the most useful for your personal development?

And for children to learn for their future?

Eurobarometer, 2012

The answers to these questions allow the importance of languages to be evaluated in terms of their present and future use according to the spontaneous opinion of those surveyed.

b. Estimated importance

A second procedure for assessing the international weight of languages consists of making a rough estimation or guess. To do this, a particular score can be attributed to each language according to a previously established scale: for example, from 0 to 5 or from 0 to 100. For the construction of each scale, different criteria are generally taken into account which are, in turn, quantified with the goal of building a final overall score. An example of this procedure is that followed by George Weber (1997) to classify the ten most influential languages of the world. He started with six factors to which he gave a score whose sum could reach a maximum of 38 points: for the economic power of the countries where the language is spoken, 8 points; for the number of areas of activity in which the language is important, a maximum of 8 points; for the number and population of the countries that use the language, 7 points; for the number of speakers as a second language, a maximum of 6 points; for the "socio-literary prestige" [sic] of the language, a maximum of 4 points; for its official status at the United Nations, 1 point. Thus, the estimation of the importance supposes the systematic incorporation of factors like those mentioned in earlier chapters. And those factors become more relevant when subjected to more stringent calculations.

c) Calculated importance

When the analysis is carried out based on parameters, indicators, and indexes, treated by means of mathematical models and formulas, the calculation of the importance of languages is addressed. This calculation makes it possible to establish classifications based on precise and objective data. This intended objectivity fails to avoid fundamental obstacles of a qualitative and methodological nature, such as the choice of the parameters and indicators that have to be handled for the calculation or the source of the data handled. Let's look at a couple of examples that have already been presented, although others could easily be added to these, such as the Calvet Language Barometer (Calvet & Calvet, 2022) or Kai L. Chan's Power Language Index (PLI) (2016).

In 1993, Dutch sociologist Abram de Swaan proposed the calculation of a "Q" index to determine the value of languages in communication, considering their potential to relate some speakers to others. The Q value provides a comparative criterion to distinguish between languages on the rise and those in decline. The importance of a language depends, then, on its relative position within a global constellation of languages. De Swaan proposes to calculate the "prevalence" of a language, considering the number of speakers competent in it, divided by the total number of speakers in the constellation. This measures the proportions of people with whom a direct contact through a given language is possible. Along with this, the degree of "centrality" of a language is defined by the number of multilingual speakers who are competent in a language, divided by the total number of multilingual speakers in its constellation. The Q value or communication value of a language is the product of the "prevalence" and "centrality" of a language in a given constellation.

For its part, the index of the international importance of languages proposed by Marqués de Tamarón, applied by Jaime Otero Roth and later by Francisco Moreno-Fernández and Héctor Álvarez Mella (2022), numerically and comparatively represents the internationality of languages based on six quantitative indicators. The index is constructed from the number of native speakers of a language, the number of countries where the language holds official status, the Human Development Index (HDI) of those countries, their exports, the number of translations from which it is a source language, and its official status at the United Nations. These six components make it possible to represent different dimensions of internationality: demographic, political, societal, economic, cultural, and diplomatic. The methodology is not exempt from difficulties, such as deciding the source from which to take the number of speakers or considering that the choice of an indicator is not independent of the choice of the rest, since some components compensate or complement the possible limitations (or counterbalance the weights) of the others. In fact, the research itself reflects an interesting sequence of methodological decisions.

From the calculation of these indices, different comparisons and estimations can be made. These graphs compare the relative positions of languages according to the indexes of importance of languages (ILI) from 1995 and 2015, on the one hand (graph 7.8.1), and from 2015 and 2020 on the other (graph 7.8.2) (Moreno-Fernández and Álvarez Mella, 2022).

This graphic representation allows for comparison of the evolution of the index of each language at the three moments considered. The languages located to the right of the dotted line are those whose index presents values that have improved with regard to the earlier analysis, whereas those located to the left are those whose position has worsened. Between ILI1995 and ILI2015 (graph 7.8.1), only Spanish, Hindi, and especially Chinese improved their relative values. Their repositioning is due in part to methodological aspects that affect the calculation, such as the way of assigning an HDI to each language, but also to demographic growth and the economic and social improvements that took place in Latin America, India, and China during the reference period.

The comparison between ILI2015 and ILI2020 (graph 7.8.2) shows minor changes in the relative positions of the languages which can be seen from the

248 Applications of Demolinguistics

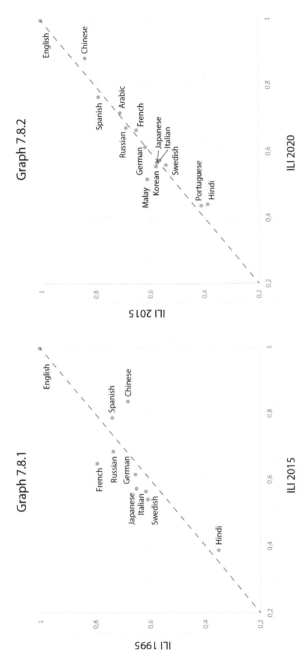

GRAPH 7.8 Comparison of the relative positions of languages according to their IL from 1995 to 2015 (graph 7.8.1) and from 2015 to 2020 (graph 7.8.2).

fact that most of the points touch the diagonal line or are very close to it. On the side of the languages that improve their position (right), the indices of Hindi and Chinese stand out as rising. On the other hand, Spanish, the other language that had improved its index between 1995 and 2015, loses weight, conditioned by the slowdown in the social and economic development of Latin America (Carrera & Domínguez, 2017; CEPAL, 2017).

The information collected by projects such as those mentioned earlier in this section finds very diverse applications. Knowing the international weight of a language, even if it is relative or approximate, can be of value in various fields, including:

i. The political recognition of linguistic realities.
ii. International relations.
iii. Decisions on official and working languages in international organizations.
iv. The public use of some languages or others.
v. Decisions in cultural industries (editions, translations, distributions).
vi. The information and entertainment audiovisual media market (dubbing and subtitling).
vii. Opening international markets according to language affinities.
viii. Forecasting and organizing the educational offering of foreign languages in each country.

As is expected and even reasonable, such proposals have been reviewed critically (Calvet, 1974; Junyent, 1993; Del Valle, 2013), generally with the aim of discovering and denouncing the intentions of the groups with power. Such external criticism is not incompatible with the development of a "critical demolinguistics" that makes use of its instruments to establish and verify its comparison criteria, to discover realities hidden for unpredictable interests, or to search for objective evidence on trends in the sociopolitical evolution of languages and their communities.

Criticism should not ignore, however, that these analyses contribute to highlighting facts of reality that are little valued and sometimes unnoticed. In the case of the Spanish language, analyses revealed, for example, the high proportion of Spanish speakers in Belize, the linguistic complexity of Equatorial Guinea, the solid implantation of the Spanish language in Puerto Rico, the relative educational weight of indigenous languages in Peru and Bolivia, and the large percentage of speakers with native command of Spanish in the Hispanic territory overall (Moreno-Fernández & Otero, 1998, 2006, 2009). The causes for all this deserve deeper historical, cultural, sociological, and ideological analysis, and demolinguistics contributes decisively to its development.

Summary

One of the big questions raised by demolinguistics is the purpose with which its databases, calculations, and analyses are organized, which places us in the field of applications, of great interest for any demographic study. The applications of demolinguistics, as is the case for demography, have a marked sociopolitical nature. Demolinguistic analyses help us to know a fundamental dimension of populations: that related to the language(s) or variety(ies) with which they communicate. This dimension is clearly appreciated in the fields of public communication, internal and external community relations, administration, justice, education, and the social and cultural life of a community. The applications of demolinguistics, therefore, are of interest to politics, insofar as it regulates the social life of populations, and to the planning of services of all kinds.

Taking the action of demolinguistics to specific spaces, it is possible to observe applications according to the kinds of contexts in which the languages are used and according to the social nature of those same languages. Thus, the demolinguistic analysis of indigenous minority languages allows us to achieve a very important objective: to know the degree of vitality of the languages. It is evident that the maintenance, displacement, or substitution of languages cannot be exclusively explained from data on the speaker populations, but the number of speakers or generational transmission are essential factors in any possible explanation. Once the vitality of the languages is known, individually or in the form of atlases or catalogs, it is possible to think of tackling more complex and ambitious objectives: the revitalization of languages or reversal of their decline.

In the field of minority languages, the contexts of local languages can be distinguished from those that correspond to the languages of social groups and immigrant languages. Each of these contexts meets different conditions and, therefore, the data that demolinguistics provides can find diverse applications, such as the knowledge and preservation of local languages, the official protection of the languages of groups, such as sign language or Romani, and educational planning for young immigrants according to their linguistic origins and their educational levels.

Demolinguistics, on the other hand, also finds sense in analyzing the contexts of regional minority languages in which nationalist demands become more intense and conscious. This forces states to act through policies which, in some way, coordinate regional interests with state ones, and the needs of the speakers of the majority languages with those of the minority ones, which often do not enjoy sufficient presence within their geosocial domain. In such contexts, the organization of educational systems is a critical element, as well as the presence of the languages in public media and social communication.

Finally, demolinguistics is a fundamental component of the analysis of the international weight or importance of languages. To this end, the factors involved in the analyses are very diverse, but among these, those related to the composition and size of the population of speakers are crucial. The applications of these analyses are also evident in the fields of politics, services, commerce, and culture.

References

Ambadiang, Theophile and Isabel García Parejo (2006): "La cultura lingüística y el componente cultural en la enseñanza de lenguas no maternas: observaciones sobre algunos paradigmas de la competencia cultural". *Didáctica (Lengua y Literatura),* 18: 61–92.

Auer, Peter and Frans Hinskens (1996): "The convergence and divergence of dialects in Europe. New and not so new developments in an old area". *Sociolinguistica,* 10: 1–30.

Bakker, Peter (2001): "Romani in Europe". In G. Extra and D. Gorter (eds.), *The Other Languages of Europe.* Clevedon: Multilingual Matters, pp. 293–313.

Bakker, Peter and Hristo Kyuchukov (eds.) (2000): *What is the Romani Language?.* Hatfield: University of Hertfordshire Press.

Bayona-i-Carrasco, Jordi, Isabel Pujadas Rúbies and Rosalía Avila Tàpies (2018): "Europa como nuevo destino de las migraciones latinoamericanas y caribeñas". *Biblio3W: Revista Bibliográfica de Geografía y Ciencias Sociales,* XXIII: 1.242. Barcelona: Universidad de Barcelona.

Brenzinger, Matthias, Tjeerd de Graaf, Arienne Dwyer, Colette Grinevald, Michael Krauss, Osahito Miyaoka, Nicholas Olster, Osamu Sakiyama, María Villalón, Akira Yamamoto, Ofelia Zepeda (2003): *Language Vitality and Endangerment: UNESCO Ad Hoc Expert Group Meeting on Endangered Languages.* Paris: UNESCO.

Breton, Roland (2008): *Atlas des minorités dans le monde: panorama des identités culturelles et ethniques.* Paris: Autrement.

Bromham, Lindell, Russell Dinnage, Hedvig Skirgård, Andrew Ritchie, Marcel Cardillo, Felicity Meakins, Simon Greenhill, and Xia Hua (2021): "Global predictors of language endangerment and the future of linguistic diversity". *Nature Ecology & Evolution,* 6: 163–173.

Calvet, Alain and Louis-Jean Calvet (2022): *Baromètre Calvet des langues du monde.* Paris: Ministère de la Culture.

Calvet, Louis-Jean (1974): *Linguistique et colonialismo: petit traité de glottophagie.* Paris: Payot.

Calvet, Louis-Jean (1999): *Pour une écologie des langues du monde.* Paris: Plon.

Campbell, Lyle (2017): *About the Endangered Languages Project.* http://endangeredlanguages.com/about/ Online resource.

Carrera Troyano, Miguel and Rafael Domínguez Martín (2017): "Reducción de la pobreza en Brasil y México: crecimiento, desigualdad y políticas públicas". *Revista de Economía Mundial,* 45: 23–42.

Casesnoves, Raquel-Ferrer and David Sankoff (2006): "El proceso de inversión de la sustitución lingüística: modelos de transmisión, escolarización y asimilación para proyecciones demolingüísticas". In M. Sedano, A. Bolívar, and M. Shiro (eds.), *Haciendo lingüística: homenaje a Paola Bentivoglio.* Caracas: Universidad Central de Venezuela, pp. 717–736.

CEPAL (2017): *Estudio económico de América Latina y el Caribe 2017: la dinámica del ciclo económico actual y los desafíos de política para dinamizar la inversión y el crecimiento.* Santiago: CEPAL.

Chan, Kai L. (2016): *Power Language Index: Which are the World's Most Influential Languages?.* Fontainebleau: Institut Européen d'Administration des Affaires. Accessible at http://www.kailchan.ca/wp-content/uploads/2016/12/Kai-Chan_Power-Language-Index-full-report_2016_v2.pdf

Council of Europe (1992): *European Charter for Regional or Minority Languages*. Strasbourg: Council of Europe.

De Laurentiis, Antonella (2019): "'Unidad en la diversidad': el valor económico de la lengua española". In M. Colucciello, G. D'Angelo, and R. Minervini (eds.), *Ensayos americanos*. Bogotá: Penguin Random House Grupo Editorial, pp. 343–370.

De Swaan, Abram (1993). "The evolving European language system: a theory of communication potential and language competition". *International Political Science Review*, 14: 241–255.

De Vries, John (1994): "Canada's official language communities: an overview of the current demolinguistic Situation", *International Journal of Sociology of Language*, 1994: 37–68.

Del Valle, José (2013): *A Political History of Spanish: The Making of a Language*. Cambridge: Cambridge University Press.

Eberhard, David, Gary Simons, and Charles D. Fennig (eds.) (2022): *Ethnologue: Languages of the World*, 245th ed. Dallas: SIL International. Online version: http://www.ethnologue.com.

Escobar, Anna María (2014): "Haciendo visible lo invisible: contacto de lenguas e instrumentos de vitalidad lingüística". In L. Zajícová and R. Zámec (eds.), *Lengua y política en América Latina: perspectivas actuales*. Olomouci: Univerzita Palackého., pp. 149–175.

Essegbey, James, Brent Henderson, and Fiona McLaughlin (eds.) (2015): *Language Documentation and Endangerment in Africa*. Amsterdam: John Benjamins.

Eurobarometer (2006): *Los europeos y sus lenguas*. Special 243. European Commission. https://europa.eu/eurobarometer/surveys/detail/518 Online resource.

Eurobarometer (2012): *Los europeos y sus lenguas*. Special 386. European Commission. https://europa.eu/eurobarometer/surveys/detail/1049 Online resource.

European Commission (2020): *The New EU Roma Strategic Framework for Equality, Inclusion and Participation*. https://commission.europa.eu/publications/new-eu-roma-strategic-framework-equality-inclusion-and-participation-full-package_en Online resource.

Eurostat (2014): *EU Labour Force Survey*. https://ec.europa.eu/eurostat/web/microdata/european-union-labour-force-survey Online resource.

Eurostat (2021): *Statistics on Migration to Europe*. European Commission. https://ec.europa.eu/info/strategy/priorities-2019-2024/promoting-our-european-way-life/statistics-migration-europe_en Online resource.

Extra, Guus and Ludo Verhoeven (eds.) (1993): *Immigrant Languages in Europe*. Clevedon: Multilingual Matters.

Fardon, Richard and Graham Furniss (1994): *African Languages, Development and the State*. London: Routledge.

Ferguson, Charles (1966): "National Sociolinguistic Profile Formulas". In W. Bright (ed.), *Sociolinguistics: Proceedings of the UCLA Sociolinguistics Conference, 1964*. The Hague: Mouton, pp. 309–315.

Fishman, Joshua (1991): *Reversing Language Shift*. Clevedon: Multilingual Matters.

Flores Farfán, José Antonio (2011): "Keeping the fire alive: a decade of language revitalization in Mexico". *International Journal of the Sociology of Language*, 2011: 189–209.

Flores Farfán, José Antonio and Lorena Córdova (2012, 2020): *Guía de revitalización lingüística*. https://es.calameo.com/read/004494715731854c1d4df Online resource.

Friedman, Debra (2011): "Language Socialization and Language Revitalization". In A. Duranti, E. Ochs, and B.B. Schieffelin (eds.) *The Handbook of Language Socialization*. Oxford: Blackwell, pp. 631–647.
García Delgado, José Luis, José Antonio Alonso, and Juan Carlos Jiménez (2007, 2012): *Economía del español: una introducción*. Barcelona: Ariel.
Gómez Bautista, Alberto (2013): *El mirandés: contexto y procesos de formación de palabras*. Madrid: Universidad Complutense.
Graddol, David (1997): *The Future of English?*. London: British Council.
Graddol, David (2006): *English Next*. London: British Council.
Grin, François (2003): *Language Policy Evaluation and the European Charter for Regional or Minority Languages*. London: Palgrave.
Hammarström, Harald, Robert Forkel, and Martin Haspelmath (2018): Glottolog 3.3. Jena: Max Planck Institute for the Science of Human History.
Haugen, Einar (1938): "Language and immigration". *Norwegian-American Studies and Records*, 10: 1–43. In Haugen, Einar (1972) *The Ecology of Language*. Stanford: Stanford University Press, pp. 1–36.
Haugen, Einar (1972): *The Ecology of Language*. Stanford: Stanford University Press.
Heller, Monica and Alexandre Duchêne (2016): "Treating Language as an Economic Resource: Discourse, Data and Debate". In N. Coupland (ed.), *Sociolinguistics: Theoretical Debates*. Cambridge: Cambridge University Press, pp. 139–156.
Hervás y Panduro, Lorenzo (1800–1805): *Catálogo de las lenguas de las naciones conocidas*. Madrid: Administración del Real Arbitrio de Beneficencia.
Holliday, Adrian (2006): "Native-speakerism". *ELT Journal*, 60: 385–387.
Irvine, Judith and Susan Gal (2000): "Language Ideology and Linguistic Differentiation". In P. Kroskrity (ed.), *Regimes of Language: Ideologies, Polities, and Identities*. Santa Fe: School of American Research Press, pp. 35–84.
Junyent, M. Carme (1993): *Las lenguas del mundo: una introducción*. Barcelona: Octaedro.
Kachru, Braj (1990): *The Alchemy of English: The Spread, Functions, and Models of Non-native Englishes*. Urbana-Chicago: University of Illinois Press.
Kachru, Braj (2017): *World Englishes and Culture Wars*. Cambridge: Cambridge University Press.
Kachru, Braj, Yamuna Kachru, and Cecil Nelson (eds.) (2009): *The Handbook of World Englishes*. Oxford: Wiley-Blackwell.
Kloss, Heinz and Grant McConnell (eds.) (1974–1984): *Linguistic Composition of the Nations of the World, Vol. 2: North America*. Québec: Presses de l'Université Laval.
Kraus, Peter A. (2018): "Between minority protection and linguistic sovereignty". *Revista de Llengua i Dret*, 69: 6–17.
Lagos, Cristián (2006): "Mapudungun en Santiago de Chile: vitalidad, lealtad y actitudes lingüísticas". *Lenguas Modernas*, 31: 97–126.
Lee, Nala H. and John R. Van Way (2018): "The Language Endangerment Index". In L. Campbell and A. Belew (eds.), *Cataloguing the World's Endangered Languages*. London: Routledge, pp. 66–78.
Lewis, M. Paul and Gary F. Simons (2010): "Assessing endangerment: expanding Fishman's GIDS". *Revue Roumaine de Linguistique*, 55:103–120. http://www.lingv.ro/resources/scmimages/RRL-02-2010- Lewis.pdf.
Llera Ramo, Francisco José and Pablo San Martín Antuña (2003): *II estudio sociolingüístico de Asturias*. Uviéu: Academia de la Llingua Asturiana.
Loureda Lamas, Óscar, Francisco Moreno-Fernández, Héctor Álvarez Mella, and David Scheffler (2020): *Demolingüística del español en Alemania*. Madrid: Instituto Cervantes.

MacGregor-Mendoza, P. (2000): "Aquí no se habla español: stories of linguistic repression in Southwest schools". *Bilingual Research Journal*, 24: 355–367.

Mackey, William F. (1968): "The Description of Bilingualism". In J. Fishman (ed.), *Readings in the Sociology of Language*. Berlin: De Gruyter, pp. 554–584.

Malone, Dennis and Suwilai Premsrirat (2005): *Language Development and Language Revitalization in Asia*. Salaya: Mahidol University / SIL International.

Marqués de Tamarón (1992): "El español, ¿lengua internacional o 'lingua franca'?". *Actas del congreso de la lengua española: Sevilla, 7 al 10 octubre*. Madrid: Instituto Cervantes, pp. 189–211.

Martín Rojo, Luisa and Alfonso Del Percio (2020): *Language and Neoliberal Governmentality*. London: Routledge.

Martins, Cristina (2008): *Línguas em contacto, "saber sobre" o que as distingue*. Coimbra: Imprensa da Universidade de Coimbra.

McCallen, Brian (1989): *English: A World Commodity. The International Market for Training in English as a Foreign Language*. London: Economist Intelligence Unit.

Moreno Cabrera, Juan Carlos (2014): *El nacionalismo lingüístico: una ideología destructiva*. Barcelona: Península.

Moreno-Fernández, Francisco (2014): "Fundamentos de demografía lingüística: a propósito de la lengua española". *Revista Internacional de Lingüística Iberoamericana*, 12: 19–38.

Moreno-Fernández, Francisco (2018): "La represión lingüística del español en Estados Unidos". The New York Times, 23.06.2018.

Moreno-Fernández, Francisco and Héctor Álvarez Mella (2022): "Reexamining the international importance of languages". *HCIAS Working Papers on Ibero-America*, 1. https://journals.ub.uni-heidelberg.de/index.php/hciaswp/article/view/84517.

Moreno-Fernández, Francisco and Jaime Otero Roth (1998): "Demografía de la lengua española". In *El español en el mundo. Anuario del Instituto Cervantes 1998*. Madrid: Instituto Cervantes-Arco / Libros, pp. 59–86.

Moreno-Fernández, Francisco and Jaime Otero Roth (2006): *Demografía de la lengua española*. Madrid: Instituto Complutense de Estudios Internacionales.

Moreno-Fernández, Francisco and Jaime Otero Roth (2009): *Atlas de la lengua española en el mundo*. 3rd ed. Barcelona: Ariel.

Moseley, Christopher (ed.) (2010): *Atlas of the World's Languages in Danger*. 3rd ed. Paris: UNESCO Publishing.

Mufwene, Salikoko (2001): *The Ecology of Language Evolution*. Cambridge: Cambridge University Press.

Mufwene, Salikoko (2017): "Population Movements, Language Contact, Linguistic Diversity, Etc. A Postscript". In E.A. Albaugh and K.M. de Luna (eds.), *Tracing Language Movements in Africa*. Oxford: Oxford University Press, pp. 387–414.

Mufwene, Salikoko and Cecile Vigouroux (2020): "Do Linguists Need Economics and Economists Linguistics?". In S. Mufwene and C. Vigouroux (eds.), *Bridging Linguistics and Economics*. Cambridge: Cambridge University Press, pp. 1–55.

Mühlhäusler, Peter (1996): *Linguistic Ecology: Language Change and Linguistic Imperialism in the Pacific Region*. London: Routledge.

Neri, Lourdes (2011): "El desplazamiento de la lengua totonaca en la comunidad de Mecapalapa, Pantepec, Puebla". In R. Terborg and L. García Landa (eds.), *Muerte y vitalidad de lenguas indígenas y las presiones sobre sus hablantes*. México: UNAM, pp. 153–176.

Paolillo, John and Anupam Das (2006): *Evaluating Language Statistics: The Ethnologue and Beyond*. Montréal: UNESCO Institute for Statistics.

Pohl, Jacques (1972): "Demolinguistique et problemes des langues". *Monda Lingvo-Problemo*, 4: 129–141.
Potowski, Kim (ed.) (2018): *The Routledge Handbook of Spanish as a Heritage Language*. London: Routledge.
Quarteu, Reis and Xavier Frías Conde (2002): "L mirandés: ua lhéngua minoritaira an Pertual". *Ianua: Revista Philologica Romanica*, 2: 89–105.
Reques Velasco, Pedro (2011): *Geodemografía: fundamentos conceptuales y metodológicos*. Santander: Universidad de Cantabria.
Reyhner, Jon, Gina Cantoni, Robert N. St. Clair, and Evangeline Parsons Yazzi (eds.) (1999): *Revitalizing Indigenous Languages*. Flagstaff: Northern Arizona University.
Ribeiro, Darcy (2007): *As Américas e a civilização: proceso de formação e causas do desenvolvimento desiguel dos povos americanos*. São Paulo: Companhia das Letras.
Rowland, Donald (2003): *Demographic Methods and Concepts*. Oxford: Oxford University Press.
Simons, Gary F. and M. Paul Lewis (2011): "Making EGIDS assessments". Unpublished working paper.
Švejcer, Aleksandr (1986): *Contemporary Sociolinguistics: Theory, Problems, Methods*. Amsterdam: John Benjamins.
Teillier, Fernando (2013): "Vitalidad lingüística del Mapudungun en Chile y epistemología del hablante". *Revista de Lingüística Teórica and Aplicada*, 51: 53–70.
Terborg, Roland and Laura García Landa (eds.) (2011): *Muerte y vitalidad de lenguas indígenas y las presiones sobre sus hablantes*. México: UNAM.
UNESCO (1996): *Universal Declaration of Linguistic Rights*. Barcelona: UNESCO.
UNESCO (2001): *Universal Declaration on Cultural Diversity*. Paris: UNESCO.
United Nations (2019): *UN Department of Economic and Social Affairs Population Division Databank*. New York: UN.
Vázquez Sandrin, Germán and María Félix Quezada (2015): "Los indígenas autoadscritos de México en el censo 2010: ¿revitalización étnica o sobreestimación censal?". *Papeles de Población*, 21: 171–218.
Weber, George (1997). "Top languages: the world's 10 most influential languages". *Language Today*, 2: 12–18. Reprinted in *American Association of Teachers of French National Bulletin*, 24: 22–28.
Wolff, Alexandre (2019): *La langue française dans le monde 2015–2018*. Paris: Gallimard.
Wolff, Alexandre and Aminata Aithnard (2014): *La langue française dans le monde*. Paris: Nathan.
Woolard, Kathryn (1998): "Introduction: Language Ideology as a Field of Inquiry". In B.B. Schieffelin, K.A. Woolard, and P.V. Kroskrity (eds.), *Language Ideologies: Practice and Theory*. Oxford: Oxford University Press, pp. 3–50.
World Health Organization (2021): *World Report on Hearing: Executive Summary*. Geneva: WHO.
Yin, Ma (ed.) (1989): *China's Minority Nationalities*. Beijing: Foreign Language Press.

CONCLUSION

One of the first and most prominent experts in demolinguistic issues, John De Vries, explained in 1987 how the study of minority languages had developed since Uriel Weinreich published his well-known book *Languages in Contact* (1953) and Einar Haugen his guide on studies of bilingualism (1956). Curiously, the trends pointed out by De Vries are still valid *mutatis mutandis* and let us glimpse the discipline's future trajectory.

First of all, demolinguistic study, without having lost interest among linguists, has attracted specialists from very diverse fields: ethnography, sociology, anthropology, history, political science, economics, statistics, and demography itself. Many are experts in social sciences who make valuable contributions to this field, which has resulted in a proliferation of interdisciplinary approaches. However, this hasn't prevented many experts from working without (the benefit of) interdisciplinary dialogue.

Secondly, the proliferation of institutions, organizations, and groups interested in linguistic diversity, including its demographic dimension, deserves mention. In addition to the study centers already established in the 1980s in Canada, Belgium, Sweden, and the United States, one must consider the contributions of statistics institutes and census offices, and the initiatives for the inventory or analysis of world languages, as well as those organizations concerned with the sociocultural dimension of the peoples of this planet, championed by UNESCO and other bodies of the United Nations Organization.

Language Demography has presented theories, methods, and works evolving from macrodemolinguistic, microdemolinguistic, and even nanodemolinguistic approaches. Throughout all of them, underlying conceptual pitfalls and formal methodological difficulties have been identified, but even so, we've demonstrated the projection of demolinguistics into different spaces and levels of the sociolinguistic reality of many populations of the world. This is because demolinguistics allows for the description and analysis of minority languages of an ethnic nature, regional and immigrant minority languages, and local and social minority varieties, together with majority, national, and transnational languages. These works are carried out both independently for each language and population, and by contrasting or comparing groups of speakers of the same (bilingual or multilingual) communities. The common methodological space of all this, as well as the meeting point between linguistics, demography, statistics, and politics, is found in censuses and surveys as they are carried out and analyzed.

Demolinguistics does not aspire to unify or homogenize the ways of understanding the reality of communities of speakers, nor the ways in which bilingualism occurs, nor the evolution of the vitality of each language in its respective contexts. This is not, therefore, a proposal of an epistemological integration of well-differentiated disciplines such as anthropology, ethnography, ecology, sociology, economics, law, or linguistics. Instead, it emphasizes the existence of a common denominator for all of them, which is none other than the demography of languages, insofar as all of these disciplines are interested in phenomena of population dimensions. That denominator receives here the form of the foundations of demolinguistic analysis:

$$\frac{\text{Ethnography} + \text{Ecology} + \text{Sociology} + \text{Linguistics} + \text{Economy}}{\text{Demolinguistics}}$$

Using Coleman's boat to represent the relationship between the different areas concurring in the field of demolinguistics and the interactions produced among them at different levels, we can see how interest in linguistic vitality, in its most general sense, has shifted to an interest in the relations between transnational languages. Therefore, on a more specific level, it is possible to appreciate the evolution from the interest in territorial phenomena to an interest in the population processes derived from mobility which would include multilingualism, super-diversity, and the commodification of languages.

From this perspective, the study of the vitality of minority communities and languages has broadened its horizons to other communities of speakers, whether minority or not, and the concern for minority identity and nationalism has extended to complex and transversal identities, as well as to transnational phenomena.

The future of demolinguistics will undoubtedly be linked to the evolution of its basic disciplines (demography, linguistics, ethnography, sociology...), the ways in which they interrelate, and technological developments involved in the collection, storage, and retrieval of data. At the same time, demolinguistics' ability to influence areas outside of research will depend to a large degree on the quality and accuracy of demolinguistic projections, which will be assessed according to their applicability. It could be said, then, that interdisciplinarity, the quality of the information, and applicability must be the factors that set the future course of demolinguistics.

Given the benefit of potential applications of demolinguistics across different fields, it might seem convenient to separate an "applied demolinguistics" from those works oriented toward mere description. However, this would misinterpret the deepest meaning of demolinguistics, because description is worthless when separated from its applications. Therefore, it could be said that demolinguistics is either applied or it ceases to be demolinguistics at all.

References

De Vries, John (1987): "Problems of measurement in the study of linguistic minorities". *Journal of Multilingual and Multicultural Development*, 8: 23–31.
Haugen, Einar (1956): *Bilingualism in the Americas: A Bibliography and Research Guide*. Tuscaloosa: University of Alabama Press.
Weinreich, Uriel (1953): *Languages in Contact*. New York: Linguistic Circle of New York.

INDEX

Note: Locators in *italics* refer to figures, graphs and maps and those in **bold** to tables.

acquisition of second languages (ASL) 38–39
administrative registers 95–96, **121**
age 66–67, 184
Agglomerated Endangerment Scale (AES) 224–226
alphabets 31
analytical demography 8
anonymity 241–242
anthropology 2
applications *see* demolinguistic applications
Asturian **242**, 243
asylum seekers 237–238
authenticity 241–242
Automated Similarity Judgement Program (ASJP) 29

Bable **242**, 243
bar graphs 201, *204–205*
Barni, Monica 177
Basque 23–29, 179–180
Bernstein, Basil 44–45
biases in demographic analyses 196–197
bilingualism: categories of bilingual speakers 45–46; domains of language use 47–48; environmental 46; language vitality 140, 141; minority languages 49–52; mixed marriages 74–75; surveys 105–106; terminology 10, 116; treatment in censuses 131–133

Billari, Francesco 210
birth language 37–39; *see also* first language
birth rate 182, 183
Blum, Alain 70
borders, and linguistics 33–34
Bourgeois-Pichat, Jean 8–9
Britannica Book of the Year 115

Cabré, Anna 23–24, 189–190
Caldwell, John 87
Calvet, Alain and Louis-Jean 140–142
cartography 199, 210
Catalan 31, 189–190
catalogs of languages 80, 116–120, **122**, **125**
censuses 18; as data source 96–99, **98**, *100*, **121**; first language 38–39; link to surveys 109–110; microcensuses 110; treatment of non-national languages 131–133
Central Intelligence Agency 115
Chan, Kai L. 174
China, precursors of demolinguistics 17–18
Chinese 28–29, 31, 142
civil registers 95
civil status 73–75
Coleman diagram 210, 257
communities: and linguistics 34–36, 52; population 64–65

competence in language 42–44, 145–146
computer-assisted telephone interview (CATI) 103
confirmation bias 196
creole language 26, 27–28, 175
cultural indicators **124–125**
culture, and language 161–164

data *see* demolinguistic data and sources
De Vries, John 173–174, 175, 256
deaths *see* mortality rate
deficit theory 44–45
demographic aging 184
Demographic and Health Services (DHS) 114
demographic indicators 79–80, 182–184
demographic projections 189–193, 224–226
demographic surveys 101–112
demographic transition 86–87
demography: definitions and types 6–8; historical context 6; linguistic questions 3–5; over space and time 7
demography for linguists 62–63; composition 65–77; demographic changes 78–86; from facts to theories 86–87; population 63–65; population distribution 77–78; *see also* linguistics for demographers
demolinguistic analyses: errors, biases, and changes in criteria 193–199; graphic representations 199–215; objectives and levels 171–176; qualitative and quantitative analysis 176–181; statistical elements of demography 181–193
demolinguistic applications 219–221; ethnic, local, and social minority languages 221–235; future of 258; Immigrant Minority Languages 235–238; regional and national languages 238–243; Transnational Majority Languages 243–249
demolinguistic data and sources 91, **121**; administrative registers 95–96; censuses 96–99, **98**, *100*; data 91–93; encyclopedias, catalogs, and other sources 115–120; international and digital sources 112–115; sources 93–95; surveys 101–112
demolinguistic factors 167; dependent and independent 131; explanatory factors 149–165; speaker profiles 143–149; speakers and their communities 130–143

demolinguistics 2–5, 8–10; denominations for 11–17; future of 256–258; and geography 10–11; micro and macro 147; precursors of 17–20; terminology 9, 11–12, 21; *see also* linguistics for demographers
descriptive demography 8
dialect 27
dialectology 20
digital communication 164–165, *166*
digital data sources 112–115, **122**
diglossia 48–49

ecological linguistics 2
ecology of languages 138–139
ecology of pressures 227–228
economic context: languages and the economy 158–161; socioeconomic status 75–77
economic factors in language vitality 139
education level 72–73
educational systems: immigrant minority language instruction (IMLI) 157–158; languages in 154–157
elaborated code 44–45
employment status 75–77
encyclopedias 115–116, **122**
endangered languages 113, 221, 224–229; *see also* language vitality
endogamy 74
English: international use of 52; as lingua franca 154; meaning of demolinguistics 12, *13*
entropy 141–142, **142**
environmental bilingualism 46
errors in demographic analyses 193–196
Escobar, Anna Maria 227
ethnic minority language (EtML) **150**, 165
ethnicity: censuses 109; demolinguistic analyses 185; ethnic considerations in linguistics 46–53; migrations 81–86; population composition 68–72; subpopulations 65; treatment in censuses 134
ethnography, and linguistic diversity 2
Ethnologue catalog 30–31, 80, 116–117, 135
European Union: characterization of countries 70; educational systems 154, 155, *155–156*; immigrant groups 237–238; immigrant minority language instruction (IMLI) 157–158; regional data 113; Roma population 235;

Index **261**

treatment of non-national languages 131–132
Eurostat 113
exogamy 74
Expanded Graded Intergenerational Disruption Scale (EGIDS) 53–54, *55*
explicative demography 8
Extra, Guus 177

family: civil status 73–74; definitions and types 62; demographic statistics 63; population distribution 77–78
fecundity 79
fertility rate: as demographic indicator 79, 182; replacement level 183–184; sustainability of languages 138
first language 37–39; language spoken at home 38–39, 47–48, 103, 107, 133–134; in surveys 103, 107
Fishman, Joshua 53
'foreign language' acquisition 40–41; *see also* bilingualism
French: international use 52; as lingua franca 154; linguistic distances 28–29; meaning of demolinguistics 12–15, *14*
future of endangered languages 224–226

Gaunt, John 6
gender 67–68
gender ratio 182–183
generations: age 66–67; inter/intragenerational change 198; migrations **84**
geodemolinguistics 8–10
geographic information systems (GIS) 199
geography: borders 33–34; communities 34–36; demography across space and time 7; and demolinguistics 10–11; linguistic communities 64–65; world map of minority languages 224–225
glossaries for demographic knowledge 62
Glottolog 117, 224
glottonymy 31–32, **32**
graphic representations 199–215
gross domestic product (GDP) 159, 161
Guiter, Henri 29

habitual language *see* first language
heritage languages 39–41, 43
Hervás y Panduro, Lorenzo 19
Hindi 31
hindsight bias 196
histograms 201–203, *204*

historic demography 7
historical context: demography 6; linguistic distances 28–30; precursors of demolinguistics 17–20
home: configuration of households and families 78; language spoken at 38–39, 47–48, 103, 107, 133–134
household structures 77–78
Human Development Index (HDI) 247

immigrant minority language instruction (IMLI) 157–158
Immigrant Minority Languages (ImMLs) **150**, 221, 235–238
immigration *see* migrations
importance of languages *see* international weight of languages
indigenous languages: data sources 119, **126**; linguistic diversity 1–2; subjective vitality questionnaires (SVQs) 110–112; surveys 105–106; vitality and sustainability 138–143, 221–224
individual factors *see* personal factors (demographic statistics)
infant mortality 80
inherited languages 39–41
Integrated Public Use Microdata Series-International 114–115
intercensal surveys 110
International Data Base (IDB) 113–114
international data sources 112–115, **122**
International Organization for Migration (IOM) 113
International Standard Classification of Education (ISCED) **157**, 157–158
International Union for the Scientific Study of Population 114
international use of languages 52, 150–154
international weight of languages **124**, 163, 188, 243–249
Internet World States 115

Japanese 28–29, 142

Kloss, Heinz 28
knowledge of languages 41–45
Krauss, Michael 1
Krzyzanowski, Michal 148

Lagos, Cristián 172–173, 222
language catalogs 80, 116–120, **122**, **125**, 224
language loyalty 51–52

language vitality 53–56; demographic projections 189–193, 224–226; studies of 221–224; subjective vitality questionnaires (SVQs) 110–112
languages: culture and science 161–164; demographic processes 9–10; and the economy 158–161; in educational systems 154–157; exemplary use of 26; number spoken across the world 32–33; numbers of native speakers 135–138, **137**; standardization and context 25–26, 27–28; types of linguistic varieties 26–27
Latour, Bruno 175
learned languages 39–41
learners of foreign language cluster (LFLC) 146, 147–149
Lee, Ronald 87
lexical distance 29
Lieberson, Stanley 198
life expectancy at birth 183
limited skills cluster (LSC) 146, 147, 148
line graphs 200, *201*
linear expression mapping 211, *212*
lingua franca 154, 176
linguistic attitudes 49
linguistic community 35, 189
linguistic community of potential users (LCPU) 146
linguistic conduct 48–49
linguistic demography 9; and demolinguistics 11–12; English terminology 12; French terminology 12–15; Spanish terminology 15–17; *see also* demography for linguists
linguistic distances 28–30
linguistic diversity 1–2, 198
linguistic revitalization 228–229
linguistics for demographers 23–24; fundamental linguistic concepts 25–33; geographic considerations 33–36; language vitality 53–56; psychosocial considerations 36–46; social and ethnic considerations 46–53; *see also* demography for linguists
local minority language (LoML) **150**, 165

macrodemolinguistics 171, 172, 174
main language *see* first language
Malthusian theory 86
Mandarin Chinese 31, 142
Mapudungun 172–173
marriage 73–75

methodology *see* demolinguistic data and sources
Mexico, languages spoken in 221–223
microcensuses 110
microdemolinguistics 171–174
migrations 81–86; data sources 95–96, 109, **123**; growth rate 187; immigrant minority language instruction (IMLI) 157–158; immigrant minority languages (ImMLs) **150**, 221, 235–238
migratory balance 182
migratory registers 95–96, 109
minority languages: data sources 119; demolinguistic analyses 199, 221–235; linguistics for demographers 49–53; vitality and sustainability 138–143
Mirandese 230–231
mortality rate 80, 182
mother tongues 37–39; speaker profiles 143–149; use of term 116; *see also* first language
motivated reasoning 196
Mufwene, Salikoko 227–228
multicultural societies 70, 134, **135**
multilingualism: definition 41; language vitality 140, 141; surveys 105–106

Nahuatl 175–176
nanodemolinguistics 172
national majority languages (NaMaLs) **150**, 239
Nationalencyklopedin 115
nationalism 240–241
nationalities 184–185
native languages *see* first language; indigenous languages
native skills cluster (NSC) 146, 147
native speakers 37–39, 143–149; *see also* first language
neo-speakers 53
Newell, Colin 9

observer's paradox 175
occupational status 75–77
official languages 150–154

Palenquero 231–232
personal factors (demographic statistics) 63; age 66–67; demolinguistic analyses 182–184; education level 72–73; employment status 75–77; race, ethnicity and religion 68–72; sex 67–68
pie charts 201, *203*, *205*

plurilingualism 41
point expression mapping 211
political factors in language vitality 139, 240–241, 244
Popper, Karl 196
population 63–65; comparisons 187–189; composition 65–77; demographic changes 78–86; demographic projections 189–193; demographic transition 86–87; demolinguistic analyses 186–187; distribution 77–78; growth rate 186–187
population censuses *see* censuses
population pyramids 206, *207–209*, *223*
Population Reference Bureau 114
Power Language Index 174
prejudices in demographic analyses 196–197
Pressat, Roland 193–194
prestige in languages 48–49
proficient speakers 42–44, 145–146
pseudo-speakers 53
psychosocial considerations in linguistics 36; bilingualism 45–46; heritage languages and learned languages 39–41; knowledge of languages 41–45; mother tongues and native speakers 37–39
pyramids of speaker populations 206, *207–209*, *223*

qualitative demography 7, 176–181
quantitative demography 7–8, 176–181
quasi-speakers 53
questionnaires 101–112

race: demolinguistic analyses 185; population composition 68–72; treatment in censuses 134
radar charts 203, *206*
regional minority languages (RMLs) **150**, 229–231, 238–243
religion 68–72
replacement level fertility 183–184
restricted code 44–45
revitalization of languages 228–229
Roma population 234–235
Romanian 33–34
Rosetta Project 226
Rowland, Donald 176, 187, 219
Russian 34, 142

Scholfield, Phil 177
school: education level 72–73; language spoken at 47–48

science, and language 161–164
second language: acquisition of 38–39; treatment in censuses 131–133; *see also* bilingualism
semilingual speakers 53
sex 67–68
sex ratio 182–183
sign languages 233
social considerations in linguistics 46–53
social factors (demographic statistics) 63; civil status 73–75; socioeconomic status 75–77
social group languages 232–233
social minority language (SoML) **150**
sociodemographic factors in language vitality 139, 143–149
socioeconomic indicators **124–125**
sociolinguistics 20
Spanish: in Basque Country 179–180; demolinguistic analysis 144–145; and the economy 159–161; fertility 79; German users of 238; indigenous languages 221–223; as lingua franca 154, 176; meaning of demolinguistics 15–17, *16*; political context 32; terminology 50–51
speakers: definitions 131; as demolinguistic factor 130–143, 167; on digital platforms *166*; explanatory factors 149–165; mother tongues 37–39, 116; profiles 143–149; pyramids of speaker populations 206, *207–209*
speech communities 35–36; size of 135–138, **137**
spider charts 203, *206*
standard language 25–26, 27–28
STATISTA 114
Stewart, William 53
subjective vitality questionnaires (SVQs) 110–112, **111–112**
subpopulations 65
Survey on Language, Religion and Culture (LRCS) 103
surveys 101–112, **121**; *see also* censuses
sustainability of languages 138–139, 189–193; *see also* language vitality
Swahili 136

theoretical demography 8
'third culture' 84
translations 162–163
transnational majority languages (TrMaLs) **150**, 243–249

Ukrainian 151
uncertainty principle 175
UNESCO 80; *Atlas of Endangered Languages* 113, **125**, 221; data provided by 113, 119; demolinguistic analyses 180–181; educational systems 157; language vitality 54, **56**; translations 162–163; world map of minority languages 224–225
United Nations: demographic information 112–113, 114, 119; Development Program (UNDP) 165; official status of languages 153–154
United States: Census Bureau 113–114, 133–134; official languages 151, *152*
Urdu 31

vehicular language 36
vehicularity of languages 136, 140–142

Velasco, Reques 210
vitality *see* language vitality

weighting (demolinguistic analyses) 188–189, 243–244
Wikipedia 115–116, 165, *166*
Wodak, Ruth 148
Woolard, Kathryn 241–242
Woolgar, Steve 175
World Bank 113
World Factbook 115
World Health Organization (WHO) 233
World Population Data Sheet 114
Wu Chinese 28, 31

YouTube 165, *166*

zonal expression mapping 211–215, *213–214*

Milton Keynes UK
Ingram Content Group UK Ltd.
UKHW022030090823
426623UK00005B/13